BRITISH TRADE UNIONISM

BRITISH
TRADE UNIONISM
A SHORT HISTORY

by
ALLEN HUTT

with concluding chapter
by
JOHN GOLLAN

1975
LAWRENCE & WISHART
LONDON

First published. 1941
Second (revised) edition 1942
Third (revised and enlarged) edition 1945
Fourth (revised and enlarged) edition. . . . 1952
Fifth (revised and enlarged) edition 1962
Sixth edition (concluding chapter by John Gollan) 1975

ISBN 85315 297 7 (hardback)
85315 320 5 (paperback)

Printed in Great Britain by
The Camelot Press Ltd, Southampton

CONTENTS

Chapter 1 : The Unions as " Schools of War " (1800-50)

The British working class were, as Marx said, the " first-born sons of modern industry." So they were naturally the pioneers of trade unionism, the organisation of the economic struggle of the new class of working men against the new class of capitalist employers, against the competition " of all against all which reigns in modern civil society."[1] Here lay the social significance of the formation of trade unions and the conduct of strikes against the low wages, long hours and abominable conditions which marked the early years of the factory system. Said Frederick Engels, observing these things on the spot, and in their full flower :

> What gives these unions and the strikes arising from them their real importance is this, that they are the first attempt of the workers to abolish competition. They imply the recognition of the fact that the supremacy of the bourgeoisie is based wholly upon the competition of the workers among themselves, i.e. upon their want of cohesion. And precisely because the unions direct themselves against the vital nerve of the present social order, however one-sidedly, in however narrow a way, are they so dangerous to this social order.[2]

The attempt to abolish competition among the

[1] Engels, *Condition of the Working Class in England*, p. 75.
[2] *Ibid.*, pp. 218-19.

workers was clearly expressed in the aims of the early unions. Thus the initiation oaths of the Friendly Society of Coal Mining (1831) included the following : " I never will instruct any person into the art of coal mining . . . except to an obliged brother or brothers or an apprentice ; . . . I will never take any more work than I can do myself in one pay . . . ; I will never in a boasting manner make known how much money I get, or in how short a time." Rule XLIV of the Grand National Consolidated Trades Union (1834) read : " That every member of this Union do use his best endeavours . . . to induce his fellows to join the brotherhood, in order that no workmen may remain out of the Union to undersell them in the market of labour."

By the end of the eighteenth century trade unions had begun to take root, in the shape of local trade clubs which usually met in public-houses and bore a marked social character (liquor was an important item in the official expenditure). For the most part, these trade clubs had developed among the artisan " aristocracy," the skilled handicraftsmen whose methods of work and conditions the industrial revolution had yet left substantially untouched ; the compositors, coopers, carpenters and joiners, cabinetmakers, shipwrights, papermakers, and so forth. But from 1792 they had begun to spread among the key section of the new factory workers, the Lancashire cotton spinners ; and this potential threat to the rising capitalist employers, coupled with the panic induced among the ruling class by the French Revolution, set the stage for the hurried passage through Parliament in 1799-1800 of the notorious Combination Acts, with which the present outline may really begin.

The work of that famous statesman William Pitt and sanctimonious slave-emancipating Wilberforce,

aided by a contemporary Tory worthy named Sir John
Anderson, these Acts, historians have said, " remain
the most unqualified surrender of the State to the
discretion of a class in the history of England." They
" gave the masters unlimited power to reduce wages
and make conditions more severe. They established
the new industry on a basis of . . . serf labour and
low wages."[1] Especially monstrous in this union-
outlawing measure was a clause compelling defendants
to give evidence against themselves and their associates ; not less so the fact that, though the Acts were
nominally directed equally against combinations of
masters, no single case was recorded of their being
so used, although they served to send thousands of
workers to gaol. " Could an accurate account be
given," wrote reformer Francis Place, " the gross
injustice, the foul invective, and terrible punishments
inflicted would not, after a few years have passed
away, be credited on any but the best evidence." It
was the " cruel . . . almost incredible " sentences
passed on compositors of *The Times* in 1810 by the
Common Serjeant of London, Sir John (" Bloody
Black Jack ") Sylvester, that induced Place to devote
himself to securing the repeal of the Acts ; though it
was in the new textile industries that the weight
of the Acts was chiefly felt, and the trade clubs
of the artisans, especially in London, were half
tolerated.

During the quarter of a century that this reign of
anti-union terror lasted, trade unionism was really
born. A wider unity, a more universal solidarity,
began to supplant the parochial vision of the local
trade club. Driven underground, the unions perforce
became conspiratorial bodies, binding their members
by oath, employing initiation ceremonies and the

[1] Hammond, *The Town Labourer*, pp. 113, 141.

whole ritual of the secret society. But these illegal
unions, with a whole fifth column of police spies
despatched from the Home Office to bring them to
destruction, carried out the first series of widespread
strikes, or " turnouts " as they were then generally
called, in the new industries ; outstanding among
these strikes were those of the Scottish weavers (1812),
the Lancashire spinners (1818), the miners on the
North-East coast (1810), in Scotland (1818) and South
Wales (1816) ; the last-named included the ironworkers, and succeeded in defeating a wage reduction.
Interesting as a sample of the methods employed was
the " brothering " of the North-East coast miners,
" so named because the members of the union bound
themselves by a most solemn oath to obey the
orders of the brotherhood, under the penalty of
being stabbed through the heart or of having their
bowels ripped up."[1]

The advance of unity through these bitter years
was seen in the emergence of the first complete
national unions (for example, the Calicoprinters, the
Ironfounders,[2] and the Papermakers), the national
organisation of strike solidarity in a given trade (the
Ropemakers), and the drawing together of different
trades.   The extant records show how these struggling
unions were constantly assisting each other by strike
donations ; and the brilliant wire-pulling of Francis
Place for the repeal of the Combination Acts in 1824-5
would not have succeeded without the wide agitation
conducted by the delegate bodies representing the
different trades set up by the unions in London,
Glasgow, Manchester and elsewhere. Of special
importance were the London trades delegates, led by

[1] Webb, *History of Trade Unionism* (1920 ed.), p. 90.
[2] The Friendly Society of Ironfounders, founded 1809, is now fused
in the National Union of Foundry Workers.

John Gast of Deptford, energetic secretary of the Shipwrights.

Repeal of the " partial and despotic " Combination Acts by no means gave full and unqualified freedom to trade unionism ; but it was quite enough to open the floodgates. A Sheffield newspaper commented that the workers were overtaken by " a rage for union societies." National unions that survived to our own day were formed, like the Steam Engine Makers (1824) and the General Union of Carpenters and Joiners (1827).[1] A storm of strikes swept over the country, affecting alike the artisans and the factory workers. The London shipwrights and coopers engaged in stubborn battles, as did the Glasgow cotton operatives and the Bradford woolcombers. In 1826 Lancashire was convulsed by repeated strikes of cotton spinners and miners, seeking to resist the reductions that the employers were enforcing as a result of the severe slump that had followed the commercial crash of the previous year.

Those were stormy days, and strikes, especially in the coalfields, were civil wars in miniature, put down with every show of violence. Durham was in a turmoil in 1831-2, and marines and cavalry were drafted in to break the strikes and the union, led by the legendary Tommy Hepburn. Troops were also called upon to assist the great Welsh ironmasters in 1831, when they locked out all the members of the Union Club, first solid organisation of the miners and ironworkers ; this was headed by " Dick Penderyn," also a legendary figure, who paid with his life on the gallows for his courageous leading of these Welsh trade unionists in insurrectionary battle, arms in hand, against their oppressors. When the suppres-

[1] Now part of the Amalgamated Engineering Union and the Amalgamated Society of Woodworkers respectively.

sion of the Union Club made open unionism for a
time impossible there emerged a secret terrorist body,
calling themselves the Scotch Cattle (they used a
bull's head and horns as a symbol), who attended to
" traitors, turncoats and others " in the valleys of
Wales and Monmouthshire. Nor was this an isolated
example of the tyranny and terror of their capitalist
masters driving trade unionists to reply with their
own terror. That the Glasgow cotton-spinners, whose
union had been formed secretly in 1816, organised
the burning down of the mills of obnoxious employers
and the killing of " knobsticks " (blacklegs) was
revealed in the famous trial in 1838 of Thomas
Hunter and four other leaders of the union.[1] Or,
from a slightly different angle, we may cite the
Manchester brickmakers' strike of 1843. In that
strike one brickworks was stormed by strikers, armed
with muskets, who fought a pitched battle with the
armed guards of the employers. Though exposed to
a heavy fire from an enemy under good cover the
strikers did not give way until they had smashed up
the works ; then, their ammunition exhausted, they
retired, still under arms and in good order, to Eccles,
three miles from Manchester, though many of them
were severely wounded.[2]

Talk about the " evil " of class hatred would have
seemed absurd to the pioneers of trade unionism.
" Hatred . . . of the general oppression by the
dominant classes blazes out in the trade union records
of the time."[3] Nor was this a blind, instinctive
hate. It was realised that " in our present society "
the worker " can save his manhood only in hatred

---

[1] Of Hunter and his comrades the Webbs tell how " the whole
body of working class opinion was on their side, and the sentence of
seven years' transportation was received with as much indignation
as that upon the Dorchester labourers " (op. cit., p. 170).

[2] Engels, op. cit., pp. 226-7.   [3] Webb, op. cit., p. 174.

and rebellion against the bourgeoisie "; and the " unions contribute greatly to nourish the bitter hatred of the workers against the property-holding class."[1] A contemporary militant put it thus, in a letter to one of the principal working-class papers of the day :

> The great advantage of a strike is that it increases the enmity between labourers and capitalists, and compels workmen to reflect and investigate the causes of their sufferings. . . . The fruit of such reflections would be a violent hostility against the capitalist class ; and the new converts would be prepared to second the efforts of emancipation made by labourers in other quarters of England.[2]

Strikes, wrote Engels, " are the military school of the working-men, in which they prepare themselves for the great struggle which cannot be avoided. . . . As schools of war, the unions are unexcelled. In them is developed the peculiar courage of the English."[3]

The primary lesson taught in these " schools of war " was that to organise individual trades, to act sectionally, was not enough. The far-flung detachments of the working class needed to be embodied in one united army. From the *trade* union men sought to go further, to the *trades* union ; from the union of the workers in one trade to the union of the workers in many, or all, trades. It was the textile factory

[1] Engels, *op. cit.*, pp. 212, 219.
[2] *Poor Man's Guardian*, August 30th, 1934.
[3] Engels, p. 224. Engels added " that courage is required for a turnout, often indeed much loftier courage, much bolder, firmer determination than for an insurrection, is self-evident. . . . And precisely in this quiet perseverance, in this lasting determination which undergoes a hundred tests every day, the English working-man develops that side of his character which commands most respect. People who endure so much to break one single bourgeois will be able to break the power of the whole bourgeoisie."

workers who led in learning this lesson from the
repeated failure of sectional strikes, however stubbornly fought. Arising out of the Lancashire spinners'
strikes of 1818 and 1826 attempts were made to found
a wider organisation, without lasting effect ; though
the first effort, despite the existence of the Combination Acts, brought together delegates of fourteen
trades in Manchester who agreed to form a General
Union of Trades, or Philanthropic Society (this title,
and its picturesque alternative the Philanthropic
Hercules, presumably intended as a legal cover),
counting among its aims :   " no trade to strike
without informing and obtaining consent from the
other trades " ; and, despite its fleeting and uncertain
existence, this body branched out to London, where
John Gast was its chairman.[1]

The third attempt, made in 1830 following a particularly long and bitter strike of spinners in Ashton
and Hyde, marked an important step forward.   In
that year was established the National Association
for the Protection of Labour, led by John Doherty,
outstanding trade union fighter of Lancashire, a
talented writer and organiser ; it was he who, in
1829, had been instrumental in forming the cotton
spinners' first national organisation, the Grand
General Union of the United Kingdom, at a widely
attended and admirably publicised delegate conference in the Isle of Man.   The National Association
aimed at concerted resistance to wage-cuts ; and it
soon registered a total of 150 affiliated trade unions,
mainly among textile workers in Lancashire and the

---

[1] The influence of these broadening conceptions of trade union
unity in London was later seen in the establishment (in 1825) of
the first general union organ, the *Trades Newspaper and Mechanics'
Weekly Journal*, managed by a committee of eleven delegates from
different London trades, over which Gast presided (Webb, *op. cit.*,
p. 111).

Midlands ; mechanics, miners, potters and other trades were likewise represented, and the affiliated membership is reported to have reached 100,000. But though the Association terrified the ruling class (on resigning, Home Secretary Sir Robert Peel left the job of smashing it as his principal legacy to his successor), it was in fact a loose federation, with small funds, and a limited and defensive policy. Its two years of life represented a big advance, but there were much bigger advances ahead.[1]

Meantime the country was in the throes of the parliamentary reform crisis, which, after bringing it to the brink of civil war, resulted in the passage of the Reform Act of 1832. The most far-seeing trade unionists had no illusions about the alliance between the workers and the middle class which won reform. (Francis Place records John Doherty telling him that the Reform Bill could bring no good to the working man, and that the people ought to compel the Government by force to do what was right.) To the mass, however, parliamentary reform appeared the panacea for their ills ; in London, for instance, the National Union of the Working Classes and Others—a suitably symbolic title—had been formed in 1831 as the Metropolitan Trades Union, to which many unions affiliated. But the Reform Act speedily showed, since its sole beneficiaries were the middle class, the manufacturing capitalists, that the workers had been cannon fodder, not allies. The consequent dis-

[1] In defiance of the law the National Association first issued as its organ an unstamped weekly, the *United Trades Co-operative Journal*. When the authorities intervened, a legal stamped weekly, the *Voice of the People*, was started, with Doherty as editor. Though priced sevenpence this is said to have reached the immense circulation (for those days) of 30,000 copies a week. In addition to reports of the Association's activities, much space was given to political news, to the question of Irish freedom, and to news of revolutionary events abroad.

illusionment with " politics " (i.e. parliamentarism) brought revolutionary repercussions among the trade unions.

Already a new note had been struck with the foundation, at the height of the reform agitation, of the first national industrial union, transcending all craft divisions. This was the Operative Builders' Union, which rapidly gained the then remarkable membership of 40,000. In pursuit of its aim " to advance and equalise the price of labour," it was soon conducting a whole series of determined strikes, notably in Lancashire and London. The masters replied with lockouts and the notorious " document," requiring their men to abjure trade unionism as a condition of employment.

Nor was this activity confined to the builders. There was a rising wave of strikes in other industries ; the cotton-spinners in particular were on the move, planning a " universal strike " for an eight-hour working day, to date from March 1st, 1834. Into the midst of this upsurge there entered the great Utopian Socialist Robert Owen and his friends ; and their propaganda for a new social order took the unions by storm. Owen intervened in two vital working-class conferences in the autumn of 1833. First came the congress of the Builders' Union (the " Builders' Parliament "), held at Manchester and attended by 500 delegates. Then at London, in October, delegates of trade unions and co-operatives gathered to discuss amalgamation. On both occasions close attention was paid to Owen's plea for ensuring a peaceful transition from capitalism to Socialism by transforming the unions into co-operative productive societies (the builders decided to form a productive guild), but it became clear that the general trend was social revolutionary.

Of the London congress James Morrison—a young and self-taught Socialist building worker who edited *The Pioneer*, weekly organ of the Builders' Union —wrote " the crisis of our condition is at hand—close upon us. The contest affects all alike ; and woe unto the man who deserts his post. The question to be decided is, Shall Labour or Capital be uppermost ? " The *Poor Man's Guardian* (October 19th, 1833) wrote that the reports of the delegates to the London congress " show that an entire change in society—a change amounting to a complete subversion of the existing ' order of the world '—is contemplated by the working classes. They aspire to be at the top instead of at the bottom of society—or rather that there should be no bottom or top at all ! " The paper went on to contrast this revolutionary aim with the " paltry objects " of former trade unions, which " did not aim at any radical change ; their tendency was not to alter the system, but rather to perpetuate it, by rendering it more tolerable " ; and it spoke of the " silent but rapid progress of a grand national organisation which promises to embody the physical power of the country."

The return of the delegates from the London congress to their districts turned the mounting tide of trade unionism into a flood which swept the country from end to end in a manner beyond all precedent. No fewer than 800,000 workers were thus speedily organised, claimed Owen's paper, *The Crisis*. Evidently the " grand national organisation " of which the *Poor Man's Guardian* had spoken was casting its shadow before. That shadow was shortly to be given substance. In February 1834 union delegates again assembled in London and, meeting behind closed doors, finally constituted the Grand National Consolidated Trades Union, the first, and the greatest, example of the One Big Union. Its aim was expressed in its Rule XLVI :

> Although the design of the Union is, in the first instance, to raise the wages of the workmen, or prevent any further reduction therein, and to diminish the hours of labour, the great and ultimate object of it must be to establish the paramount rights of Industry and Humanity, by . . . bringing about A DIFFERENT ORDER OF THINGS, in which the really useful and intelligent part of society only shall have the direction of its affairs.

In an astonishingly short time the G.N.C.T.U. counted a membership of half a million, enrolling adherents by scores of thousands in every branch of industry ; the experience of two organisers visiting Hull, who made 1,000 members in a single evening, was typical ; whole tracts that had hitherto been barren of trade union organisation suddenly proved fertile ; agricultural labourers were organised *en masse*, in the English counties, in Scotland (where the Perthshire ploughmen and the Dundee shearmen were reported as forming unions), and in the then rural suburbs of London ; women workers were drawn in in large numbers—Rule XX providing specifically that " Lodges of Industrious Females shall be instituted " ; non-manual workers even swelled the surging throng, the Grand National issuing a special appeal " to the Shopmen, Clerks, Porters and other industrious non-producers."

Scarcely had the Grand National assumed concrete shape than it was involved in a flood of strikes and lockouts all over the country on questions of wages, hours and the right to union membership. Chief among these were the strikes of the hosiers in Leicester, of engineers, calico-printers and cabinet-makers in Glasgow, of tailors in London. Specially

important, too, was the lockout of builders in the
metropolis, arising from a dispute as to the beer
Cubitt's men were to have on the job (they refused
non-union liquor), and marked again by the pre-
sentation of the " document." Nation-wide attention
centred on a long-drawn lockout of 1,500 men, women
and children at Derby for refusing to give up the
union. The cotton-spinners' movement flared up in
a remarkable popular uprising at Oldham, where
every mill struck and stormy demonstrations demanding the eight-hour day, in which women played a
prominent part,[1] were accompanied by fierce fights
with the police.

These events induced panic among the ruling class,[2]
who found their own dictatorship confronted by the
potentially dictatorial power of the working class.
As James Morrison had written :

> The growing power and growing intelligence of trades
> unions, when properly managed, will draw into its
> vortex all the commercial interests of the country and,
> in so doing, it will become, by its own self-acquired
> importance, a most influential, we might almost say
> dictatorial part of the body politic.[3]

Accordingly the authorities struck hard, and at the
weakest link in the G.N.C.T.U. chain, the organisation
of the agricultural labourers. In Dorset, where conditions were specially bad, two brothers in the village
of Tolpuddle, George and James Loveless, had got
in touch with the Grand National and were forming a
Friendly Society of Agricultural Labourers, employing

[1] Reports in *The Times* mentioned the activity of the Lodge of
Female Gardeners and the Lodge of Ancient Virgins, which may very
well have been " Lodges of Industrious Females " of the G.N.C.T.U.

[2] Dr. Arnold, the " enlightened " educational reformer and head-
master of Rugby, wrote to a friend at this time : " you have heard,
I doubt not, of the Trades Unions ; a fearful engine of mischief,
ready to riot or to assassinate ; and I see no counteracting power."

[3] *The Pioneer*, May 31st, 1834.

the customary initiation ceremonies and oaths. The
Lovelesses and four others were hastily framed on a
preposterous charge of administering illegal oaths
(under a special Act of 1797 passed in connection with
the Mutiny at the Nore), haled before the Dorchester
Assizes and, after an entirely monstrous trial, sentenced
to seven years' transportation.

This famous case of the Tolpuddle Martyrs produced
an instant protest campaign of nation-wide dimen-
sions, in which the Grand National was warmly
seconded by important unions in the north which
remained outside its ranks ; over a quarter of a
million signatures were obtained to a petition for the
release of the Tolpuddle men, and the agitation
culminated in London's first monster working-class
demonstration. Despite formidable police and military preparations between 100,000 and 200,000
demonstrators, representing every trade, each mar-
shalled behind thirty-three different banners, marched
to Copenhagen Fields, a piece of open land then
existing near King's Cross. The building trades
struck work to take part.

But while the G.N.C.T.U. could thus successfully
conduct an impressive protest campaign (which led
eventually to the release of the Tolpuddle Martyrs),
it proved unable to accomplish the more positive
tasks of leadership to achieve the " different order of
things." It was the first great example of what we
nowadays call Syndicalism, the belief that trade union
action alone can overthrow capitalism, employing the
general strike—or " national holiday " as it was then
termed—as a peaceful, passive resistance weapon ;
" this inert conspiracy of the poor against the rich,"
said a Scottish working-class paper.[1] Even from
this standpoint the Owenite Executive of the Grand

[1] *Glasgow Liberator : Trades Union Gazette*, February 1st, 1834.

National, faced with the torrent of sectional disputes described, failed to ride the whirlwind and direct the storm. A public statement was issued deprecating all industrial disputes, and sanction for strikes was refused (as in the case of the London shoemakers, who thereupon voted to secede from the G.N.C.T.U. and struck on their own). Such a policy inevitably induced the rapid disintegration of the union, which did not outlast the year.

The passing of this revolutionary-aimed mass unionism—and there was to be no further organisation of the unskilled labouring mass for nearly half a century—left its mark, notably in the building trades. But the following great stage in working-class development, the revolutionary political movement of Chartism (1837-48), was not of a trade union character, though many trade unionists played an active part in it. The story of the fight for the People's Charter falls outside the scope of this study.[1] Here it must suffice to say that the shock troops of Chartism were the textile factory workers and the miners ; the unions of the former favoured by overwhelming majorities the turning of the Lancashire General Strike of 1842 into a political rising for the Charter ; while Chartists played a leading part in the formation of the first national coalfields organisation, the Miners' Association, in 1841. But Chartism tackled too late the vital problem of rooting itself firmly in the relatively strong craft unions, the " pompous trades and proud mechanics " as Chartist leader Feargus O'Connor called them.

The strike of 1842 was Chartism's highest point, save for its final burst in Europe's revolutionary year 1848. Thereafter the trade union development which

[1] The best introduction is Salme A. Dutt's *When England Arose* (Key Books No. 6).

took place diverged more and more from any aiming at radical change. Union development in the mid-forties was important, too. The Miners' Association reported a membership of 100,000 in 1844, and made the coalfields ring by its employment of a brilliant Chartist solicitor, W. P. Roberts, to fight the tyranny of local magistrates and truck firms. In that year, too, the five-months' strike of the Durham miners was at once the most sensational and the most heroic struggle that the coalfields of this country had yet seen. It was fought with the utmost brutality on the part of the owners ; in the course of it every one of the 40,000 strikers was evicted " with revolting cruelty. The sick, the feeble, old men and little children, even women in childbirth, were mercilessly turned from their beds and cast into the roadside ditches " [1]; and the reigning Lord Londonderry, leading coalowner, issued a notorious manifesto denouncing " the senseless warfare of the pitmen against *their proprietors and masters.*"

During the same period union organisation was revived and strengthened among the potters and the cotton-spinners (1843), while the compositors amalgamated their local unions into the National Typographical Society (1845).[2] In that last year, too, there was formed a new general organisation, the National Association of United Trades. From this the larger unions tended to hold aloof, and it became a rallying centre for the smaller and less well-organised trades. Not setting up to be more than a strictly federal body, the Association also specifically eschewed the revolutionary aims of the Grand National, stressing

[1] Engels, *op. cit.*, p. 256.
[2] This national union only survived for a couple of years, then dividing into the metropolitan and provincial unions that we have to-day (the London Society of Compositors and the Typographical Association).

instead " the importance of, and beneficial tendency arising from, a good understanding between the employer and the employed."[1]   Clearly the tendency " not to alter the system, but rather to perpetuate it, by rendering it more tolerable " (so denounced by the *Poor Man's Guardian* a dozen years before) was again in the ascendant.

[1] Webb, *op. cit.*, p. 189.

Chapter 2 : " Defence Not Defiance "
(1850-80)

THIS mid-Victorian period of trade unionism was essentially that of the definitive national organisation of the " pompous trades and proud mechanics," the skilled minority of the working class. " Defence not defiance " became the union motto—to defend the vested interest of the craftsman, not to defy the employing class with the organised might of the whole working class ; similarly the line " a fair day's wage for a fair day's work " implied the full acceptance of the existing order, subject to specific and limited reform, to getting the best that could be got within its framework.

There was nothing accidental about this development. By the end of the 'forties British capitalism had been able to break down all barriers to its full growth. The triumph of Free Trade meant complete freedom for capital. There was industrial and commercial expansion on an unparalleled scale, " leaping and bounding " (in Gladstonian phrase), returning profits not of tens but thousands per cent.,[1] confirming Britain, the " workshop of the world," in its privileged position of industrial monopoly. Thus it was both possible and necessary for substantial concessions to be made to the two main groups upon whom this prosperity depended, the textile factory workers

[1] Webb, *The Decay of Capitalist Civilisation*, p. 81.

(who were greatly benefited by the Ten Hour Act of
1847) and the skilled artisans in the metal-working
and building trades. The consolidation in this way of
an " aristocracy of labour " over and above the main
mass of the working class was fully reflected in the
new character of trade unionism.

First of the " new model " was the Amalgamated
Society of Engineers, established in 1851 after some
years of gradual getting together of the numerous
small and mostly local craft societies in the industry.
These coalesced around the largest among them, the
Journeymen Steam-Engine, Machine-Makers and Mill-
wrights Friendly Society (an 1826 foundation), two
of whose prominent members, William Newton and
William Allan, were the principal protagonists of
amalgamation. Allan, a Crewe railway shopman,
became the first secretary of the A.S.E., bequeathing
to that body its tradition of cautious administration
and almost miserly care for its funds.

This new " Amalgamated " unionism—the name
became a programme—marked a decisive break from
the " schools of war " described by Engels. For the
old militancy it substituted the policy of co-operation
with the employers, asking no more for the working
man than " a fair and legitimate share of the profits
of his toil."[1] Strikes were frowned upon. The funds
that were accumulated from high contributions were
employed to finance a wide series of provident benefits,
and the amalgamated unions functioned substantially
as trade friendly societies. The A.S.E. figures afford
a typical picture ; from 1851-89 these showed that
while the union's expenditure on the various friendly
benefits (sick, funeral, out-of-work, superannuation,

[1] A phrase from a pamphlet by William Graham, a stonemason,
published in 1868 ; quoted in Rothstein, *From Chartism to Labourism*,
p. 200.

etc.) was £2,987,993, on strikes it was only £86,664.[1]

As a natural accompaniment of this, the loose structure of the old fighting unions, with the wide autonomy enjoyed by the local lodges, was changed for the elaborately centralised structure of a business organisation. Thus decisive power now resided in the national executive body and, by the same token, effective authority was placed more and more in the hands of the permanent officials, the head office administrators required by the " new model " unionism, whose emergence as a regular corps set apart from their members was a fact of first-rate importance. First symptom of this was the informal and influential London grouping of union general secretaries, christened " the Junta " by the Webbs, which included Allan (Engineers), Robert Applègarth (Carpenters and Joiners), Daniel Guile (Ironfounders), Edwin Coulson (Bricklayers) and George Odger (Ladies' Shoe-makers).[2]

It must not be supposed that this period was free from strikes. Quite the contrary ; and it was remarkable for the growing use by the employers of the lock-out, found a convenient instrument for " solving " problems of over-production. When it was but a year old the A.S.E., fighting against overtime and piece-work, was involved in a lockout of engineers in London and Lancashire, which ended with the employers reviving the hated " document " ; this, however, the men signed only under duress and did not abandon the union.

The principal issue of the disputes of this time was

[1] George Howell, *Trade Unionism New and Old* (1900 ed.), pp. 126-7.

[2] Odger was not a general secretary, and his union was a small, old-fashioned local craft union ; he was a notable figure for his general activity in London, both as a trade unionist and as a Radical politician.

the shorter working day—nine hours instead of ten. A Nine Hours Movement developed in the building trades over a period of years ; it came to a head in the lengthy London strike and lockout of 1859-60, when the employers were defeated in their attempt to enforce the " document," though the shorter hours were not then won. This dispute was noteworthy for the solidarity shown by unions outside the building trade (the A.S.E. created an immense sensation by three separate weekly donations of £1,000 each) and for its sequel in the establishment of the Amalgamated Society of Carpenters and Joiners. Formed directly on the engineers' model, this shortly became, under its secretary, Robert Applegarth, second only to the A.S.E. itself in membership and funds.

Nor did the Nine Hours Movement stop there. In 1871 the engineers on the north-east coast embarked on a five months' strike which, despite the apathy of their national executive, not only won the nine-hour day for the district but gave powerful impetus for its successful achievement in other places and other trades. It was significant that organisation in the north-east was at a very low level when the strike began, and the success was due to the uniting of the various trades, unionists and non-unionists alike, around an *ad hoc* body, the Nine Hours League, led by John Burnett, a local A.S.E. militant who in 1874 succeeded Allan as general secretary.

Shorter hours were also the concern of the cotton factory workers and the miners. In the 'fifties the Lancashire cotton operatives began to form their present craft " Amalgamations," or federations of local craft unions (spinners, weavers, etc.). To interpret the immensely complicated piece price-lists which came to govern cotton wages, there grew up an extraordinary mandarinate of union officials, appointed by competitive examination for their mathematico-technical ingenuity and as willing to serve the employers as they were their own members.[1] In the 'seventies a strong movement for a nine-hour day developed and secured the compromise of a 56½-hour week. As for the coalfields, where the powerful Miners' Association had faded out in the early 'fifties, organisation picked up with the formation in 1863 of the National Miners' Union, led by Alexander Macdonald, a remarkable Scottish ex-miner turned successful business man who in 1874 was elected (together with Thomas Burt of Northumberland) one of the first two Liberal-Labour M.P.s. There were constant struggles over the right to appoint checkweighers, partially conceded in the Mines Act of 1860. Throughout the 'sixties there was a series of miners' strikes and lockouts, the latter being an especial fancy of the Yorkshire coalowners ; and in North Wales in 1869 four persons were killed, twenty-six wounded when the troops fired on a crowd of demonstrating miners. As a rival to the National Union an Amalgamated Association of Miners was formed in Lancashire, spreading to South Wales and the Midlands. Between the two some 200,000 miners were organised. Through the National Union in particular the demand for an eight-hour day underground was voiced ; in one coalfield (Fife) the direct action of the men secured this.

Though amalgamated unionism eschewed political independence and sought co-operation with the employers, it nevertheless engaged in important battles with the governing class and the State on certain broad democratic issues. First came the fight for freedom of organisation, for the unfettered legal status of trade unions, which the Acts of 1824-5 had not

[1] Webb, *History of Trade Unionism*, p. 479.

positively secured. Unions still had no legal protection for their funds, strikers could still be (and were) gaoled for " conspiracy " and " intimidation," the Master and Servant Act was rigorously applied.[1] Some incidents in Sheffield (where the local trade clubs of the cutlery crafts went in for " rattening "—a hangover of the old tradition of terrorising blacklegs) were made the excuse for the appointment of a Royal Commission on trade unions in 1867, and stiffer anti-union legislation was feared. Allan, Applegarth and their friends thereupon established the Conference of Amalgamated Trades (in effect a committee of themselves) and set to work to influence the Commission.

At this point the second fight, for extension of the franchise, showed its importance. The Reform Act of 1867, which gave the vote to the workers in the towns, was the result of a wide agitation by the National Reform League, a body inspired by the First International (see below) and largely influenced by Marx himself.[2] Trade unionists were the shock troops of the League, as in the famous battle of Hyde Park in 1866, when a crowd of 200,000 broke the railings down and the Guards were called out, or in the many demonstrations where union banners led the way, the Carpenters bearing the slogan : " Deal With Us on the Square. You Have Chiselled Us Long Enough."

With the trade unionists enfranchised, some concessions had to be made ; but while the Trade Union Act which emerged in 1871, after much ministerial shuffling, improved the juridical status of the unions, new and severe legal blows were struck at all normal

[1] This monstrous piece of class legislation made breach of contract by a worker a criminal offence, punishable by imprisonment up to three months, whereas a defaulting employer committed only a civil offence, punishable by a small fine.

[2] Karl Marx, *Letters to Kugelmann*, pp. 33, 40.

strike activity, like picketing (so that, to give one out of many cases, a group of women in South Wales were gaoled simply for saying " bah " to a blackleg). Five more years of struggle were necessary, together with the decisive intervention of the trade union vote against the Government in the General Election of 1874, before an acceptable amending Act was finally passed in 1876.

The third fight was on the international field, for solidarity with democratic movements abroad, and against reactionary intervention—or " non-intervention "—by Britain. By impressive mass meetings British trade unionists demonstrated their support for the North in the American Civil War, despite the desolation of Lancashire by the cotton famine resulting from the Northern blockade. The national struggles of the Polish and Italian peoples also had full backing ; when Garibaldi visited London he received a tremendous popular welcome, and many trade unionists played a prominent part in the National League for the Independence of Poland. From these quarters came active participation in the historic International Workingmen's Association when it was founded in London under Marx's direct leadership. Many unions and their branches affiliated to the International, and union leaders, like Applegarth, sat for a time on its General Council, of which George Odger was the first president. The International was heartily endorsed by the Trades Union Congress at its second meeting, in Birmingham, in 1869 ; and it played a highly practical part in stopping the import of foreign blacklegs, notably in the engineers' nine-hours strike already mentioned.[1]

[1] For the First International see *Founding of the First International* (a collection of documents), and also Lozovsky, *Marx and the Trade Unions*, especially Chaps. IV and V.

Arising out of these varied struggles there came the first permanent grouping of trade unions, first on a local and then on a national scale. The 'sixties saw the establishment and consolidation of Trades Councils in the principal cities, the London Council being a by-product of the building dispute of 1859-60. In London the Amalgamated leaders were especially strong and the Trades Council was the scene of a bitter feud between them and the leading representative of the old, aggressive but anarchic local trade unionism, George Potter, whom they denounced as a " strike-jobber." Potter, a thorough demagogue, had his importance through his founding and editing of *The Beehive*, the leading trade union weekly of the time, which was for a while the organ of the First International.

The problem of the unions' legal position, and the threat of the Royal Commission, led the Manchester and Salford Trades Council in 1868 to summon a national conference of trade unions and trades councils ; this was the first regular Trades Union Congress which, through the Parliamentary Committee that it shortly set up, led the final stages of the fight for union legalisation. Precursors of the T.U.C. were national trade union conferences called in the middle 'sixties by the Glasgow and Sheffield Trades Councils and in London by George Potter.

Though trade unionism had thus, over a score of years, registered substantial advances, the narrow craft outlook of the " new model " clearly bore within itself the elements of grave weakness. This had begun to be evident even when the boom years of the early 'seventies saw a sudden union upsurge which pushed the T.U.C. affiliations up from 375,000 to nearly 1,200,000 and reached out to the unskilled, notably the agricultural labourers. But the remarkable

organisation in 1872-3, under the leadership of Joseph
Arch, a Warwickshire farm labourer and lay preacher,
of a union totalling 100,000 members, which battled
valiantly against squire and parson, did not seriously
survive the heavy agricultural depression that soon
set in. Nor were the craftsmen likely to be held in
difficult days to unions in all of which, say the Webbs,
there was " the same abandonment by the Central
Executive of any dominant principle of trade policy,
the same absence of initiative in trade movements,
and the same more or less persistent struggle to check
the trade activity of its branches."[1]

The narrow particularism of the Amalgamated
unions was breeding new disunity. The patternmakers seceded from the A.S.E. in 1872 and throughout the metal-working trades many new craft unions
sprang up. Unedifying and demoralising demarcation
disputes between unions multiplied. A break in trade
in the mid 'seventies brought a series of bitterly fought
but uniformly defeated strikes, notably among the
South Wales miners, who were forced to accept the
sliding scale payment of wages (1875), the stonemasons (1877), the Clyde shipwrights and the Lancashire cotton operatives (1878). The last-named strike
was over the characteristic issue of over-production,
the employers demanding a wage reduction and the
operatives proposing short time ; a curiously unreal
difference for a dispute which had its violent moments,
including the burning down of the house of the
employers' president.

Just at this moment Frederick Engels was writing
that " the British Labour movement is to-day and
for many years has been working in a narrow circle
of strikes " which " cannot lead the movement one
step further," since they " are looked upon not as an

[1] Webb, op. cit., p. 319.

expedient and not as a means of propaganda but as an
ultimate aim." The exclusion of political activity by
the unions, he added, meant that there was no general
working-class movement in the continental sense.[1]
The slump of 1878-9, worst hitherto known in British
industry, signalising that the epoch of Britain's
privilege and industrial monopoly was at its end,
brought a crisis of trade unionism which gave Engels'
words new meaning.

[1] Letter to Edward Bernstein, June 17th, 1878.

CHAPTER 3: THE NEW UNIONISM (1880-1900)

THE crisis of trade unionism in the 'eighties was one aspect of the deep social crisis brought about by the ending of Britain's industrial monopoly, the dethroning of " the despot of the world market." Unbroken stagnation in the major branches of industry, poverty so widespread and grinding that a leading capitalist apologist—Sir Robert Giffen—was compelled to exclaim " no one can contemplate the present condition of the masses without desiring something like a revolution for the better," brought a breaking of the ties that had bound the working class to their masters. Socialism was re-born in Britain and the working-class movement as we know it took shape.

Amalgamated unionism was now absolutely moribund. Not only did it abandon all pretence of defending the standards of its members ; not only was it becoming, in the Webbs' phrase, " nothing more than a somewhat stagnant department of the Friendly Society movement " ; benefits were being reduced, contributions raised and many members deprived of benefit altogether. And what was the way out ? Already in 1881 Engels had publicly pointed out[1] that with the waning of Britain's industrial monopoly the unions could not maintain their

[1] In the *Labour Standard*, organ of the London Trades Council : a remarkable series collected in Engels, *The British Labour Movement*.

34

organised strength " unless they really march in the
van of the working class " ; and this meant breaking
the " vicious circle out of which there is no issue "
(of movements limited to wages and hours), ceasing
to be the " tail of the ' Great Liberal Party,' "
building out of the unions a working-men's party,
" a political organisation of the working class as a
whole," which would win power for the workers and
build a new social order.

As for the dominant leaders—the " old gang " as
they came to be called—this appeal fell on deaf ears.
Bound hand and foot to Gladstonian liberalism and
middle-class orthodoxy, the men who had succeeded
the Junta offered the movement not leadership but
abdication. They dominated the Trades Union
Congress, of which Henry Broadhurst (Stonemasons)
was secretary, and men like John Burnett (Engineers),
J. D. Prior (Carpenters), George Shipton (London
Trades Council) leading lights ; and the whole policy
of the T.U.C. in those days has been summed up in
two words—" contemptuous inactivity."[1]   Added
to which there was the point, made by Socialist
pioneers like William Morris, that the unions

> now no longer represent the whole class of workers as
> working *men* but rather are charged with the office of
> keeping the human part of the capitalists' machinery
> in good working order and freeing it from any grit of
> discontent.[2]

It was the Socialists, both the intellectual leaders
outside the unions and the younger trade unionists
who became converts, who led the fight against the
" old gang " and revolutionised trade unionism.
There was a vast difference, however, between the
criticism of the limited, negative character of the old
unions, and the reactionary, often corrupt character

[1] Webb, *op. cit.*, p. 399.   [2] *Lecture on Socialism*, 1885.

of their leaders, offered by Engels or by Socialist trade unionists like Tom Mann and John Burns of the Engineers, and that coming from the Socialist organisation then first in the field, the Social Democratic Federation.   In the one case criticism was positive, taking account of the revolutionary potentialities of trade unionism ; in the other it was negative, dogmatic and sectarian, reflecting the middle-class outlook of the Federation's pseudo-Marxist and dictatorial leader H. M. Hyndman, and so " antagonised trade unionists without drawing over any considerable percentage to the Socialist position."[1] We shall suggest below the serious effects that this sectarianism had on the future of the movement.

The T.U.C. was the battleground for the " old gang " and their challengers, first representative of the latter being a young miners' delegate from Ayrshire, Keir Hardie.   The polemic, both at Congresses and in the press, was couched in the most bitter and personal terms.   At the Dundee Congress of 1889 a climax was reached. Broadhurst hit out in a fashion that will be familiar to a generation accustomed to the anti-left outbursts of Mr. Bevin or Sir Walter Citrine.   He capped earlier sneers at Hardie (" he was not aware that Mr. Hardie had made sacrifices in this great Labour movement "), who had attacked his association with Brunner,[2] a great liberal capitalist long notorious for the scandalous exploitation in his chemical works, by denouncing

those who spread dissensions in the unions and seek to destroy unionism by vehemently attacking its prominent

---

[1] *Tom Mann's Memoirs*, p. 57. For a detailed account of the Socialist developments in the 'eighties, and a documented criticism of S.D.F. sectarianism, see Hutt, *This Final Crisis*, Pt. II, Chap. III, " The Re-birth of Socialism."

[2] Of Brunner, Mond & Co., forerunners of the modern Imperial Chemical Industries Ltd.

representatives. . . . Their emissaries enter our camp
in the guise of friends, in order that they may the
better sow the seeds of disruption. Let the workers
beware of them!

and concluded with the cry " hound these creatures
from our midst." The " old gang " were rewarded
with an overwhelming vote of Congress ; but they
were in fact on the eve of defeat.

There had already been signs that new forces were
on the move. In July, 1888, a Socialist-led strike of
the girls at Bryant and May's match factory in the
East End secured wide publicity, alike for the
shocking conditions that it exposed and for the
revelation of the number of Liberal politicians who
were concerned as shareholders. The strike was
successful. It was the " light jostle needed for the
entire avalanche to move " (Engels). The gasworkers followed. Unrest had been growing for some
time at Beckton, where the stokers worked a twelve-
hour shift and a thirteen-day fortnight. They
demanded an eight-hour shift, a twelve-day fortnight
and a shilling a shift wage increase. Led by Will
Thorne, a Beckton stoker, the men vainly sought
Liberal aid to have their case raised in Parliament,
and then turned to the Socialists. They were advised
to organise a union and given every assistance, notably
by Eleanor Marx (Karl's most talented daughter)
and her husband Edward Aveling.[1] Rapid recruitment to the new Gasworkers' and General Labourers'
Union enabled the men shortly to hand in strike

[1] The Avelings, who worked in intimate association with, and
under the guidance of, Engels, had already been working hard at
propaganda among the Radical working-men's clubs, particularly in
the East End, out of which had come, after the " Bloody Sunday "
battle in Trafalgar Square in 1887, the Law and Liberty League,
uniting Socialist and Radical working men and trade unionists in
a broad mass movement (Hutt, *This Final Crisis*, pp. 106-12).

notices ; and they were in so strong a position that the Gas Companies conceded the whole of their demands, save that the wage increase granted was sixpence a shift instead of a shilling.

Within a few days of this striking success the " stagnant pool of misery " that was London's waterfront was in violent agitation. A spontaneous strike of the men at the South-West India Dock, provoked by a dispute over the amount of extra pay due on a certain cargo, became within a week a general dockers' strike. The world was electrified by a movement that completely paralysed its greatest port. Under the leadership of Socialists—John Burns, Tom Mann, Ben Tillett, with Eleanor Marx as secretary of the strike committee—the starvelings had truly arisen from their slumbers. Among the principal demands were a minimum wage of sixpence an hour (the " dockers' tanner "), extra pay for overtime, a minimum engagement of four hours. The strike lasted for over four weeks, sustained by an unprecedented wave of international solidarity ; of the £48,000 odd subscribed to the strike funds, no less than £30,000 was telegraphed from Australia. Self-appointed mediation efforts by Cardinal Manning and Lord Buxton (the Liberal politician who had refused to help the gasmen) baulked the dockers of their full demands ; but they won their tanner, and their success brought the unskilled masses into organisation in a way unparalleled since the apocalyptic days of 1834.

The following year saw over 200,000 supposedly unorganisable labourers brought into the ranks of trade unionism, which was transformed in the process.

These unskilled (wrote Engels) are very different chaps from the fossilised brothers of the old trade unions ; not a trace of the old formalist spirit, of the craft exclusiveness of the engineers for instance ; on the contrary, a general cry for the organisation of *all* trade unions in one fraternity and for a direct struggle against capital.[1]

The Dockers' Union that was formed out of the strike extended from London to the other principal ports. The Gasworkers organised general labourers throughout the provinces, soon reporting a membership of 70,000 in no fewer than seventy trades. On the railways, one of the blackest spots for exploitation and lack of organisation, the General Railway Workers' Union arose to challenge and reinforce the hitherto feeble Amalgamated Society of Railway Servants ; its proclamation " that the union shall remain a fighting one, and shall not be encumbered with any sick or accident fund " was typical of the spirit of the New Unionism.[2] The Sailors' and Firemen's Union, founded in 1887, registered 65,000 members two years later. Organisation spread apace in the coalfields, where the Miners' Federation (formed in 1888 with an affiliated membership of only 36,000) was soon to pass the 200,000 mark, emerging as the permanent mass organisation of the country's mineworkers. With the willing aid of the new movement in the towns, unionism was revived in the countryside, the remnant of Joseph Arch's union picking up strength and new unions being formed,

[1] Letter to Hermann Schlueter, January 11th, 1890 : Marx-Engels, *Correspondence* (edited by Dona Torr), p. 463.

[2] In 1890 the A.S.R.S. was galvanised into launching its first aggressive campaign, against the appalling hours of labour then prevalent on railways. It donated £6,000 to the separate Scottish Society of Railway Servants, which conducted an unsuccessful strike for a shorter working day at Christmas of that year and was later merged in the A.S.R.S. An attempt at mass victimisation on the old London and North-Western Railway in 1896 was defeated by the union. Its membership doubled and next year it initiated the first " all grades " movement for general improvements which, however, was stonewalled by the companies.

notably in the eastern counties. In the arrogant and exclusive London printing trade the despised and disregarded machine-room labourers formed a Printers' Labourers' Union, later to grow into the formidable national body we know as Natsopa. Nor were these developments without their effect on the old craft unions, whose decline in membership was sharply reversed, a doubling or trebling of the pre-1889 figures being recorded in some cases. The old exclusiveness also began to break down ; in 1892 the A.S.E. itself revised its rules so as to open its ranks to virtually all grades of engineering mechanics. It was significant of the new solidarity that between 1889-1891 over sixty new Trades Councils were established.

The New Unionism fought its first battle within the general movement over the legal eight-hour day. This had for some time been a main point of contention between the Socialists and the " old gang " in the T.U.C., and union opinion was steadily veering in its favour. It had been proclaimed a primary slogan by the Paris Congress of 1889 which reconstituted the International,[1] and was the rallying cry which made London's first May Day (in 1890), when 200,000 demonstrated to Hyde Park, an impressive manifestation of the power of the New Unionism. This was a particular triumph for the Marxist leadership of the Gasworkers (of which Eleanor Marx was bluntly described by Engels as " the boss," and whose rules were the work of Edward Aveling) ; and this union was the centre of the Legal Eight Hour Day and International Labour League, established as a follow-up of the May Day success with a view to the eventual organisation of an independent Workers' Party on the broadest possible basis. It

[1] Commonly called the Second International, which broke up with the war of 1914.

may be noted here that a new and keen internationalism was a vital feature of the time ; once again the Gasworkers were to the fore, as their early records bear witness, and the report on Britain that they, together with the Eight Hour League, presented to the Brussels International Congress in 1891 (it was drafted by the Avelings), was " generally admitted," said Will Thorne, " to be one of the best and most valuable presented to the Congress."[1]

When the Trades Union Congress came round, in September, 1890, at Liverpool, the " old gang " had their backs to the wall. John Burns and Tom Mann were present as delegates from the haughty A.S.E., which had furthermore mandated them to vote for the legal eight-hour day. After a vehement debate the resolution on this point was adopted by 193 votes to 155 and Broadhurst, in dudgeon, resigned the Congress secretaryship. The two following Congresses substantially confirmed the Socialist victory on this issue and the Norwich Congress in 1894 adopted by 219 votes to 61, on the motion of Keir Hardie, a complete nationalisation resolution.

Naturally the challenge of the New Unionism was not taken lying down by the employers. They rallied their own forces and sought means of striking back. A new dockers' strike in 1893 against the employers' " free labour registries " was defeated. The engineering employers federated and in 1897, after a long and bitter lockout, forced upon the A.S.E. their claim to be absolute masters in their own works. In two

[1] *Third Yearly Report and Balance Sheet of the National Union of Gasworkers and General Labourers of Great Britain and Ireland* (1892), pp. 5-6. For access to the unique file of the Gasworkers' early reports now in the possession of the original union's lineal successor, the National Union of General and Municipal Workers, I am indebted to the good offices of Mr. Thorne himself and Mr. Adams, of the N.U.G.M.W. head office.

of the biggest miners' strikes of the period, that of
the Federated area in 1893 and South Wales in 1898,
troops were called out at the request of the coalowners ; on the first occasion striking miners were
fired on at Featherstone in Yorkshire, and several
killed. The South Wales strike was directed against
the sliding scale, which it succeeded in killing, and
also resulted in the establishment of the South Wales
Miners' Federation. On the other hand the gearing
of wages to profits (together with detailed conciliation machinery) was applied to the Lancashire
cotton trade in the famous Brooklands agreement
which terminated the spinners' strike of 1893.

A number of influential employers combined to
form the Employers' Parliamentary Council, a
bitterly anti-union body, which subsidised an imita-
tion Pinkerton strike-breaking agency called the
Free Labour Association, headed by a renegade
trade unionist and adventurer named William
Collison. The Council also campaigned for the
promotion of new anti-union legislation. It was well
seconded by the Courts, which began to hand down
decisions in cases affecting the rights of picketing
or boycott of non-union firms that made the whole
apparently secure legal status of the unions look
extremely uncertain and hazardous by the late
'nineties.

In this developing situation it was a major disaster
that there was a divorce between the New Unionism
and Socialism (that is, revolutionary Socialism). For
this the main responsibility fell to the sectarian
S.D.F., which had misunderstood and attacked the
New Unionism from the start ; " it insisted upon
John Burns unfurling the Red Flag in the dock strike,
where such an act would have ruined the whole
movement, and instead of gaining over the dockers,

would have driven them back into the arms of the capitalists."[1]   The S.D.F. likewise refused to enter the all-embracing workers' party which the leading advanced trade unionists established in 1893 in the shape of the Independent Labour Party ; consequently the I.L.P. soon veered to the opposite error, of unsure opportunism, which could welcome a Liberal like James Ramsay MacDonald, who carefully explained that his change-over from Liberalism to the I.L.P. meant no change in his political objects !

Of especial significance for the future was the year 1895.   It marked the peak to date of the strikes against non-unionism which were becoming a feature. It witnessed the death of Frederick Engels, presaging the tragedy of the Avelings and the suicide of Eleanor Marx three years later, which shattered the little Marxist leading group.   It saw the first large-scale General Election effort by Socialist candidates, the I.L.P. putting up 28 and the S.D.F. 5 ; all were defeated, including Keir Hardie in West Ham, which he had won three years before. Following this political setback for the Socialist-New Unionist forces reactionary elements in the T.U.C. plucked up courage and at the Cardiff Congress were able to put through a series of menacing measures.   The Trades Councils, which had fathered the T.U.C. in the 'sixties, as we have seen, were excluded.   The card vote was introduced for the first time.   Those who were not union officials or working at their trade were declared ineligible as delegates (a blow at Hardie, Burns, etc.).   The effect of this was seen in the defeat of Ben Tillett for re-election to the Parliamentary Committee and the rejection of a nationalisation resolution by 607,000 to 186,000 on a card vote ; the reactionary trend continued, and at the Birming-

[1] Engels in an interview with the *Daily Chronicle*, July 1st, 1893.

ham Congress in 1897 an invitation to an international trade union congress was rejected by
317,000 votes to 282,000.[1] Some of the new unions
underwent significant internal changes. Thus a
French observer wrote of the Dockers that " the
original militant character of the union has been
modified. . . . Strike pay plays but a small part
and its amount is not even determined. On the
other hand the funeral benefit . . . is the subject of
detailed regulations."[2]

These were years in which the increase in income
from foreign investments, the growth of imperialism,
was proceeding by giant strides ; the new colonial
monopoly was coming to replace the vanished
industrial monopoly and enabling the ruling class to
continue in a different form the policy of concessions
to special sections of the working class. Real wages
were rising up to the turn of the century. Nevertheless the trade unions were feeling their way towards
the independent political movement which the
developing employers' attack upon them was rendering
essential.

[1] Of one effort by the T.U.C. at this time much was expected in
some quarters but nothing came. That was the establishment in
1899, following the severe financial strain of the engineers' lockout
two years before, of the General Federation of Trade Unions. This
body was designed essentially as a mutual insurance society and
functioned as such, despite the vague hopes that it might become a
real trade union centre and directing authority, which the T.U.C.
was not. For some time it undertook the international representation of the British movement, but ceased to do so with the reconsti-
tution of the International Federation of Trade Unions after 1918 ;
thereafter the G.F.T.U. no longer had any sort of importance for the
general trade union movement.
[2] P. de Rousiers, *Le Trade Unionisme en Angleterre* (1897), p. 184.

CHAPTER 4 : THE UNIONS ENTER POLITICS (1900-10)

DURING the 'nineties Socialist delegates to the Trades Union Congress had persistently moved for the establishment of a Parliamentary fund, with no substantial success. In 1893 the T.U.C. accepted the proposal in principle, with the added proviso that any candidates supported by such a fund should be independent of the Liberal or Conservative Parties ; but the majority was small, and nothing was done. When the matter was raised more sharply, at the Edinburgh Congress in 1896, a motion insisting that a referendum of affiliated unions should be taken was rejected by 136 votes to 62. But the Socialists persisted and a resolution drafted by I.L.P. members was proposed by the moderate Amalgamated Society of Railway Servants at the Plymouth T.U.C. in 1899 ; this resolution directed the calling of a special conference, representing trade unions, co-operative societies and Socialist organisations, to consider means of increasing Labour representation ; it was adopted on a card vote by 546,000 to 434,000, the miners and the cotton unions notably dissenting.

The special conference met in London in February, 1900. There were present 129 delegates, from trade unions totalling a membership of 500,000 and from the Socialist bodies totalling a membership of under 70,000. It was agreed to establish a separate body called the Labour Representation Committee, as a

federation of trade unions and trades councils, co-
operative societies and Socialist organisations ; an
executive was elected, consisting of seven trade
unionists, two each from the I.L.P. and the Social
Democratic Federation, and one from the Fabian
Society, while James Ramsay MacDonald, a young
Scottish expatriate politician who had recently
exchanged Liberalism for the I.L.P. (as we have
noted) was appointed secretary.[1]

For over a year the new Labour Party, as it was
soon to be called, hung fire. It attracted no substantial affiliations and at the General Election of
1900, when it put forward fifteen candidates, only
two were elected. Then, as it were overnight, there
came a sudden change when the developing legal
attack climaxed in the famous Taff Vale decision of
July 1901. This arose out of a strike of railwaymen
on the then independent Taff Vale lines in South
Wales, which was so effective that 100,000 miners
were thrown idle, and which attracted much attention
because the Company sought to introduce Collison's
" Pinkertons " as blacklegs, an attempt that the
exceptional determination and ingenuity of the picketing prevented. Fog signals were used to warn pickets
of the approach of trains bearing blacklegs, the track
was greased on inclines so that trains were brought
to a standstill through the engine wheels slipping,
enabling pickets to uncouple trucks and let them run
back to the bottom, while unattended locomotives
were expertly put out of action. Furious, the Company
went to the High Court, secured an injunction against
the union (the Amalgamated Society of Railway
Servants), which was appealed against but upheld

[1] It has often been said that many delegates voted for the relatively
unknown MacDonald in error, thinking they were voting for James
MacDonald, seeretary of the London Trades Council, and one of the
best-known Socialist trade unionists of the day.

by the House of Lords. An action for heavy damages
was likewise successful and altogether the union was
mulcted to the tune of £35,000, of which the Company's
damages amounted to £23,000. The effect of the
decision was to destroy, by what has been called a
" judicial *coup d'état*," the entire legal rights of trade
unions as established by the Acts of 1871-6, and to
make strikes " for all practical purposes absolutely
illegal."[1]

There was consequently much excitement at the
Swansea T.U.C. in September 1901, and a union rush
to affiliate to the Labour Representation Committee
began. Affiliations jumped by 100,000 within a year,
and in 1902-3 practically doubled, the figure then
standing at nearly 850,000.[2] The time was certainly
ripe for action, for there had been signs enough of
general governing class support for the anti-union
drive typified by Taff Vale. In the winter of 1901
The Times had widely featured a long series of articles
entitled " The Crisis in British Industry," which
cynically drew on the more than dubious source of
the egregious Collison and the employers who backed
him to re-hash all the hoary allegations about trade
union " ca'canny," " intimidation " and so forth,
with the apparent aim of crabbing the unions' independent political efforts.[3]

Labour by-election successes now began to point
the way to big developments ahead, as it became clear
that the existing Tory Government had no intention
of remedying the unions' new legal disabilities. Most
striking was the triumph of Will Crooks (Coopers) at
Woolwich in March 1903, when an aggressive Labour

[1] Lord Askwith, *Industrial Problems and Disputes*, p. 92.
[2] This was the moment chosen by the S.D.F. sectarians to withdraw from the L.R.C.!
[3] Hutt : A Forgotten Campaign of *The Times* against Trade
Unionism (*Modern Quarterly*. Vol. 2, No. 1).

campaign, on a free trade programme, won victory
in a Tory stronghold. But the most startling success
was reserved for the General Election of 1906, when
the biggest Liberal landslide of all time thrust the
Tories into the wilderness. Fifty Labour candidates
were put up and, to the surprise of a political world
still quaking from the seismic shocks of the Russian
Revolution of 1905, no less than twenty-nine were
returned. Yet though the working class experienced
for a space an apocalyptic uplifting, the triumph was
not really so sensational. In many cases Liberals had
withdrawn and their votes gone to the Labour men
in straight fights.

Immediate legal redress was afforded to the unions
with the passage of the Trades Disputes Act (1906).
This absolved unions of any legal responsibility for
civil damages in respect of actions by their members
or officials in furtherance of a trade dispute, and also
expressly ensured the legality of picketing. The Taff
Vale decision was thus reversed. But thereafter the
session was one of legislative sterility and the begin-
nings of disillusionment and unrest made themselves
evident. The new political expression of trade unionism was, after all, as Lenin said in 1908, only the
" first step . . . towards a conscious class policy and
a *Socialist* Workers' Party." The lack of a clear and
firmly-grasped Socialist outlook and theory had only
too practical results ; a famous historian aptly
remarked that while the Labour M.P.s of 1906 were
completely *class* representatives (the vast majority
being of working-class origin) they were just as
completely *undoctrinal,* so that astute Liberal imperialists like Lords Grey and Haldane could boast that they
found them much more " reasonable " to handle than
if they had been gentlemen.[1] And though the battle

[1] Elie Halévy, *History of the English People : Epilogue,* Vol. II, p. 91.

for the political independence of the Labour Party
had been keenly fought at its Newcastle conference
in 1903, Keir Hardie crying to the old-time Liberal-
Labour objectors :

> The opponents of independence really meant to bring
> Labour back to a policy of weak and unprincipled
> opportunism. . . . Let them beware lest they surrender
> themselves to Liberalism, which would shackle them,
> gag them, and leave them a helpless, discredited, and
> impotent mass,

it appeared in the years that followed 1906 as if those
words of warning were being literally borne out, but
by the supposedly independent Parliamentary Labour
Party under the leadership of Hardie and MacDonald.[1]

That opening Edwardian decade of the century
saw the new imperialist system come to full fruition.
New alliances abroad, with the old enemy France and
with reactionary Russia, presaged the coming conflict
with Britain's great rival, Germany. At home wealth
accumulated while men decayed. Edward VII was
a monarch after plutocracy's own heart ; there was
wholesale ennobling of wealthy men, and the sale of
honours created a scandal. The social contrasts
appeared sharper than ever ; they were searchingly
exposed in *Riches and Poverty*, a statistical study by
L. G. (later Sir Leo) Chiozza Money, a Radical publi-
cist, which was first published in 1905 and ran through
many editions. Money showed that out of a total
population of 43,000,000 no less than 38,000,000 fell
into the category of poor—more than the total population of the country forty years before.

The condition of the working class was worsening,
both relatively and absolutely. While money wages

[1] The avoidance of any clear Socialist definition of aims on the
Labour Party's part was a feature of these years (Hutt, *This Final
Crisis*, pp. 212-13).

rose hardly at all between 1900 and 1908 (only by 1 per cent.), profits rose by 12½ per cent. Further, the cost of living was steadily rising ; in the decade ending 1910 wages expressed in terms of food prices dropped by about 10 per cent. Five out of every eight adult male manual workers earned less than the absolute minimum living wage (then generally accepted as 30s. a week) and only three out of eight were above that standard. Sweating still flourished in many trades where female labour was general, and wages as low as 8s. for a full week's work were typical ; in the case of the women chainmakers of Cradley Heath, which became a national scandal, wages were from 6s. 6d. to 8s. a week, from which deductions of 2s. or more for fuel and forge-rent were taken. After much controversy the Trade Boards Act was passed in 1909 to deal with sweating, but was at first (and for several years) only applied to four industries.

Unemployment became a pressing problem. A new note was struck by stormy demonstrations in London and Glasgow and the organisation of hunger marches. Out of a Royal Commission on the Poor Law it emerged that the outrages of Bumbledom continued to flourish, and the monstrous spirit of the New Poor Law of 1834—that to be a pauper was to be a criminal—was seen to be very much alive. Trade union concern over unemployment and demands that the Parliamentary Labour Party use more drastic methods to compel the Government to act met with angry replies from MacDonald, complaining of the " uninformed criticism " of the protesters and the " utter rubbish " of their demands.

In these circumstances the strike movement began to develop. The first was small in the numbers involved but spectacular in character, and was of importance because it showed how strike action could win recognition and improved conditions. It was the music-hall strike of February 1907, in which the artists and the whole staff of twenty-two London halls took part, and the pickets numbered over 2,500. Naturally there was wide press publicity for a strike in which a leading figure was Marie Lloyd, who staged a perfect late entrance to the official inquiry that was set up, protesting that she hadn't had any breakfast (though it was half-past eleven in the morning and Marie was dressed to kill) and joyfully slapping her counsel on the back when her evidence was concluded.

Among other disputes that year there were two particularly long-drawn-out strikes on the north-east coast against wage cuts ; one of engineers lasted for seven months, one of shipwrights and joiners nearly five. In Belfast a strike of dockers was enlarged by a sympathetic strike of carters and, in the Ulster fashion, was set upon by the authorities with the utmost violence ; more especially, no doubt, since it was led by Jim Larkin and James Connolly. Troops to the number of 10,000 were called out. There were cavalry charges, while infantry fire in the working-class districts killed many and wounded scores more.

Of main importance for the future was the railway-men's All Grades movement, which now carried forward the abortive attempt of ten years earlier to compel the companies to make general concessions in wages, hours and conditions. Once again the railway companies, living up to their reputation as Capital's diehards, refused to entertain the demands and insolently denied the men's grievances. This, although an elaborate survey conducted by the Amalgamated Society of Railway Servants revealed that over 100,000, or nearly 39 per cent., of the railwaymen worked for a standard wage of 20s. a week or less (figures later confirmed by an independent census

taken by the Board of Trade). Accordingly the
A.S.R.S. and the General Railway Workers' Union
took strike ballots ; these favoured ceasing work by
the remarkable majority of 80,026 to 1,857. When,
in November 1907, a national rail strike was at hand
Mr. Lloyd George, then President of the Board of
Trade, intervened. Eventually both sides accepted
the Governmental proposal of an elaborate system of
Conciliation Boards, both local and national. But
while the men elected union nominees as their
representatives on these boards, and small sectional
ameliorations were achieved, the major demands
remained unappeased, and in any event the obstruc-
tion and evasion practised by the companies *vis-à-vis*
the boards acted as an increasing irritant.

There followed some activity on the cotton front.
The spinners, finding the Brooklands agreement
operating to their disadvantage, had formally terminated it in 1905 ; and three years later the unsatisfactory provisional arrangements which had
taken its place led to a seven weeks' strike, which
ended in a compromise generally in the operatives'
favour. There was a fair crop of local cotton strikes,
particularly over the non-union issue, and in 1910 a
lockout followed the operatives' insistence on the
reinstatement of a grinder who was dismissed from
a Shaw mill.

Among the miners there was a good deal going
forward. In 1908 the eight-hour day had been made
statutory, and the Miners' Federation had been completed by the long-delayed adhesion of the Northumberland and Durham unions. Next year there was a
dispute in Scotland, where the owners demanded a
reduction in the percentage on basis rates from
50 to 37½. This was rejected and a Federation ballot
showed a large majority for a national strike in defence

of the Scotsmen, which Mr. Winston Churchill, who
had succeeded Mr. Lloyd George at the Board of
Trade, countered by threatening a special Act for
compulsory arbitration. Against the objections of
Robert Smillie, Scottish miners' president, agreement
was eventually concluded on a recoupment basis.

This was the general picture when, in 1909, yet
another legal onslaught was launched against the
trade unions, and directly arising out of their political
activity. Once again the blow fell on the Amalgamated
Society of Railway Servants, one of whose members
named Osborne (who happened to be of that strange
breed, a Tory working man, and certainly did not act
as a free agent) brought an action to restrain the union
from using its funds for political purposes. The Courts
granted him his injunction and in so doing offered an
interpretation of the law which appeared to render
illegal not only any political activity in the Parliamentary sense, but any union association in bodies
like Trades Councils or the T.U.C.

Other injunctions followed; but the Liberal
Government, preoccupied with Mr. Lloyd George's
celebrated Budget and the " Peers v. People " campaign, showed no anxiety to remedy this new travesty
of law which the judges had produced.[1] The immediate
effect was to give some fillip to the declining fortunes
of the Labour Party among the unions; but still
more to demonstrate to the mass of trade unionists
the kind of enemy they were up against and to fan
still further the fires of unrest.

[1] The Trade Union Act of 1913 was a tardy and grudging attempt,
of a most unsatisfactory kind, to regularise the position. Henceforth
unions had to establish separate political funds, raised by a specific
levy, and objectors were given the right to " contract-out."

CHAPTER 5 : THE GREAT OFFENSIVE (1910-14)

THE four brief years that ran from the accession of George V to the outbreak of the first World War were of outstanding importance in the history of trade unionism. They were the years of the " Labour unrest "—most widespread the country had ever known—constantly headlined in every newspaper and the staple theme of publicists of all brands. Nor was this the unrest of a working class whose conditions are being attacked and is rallying to their defence ; it was the unrest that pushes men forward to counter-attack, to open an offensive all along the line for new and positive objectives ; it was to draw the comment from Lenin[1] that :

> the masses of the English workers are slowly but surely taking a new path—from the defence of the petty privileges of the labour aristocracy to the great heroic struggle of the masses themselves for a new system of society.

Symptomatic was the remarkably rapid growth of the unions, which counted a total membership of under $2\frac{1}{2}$ millions at the beginning of this short period and nearly 4 millions at its end ; in the same period T.U.C. affiliations rose from rather over $1\frac{1}{2}$ millions to nearly $2\frac{1}{4}$ millions. The disillusionment with the Labour Party, under its I.L.P. leadership, and the fact that no authoritative revolutionary party had

[1] In an article written in 1913 ; quoted in *Lenin on Britain*, p. 130.

emerged from the Socialist sects, gave this great movement of revolt its predominantly trade union, and within the unions its rank-and-file, character.

Distrust of " politics " was heightened by the Liberal Government's attempt at what has been suggestively called the " sterilising " of the Labour movement. The Lloyd Georgian social reform policy, with its establishment of Trade Boards, Labour exchanges, National Insurance, provided large numbers of posts in the State bureaucracy which did not require the ordinary entrance examination. These posts, which were estimated to number some 4,000 to 5,000, formed a kind of " spoils system " with which to reward aspiring trade union officials, the products of University tutorial classes and so forth.[1]

The movement of 1910-14 carried forward the initiative of 1889 and the New Unionism. Again the big battles were fought by the labouring mass, with the dockers in the van ; to them being added other transport workers, miners, railwaymen. Transport trade unionism registered the biggest advances of any, gaining nearly half a million new members in these years. The organisation of general labourers also pushed rapidly ahead (thus the small Workers' Union, with only 5,000 members in 111 branches in 1910, expanded during 1911-13 to 91,000 members in 567 branches).

There were, however, important new features. The Syndicalist propaganda of revolutionary trade unionism, of which Tom Mann was the leading exponent, had considerable effect. Organisation by industry, supplanting separate organisation by craft, became the slogan of the advanced young men in the movement ; and such doctrines of wider unity and solidarity found a natural corollary in the preaching and

[1] Halévy, *op. cit.*, pp. 438-40.

practising of the sympathetic strike, with its final extension the general strike. Propagating these new lines in union policy there developed specific militant groups and movements among the rank and file. These were of particular importance among the South Wales miners, where the unofficial Reform Movement, as it styled itself, produced its own local organs and aroused frantic capitalist denunciations with the publication of a famous militant pamphlet, *The Miners' Next Step* (1912)[1]; among the railwaymen, whose union amalgamation was hailed as a victory and an example by the industrial unionists; among the craft-divided building trades, where the " amalgamationists " were an active force and a new all-in organisation, the Building Workers' Industrial Union, entered on a brief career; and among the engineers, where active spirits in the workshops, particularly on the Clyde, were spreading the new ideas that were to come to such striking fruition in 1914-18. Finally, there was a marked advance in women's trade union activity, the National Federation of Women Workers being formed to cater for women in unorganised trades, and there were a number of women's strikes. The high point was the Bermondsey women's " rising " of August 1911, when a couple of dozen separate factories spontaneously struck, and after three hectic weeks wage advances were won in eighteen of them.

Reactions of the new spirit were marked among many of the old craft unions. A lockout of boiler-

[1] The Unofficial Movement's campaign for union reorganisation and centralisation brought it into sharp conflict with the old leaders, notably Mr. William Brace and " Mabon " Abraham, who " breathed fire and blood against the frothy demagogues of syndicalism," both in the Federation and in the local coalowners' press. The Unofficial Movement was responsible for pressing the idea of the Triple Alliance of miners, railwaymen and transport workers (Ness Edwards, *History of the South Wales Miners' Federation*, Vol. I, pp. 66-78).

makers in 1910, following sporadic strikes, was an example ; for as the dispute lengthened so the votes against settlement rose. In 1911 the haughty London Society of Compositors conducted the first complete strike of its trade (newspapers excluded), and the lively daily strike sheet that the comps. produced, the *Daily Herald*, preluded its regular appearance, the following year, as the first Labour daily, conducted by George Lansbury and his friends.[1] At the turn of the year the Lancashire weavers struck against non-unionism and were locked out, a type of dispute that was to become widespread in many trades (especially building). The A.S.E. itself reacted to the pressure of events and new ideas, and in 1912 revised its rules so as to open its ranks to every worker, of whatever degree of skill, in engineering.[2]

Turning now to the major movements we may begin with the transport workers. In November 1910 the several unions of dockers and other transport men had gathered their forces into the Transport Workers' Federation. With the rising cost of living and the failure to tackle the problem of casualisation the dockers were by this time virtually no better off than they had been in 1889 ; and a strike by the seamen in June 1911 for a uniform scale at all ports and other improvements in conditions, accompanied by stormy outbursts at Southampton and Hull, produced an immediate reaction on the waterfront. The dockers and carters in Manchester struck and in July the port

[1] It was followed in November 1912 by the *Daily Citizen* as an official trade union and Labour Party organ. In contrast to the free-for-all, emotional rebelliousness of the *Herald* the *Citizen* reflected all too well the uninspiring contemporary leadership of Labour, and though the unions raised in all £200,000 of capital for it, within the first year of the war it came to an unsung end.

[2] Three years later, however, the revision was rescinded. Very few had joined in the new Class F membership that had been established.

of London was closed down by a strike exceeding in magnitude and effectiveness even its great predecessor. The dockers demanded that their " tanner " be raised to 8d., with 1s. an hour for overtime. Other demands were put forward by the stevedores, gasworkers, carters, coal-porters, tugmen, grain porters and so on.

Faced with this united movement the Port of London Authority, headed by Lord Devonport, and with the support of the Liberal Government, point-blank refused any negotiations. At the request of Mr. Winston Churchill, now Home Secretary, the War Office reinforced the London garrison and took the gravely provocative step of threatening to dispatch 25,000 troops to the docks to break the strike by doing the dockers' work.[1] Tension became acute. Daily demonstrations of the strikers on Tower Hill were of unprecedented size, the accompanying marches through the City scoring as many as 100,000 participants. Eventually the Government recoiled from action that would certainly have resulted in insurrection, persuaded the port authorities to meet the unions, and a subsequent arbitration award conceded most of the men's demands, including the basic 8d. an hour and the 1s. an hour overtime.

Parallel movements had taken place in other ports (also registering substantial gains), of which that at Liverpool almost amounted to civil war. Here there had been a general transport strike, embracing dockers, seamen, carters, tramwaymen, railwaymen, a total of 70,000 being out. Tom Mann was the leading figure and a great outcry was caused by the police brutality in charging a monster demonstration on St. George's Plateau. Warships were moored in the Mersey, their guns trained on the city. The troops were called out

[1] Webb, *op. cit.*, p. 501.

and two workers were shot when a crowd of demonstrators, said to be attempting a rescue of prisoners, were fired on. So alarmed were the authorities that the local Territorials, who included many trade unionists and who at that time kept their arms at home, were peremptorily ordered to remove the bolts from their rifles and turn them in at headquarters.[1]

The successes scored by these strikes, however, left the waterfront far from quiet. In January 1912 the Glasgow dockers struck and in May the men on the Thames and the Medway were in action again. There had been breaches of the 1911 agreement, it was claimed, and there was strong feeling on the issue of non-unionism and the recognition of the Transport Workers' Federation ticket, it being asserted that the employers were definitely discriminating against trade unionists. The strike brought 100,000 men out in London, but did not secure a wide national response, some 20,000 men only striking at provincial ports. Despite Government intervention Lord Devonport and his associates this time refused to budge an inch, simply stating that if work were resumed they would undertake to observe the 1911 agreement and to consider representations. Yet even when at the end of July the strike committee decided to call off the struggle, the dockers, though now enduring acute privation, unanimously resolved to continue ; work was, however, resumed a week later.

The big transport struggles of the summer of 1911 touched off the discontent that had been rapidly rising among the railwaymen as a result of the unsatisfactory settlement of 1907. Spontaneous and unofficial local strikes by railwaymen at Liverpool,

[1] For this interesting item of history I am indebted to the personal recollections of Mr. H. Kelly, now Education Secretary of the Liverpool Co-operative Society.

Manchester and some other centres produced a general
demand for a national strike. Uniting their forces the
executives of the railway unions thereupon dispatched
a twenty-four hours' ultimatum to the companies.
The Government intervened, and once again showed
their solidarity with the employers. The Prime
Minister (Mr. Asquith), addressing the union representatives in the most hostile and bellicose fashion,
offered a vague Royal Commission and intimated
that the Government would use military force to the
limit to break any strike. " Then your blood be on
your own head," he retorted when the empty offer
was rejected and the unions issued their orders for
the first national railway strike. " Blood " was the
operative word, for

> at the instance of Mr. Winston Churchill . . . an over-
> powering display was made with the troops, which were
> sent to Manchester and other places, without requisition
> by the civil authorities, at the mere request of the
> Companies. In fact, a policy of repression had been
> decided on, and bloodshed was near at hand.[1]

At Llanelly a strike demonstration was fired on and
among the numerous casualties two were fatal;
intense anger was aroused and the " massacre "
denounced in Parliament.

While the strike was not complete—200,000 railwaymen came out—its entire disorganisation of the
railway service was speedily bringing the whole of
industry to a standstill. The Government found itself
compelled to abandon the Churchillian shoot-'em-
down position, using as a pretext the critical international situation (it was the time of the Agadir
incident). So the railway companies were forced to
meet the unions for the first time, an inquiry was held,
and after renewed company obduracy was overcome

[1] Webb, *op. cit.*, p. 529.

by the threat of a further strike agreement was finally reached. The Conciliation Boards were reformed and permitted to have union representatives as secretaries, thus according the unions a sort of backdoor *de facto* recognition.

As a result of this strike railway trade unionism was transformed. Some idea of the fillip that was given to organisation can be got from the example of the Railway Clerks' Association, youngest of the railway unions, which had only 10,000 members in 1910, but which trebled its membership in the three years following the strike. The big event, however, was the establishment in 1913, after long negotiations, of the National Union of Railwaymen, a fusion of the A.S.R.S., the General Railway Workers' Union and the small United Pointsmen and Signalmen; the craft-conscious Associated Society of Locomotive Engineers and Firemen stood aloof. For the first time a union took its stand frankly on the principle of Industrial Unionism, declaring its object to be the organisation of every worker employed on or in connection with a railway, no matter what his grade or craft.[1] Not less significant was the structure and functioning of the constitution of this twentieth-century "New Model." It combined an elaborate representative apparatus—Annual General Meeting, Executive Committee with sectional sub-committees, District Councils—with a concentration of extensive powers in the hands of the Executive, who by rule initiate and conduct all trade movements and are not necessarily bound by any ballot vote of the members, and not least in the hands of the general officers, a

[1] Thereby challenging, not only the A.S.L.E.F., with whom a bitter feud began, but also the engineering and other craft unions catering for the mechanics in the railway shops. Demarcation disputes between the N.U.R. and the craft unions over the shopmen were to become endemic.

circumstance reflected in the long domination of
J. H. Thomas as general secretary.

The opening skirmishes of the miners' struggle
ante-dated the transport and railway strikes but did
not reach their climax till later. In the autumn of
1910 disputes over payment for abnormal places in
the pit produced a bitter strike of the 10,000 miners
employed by the Cambrian Combine in the Rhondda
Valleys. The arrogant attitude of the owners, headed
by the late D. A. Thomas (Lord Rhondda), aroused a
blaze of resentment and there were stormy demonstrations. Metropolitan police and troops were sent up
the valleys and clashed with strikers at Tonypandy.
Throughout 1911 these parts of the South Wales coalfield continued in a ferment of local strikes ; meantime
the Miners' Federation was raising nationally the
abnormal-place issue and negotiating for district
minima, but without success.

A delegate conference of the M.F.G.B. in December
1911 decided to take a ballot for a national strike to
establish the principle of a minimum wage—5s. a shift
for men, 2s. for boys ; when the vote was declared in
January 1912 it showed a majority of 445,800 to
115,271 in favour of a strike. The owners, utterly blind
to the development of opinion among the miners,
refused to accept the minimum wage as a principle
but said they were prepared to resume the discussion
of payment for abnormal places. By March 1st the
strike was complete. A million miners ceased work as
one man ; and the first national miners' strike proved
to be, not merely the vastest labour conflict ever
known up to that time in this country, but the most
thorough and sensational industrial close-down. The
Government hastily intervened, drafted a Minimum
Wage Bill, and rushed it into law by the end of
March. This measure did not meet the miners'

demands for a specified national minimum, instead prescribing machinery for the determination of district minima. A ballot favoured continuing the strike by 244,011 votes to 201,013, but a delegate conference on April 6th agreed to resume work.[1] The Miners' Federation had strikingly demonstrated its offensive power, and within a year the number of trade unionists in mining had leapt by nearly 160,000 to over 900,000. In a wider sense, as Lenin wrote :

> The miners' strike positively represents a new epoch. . . . Since the strike the British proletariat *is no longer the same*. The workers have learned to fight. They have discovered the *path* which will lead to victory. They have realised their power. . . . A change has taken place in the relation of social forces in England which cannot be expressed in figures, but which everyone feels.[2]

After the transport workers, the railwaymen and the miners had thus fought their major engagements the offensive branched out into an unprecedented series of smaller strikes affecting almost all branches of industry. The year 1913 was remarkable, to quote the official report, for its number of disputes—" far exceeding the number recorded in any previous year. Practically all the main groups of trades were affected by the increase in the number of disputes, notably the building, metal, engineering and shipbuilding, and textile trades," though no one dispute involved more than 50,000 workers. Typical of capitalist concern was the newspaper comment :

> Perhaps the most salient feature of this turmoil at the moment is the general spirit of revolt, not only against employers of all kinds, but also against leaders and

[1] On the principle that a two-thirds majority is necessary for the continuance of a strike.
[2] *Lenin on Britain*, pp. 106-7.

majorities, and Parliamentary or any kind of constitutional and orderly action.[1]

The " general spirit of revolt " seized the normally
quiescent miscellaneous metal trades of Birmingham
and the Black Country. Girl workers at Dudley,
declaring simply that they could no longer live on
their wages, came out on strike (for a minimum wage of
23s. a week). In the spring and summer of 1913 the
numbers out in various metal, tube and nut and bolt
works totalled 50,000 ; in July a ballot of thousands
to ninety-nine rejected the employers' terms, and
three contingents of strikers marched to London.
Wage increases were granted and machinery for
settling disputes established.

The most historic movement of the year did not,
however, take place in this island. It was the general
strike in Dublin in August and September, the baptism
of fire of the Irish Transport and General Workers'
Union under the revolutionary leadership of James
Connolly and Jim Larkin. This fierce struggle of 80,000
Dublin workers aroused an extraordinary response
here. Solidarity was symbolised in the enthusiastic
dispatch through the co-operative movement of a
foodship to Dublin, and in the sympathetic strikes in
which some 7,000 British railwaymen took part ; on
the other hand Labour Party leaders like Philip
Snowden went out of their way to attack the militant
union policy. The wave of unlimited police terror
launched against the Dublin strikers, an orgy of
outrage and bludgeoning that resulted in the killing
of two workers and the wounding of 400, with over
200 arrests, caused a storm of rage to sweep the working-class movement. Nor did the reaction stop at rage ;
new conclusions were drawn ; talk of arming the
workers, of general strikes and revolutionary action

[1] Quoted in Askwith, *op. cit.*, p. 347.

spread through the trade unions. Thus at the Trades Union Congress in Manchester, Robert Smillie, president of the Miners' Federation, said :

> If revolution is going to be forced upon my people by such action as has been taken in Dublin and elsewhere I say it is our duty, legal or illegal, to train our people to defend themselves. . . . It is the duty of the greater trade union movement, when a question of this gravity arises, to discuss seriously the idea of a strike of all the workers.[1]

Everything pointed to the maturing of a first-class political and social crisis in the latter part of 1914. Already in November 1913 Lord Askwith, the leading official industrial mediator, told a select audience that " within a comparatively short time there may be movements in this country coming to a head of which recent events have been a small foreshadowing." The cost of living continued to rise, and the trade union rank and file redoubled their efforts at building up union organisation, the number of strikes against non-unionism steadily increasing. This last was a special feature of the London building trades during 1913, where the strikes mostly took place against the will of the union executives and led at the beginning of 1914 to a general London lockout. The employers demanded that the unions penalise their members who might strike without executive authority, that the unions give a financial bond which would be forfeit in the event of strikes in violation of the working rules of the industry, and finally—a new edition of the " document "—that each individual worker sign a personal agreement to work quietly with non-unionists, under penalty of a pound fine. The lockout lasted for over six months, and settlement proposals were rejected by ballot ; accordingly the

[1] *Report of the Trades Union Congress*, Manchester, 1913, p. 72.

employers decided on a national lockout. They were
forestalled by the outbreak of war.

The builders' battle was only one of many. The
official figures told their own story. While the number
of disputes in 1908 averaged little over 30 a month,
rising to nearly 75 a month in 1911, in the latter half
of 1913 and the first half of 1914 the tempo literally
doubled, something like 150 strikes a month being
recorded. " British trade unionism," say the Webbs,
" was in fact in the summer of 1914 working up for an
almost revolutionary outburst of gigantic industrial
disputes."[1]   The big battalions were again making
ready for the fray. The miners were preparing new
claims for the autumn. The transport workers were
organising fast. A new forward movement by the
railwaymen, once more exasperated by the quibbling
and trickery of the companies in the operation of the
Conciliation Boards, was at hand ; and it was evident
that this would bear a political character. Transcending questions of wages and hours, the railwaymen gave
a new angle to the oft-repeated demand for the
nationalisation of the railways, hardy annual of so
many conferences. They made it clear that what they
wanted was a voice in control ; a resolution prepared
by the N.U.R. for submission to the 1914 T.U.C.
stated that " no system of State ownership of the
railways will be acceptable to organised railwaymen
which does not guarantee to them their full political
and social rights " and " allow them a due measure
of control and responsibility in the safe and efficient
working of the railway system." Finally, the agreement in the engineering industry was due to end and
wide demands on wages, hours and conditions generally were expected.

What was most significant of all about these indica-

[1] Webb, *op. cit.*, p. 690.

tions of coming struggles was that the principal combatants were forging among themselves a new and wider unity. On the initiative of the Miners' Federation—under pressure of its own rank-and-file militants —proposals had been made for the establishment of an alliance for mutual aid with the railwaymen and the transport workers. In 1914 this was agreed to by the N.U.R. and the Transport Workers' Federation, and the Triple Alliance, as it was immediately called, took shape. This powerful new alignment of forces took place on a background of steadily sharpening militant political trends among the union rank and file who, in contrast to the complacent and now hopelessly Liberalised MacDonaldite leadership of the Labour Party, realised that :

> the paths of advancement were narrow, devious and blocked. . . . There was effervescence, and behind the effervescence there were movements growing, with demands for shorter working hours, more pay and more power, both over industry and in the government of the country. The young men were ready to move. . . . There was a spirit of unrest which vaguely expressed itself in an oft-heard phrase—" wait till the autumn."[1]

It was not as if this movement, and such events as the founding of the Triple Alliance, occurred in an otherwise normal atmosphere. The Home Rule crisis, with the Tory-Ulster rebellion of March 1914, had presented the governing class with an extremely grave situation. After that wild incitement to, and preparation for, civil war by the noble landlords, the Tory politicians and the Army officers, it might well be felt that " the working class will now very quickly shake off its Philistine faith in the scrap of paper that is called English law and Constitution, which the English aristocrats have torn up before the eyes of

[1] Askwith, *op. cit.*, pp. 353, 356.

the whole people."[1] At a meeting in the City on
July 17th, 1914, Mr. Lloyd George said openly that
with Labour " insurrection " and the Irish crisis
coinciding " the situation will be the gravest with
which any Government has had to deal for centuries."[2]
A Conservative historian subsequently wrote of those
days that " if the war peril from Germany delayed
much longer to materialise, it seemed quite on the
cards that it might be forestalled by revolution . . .
it is a question whether international will not be
anticipated by civil war."[3]

In that same July of 1914 there came another
instance of the new spirit, and in a highly inconvenient
quarter. There was a strike at Woolwich Arsenal for
the reinstatement of a dismissed worker. But the
problems that looked so lowering and full of menace
to the existing order that July vanished—or so it
seemed—in the early days of August. At the beginning of that month there were 100 strikes in progress ;
at the end of the month only twenty. The war with
Germany had " materialised " in time to dissipate
an internal crisis as well as to attempt the solution
of an external one.

[1] *Lenin on Britain*, p. 58.
[2] Quoted in Halévy, *op. cit.*, p. 478.
[3] Esmé Wingfield-Stratford, *The Victorian Aftermath*, p. 310.

CHAPTER 6 : " PART OF THE SOCIAL MACHINERY OF THE STATE " (1914-18)

THE first World War marked a decisive break for the trade union movement and introduced an entirely new period. It brought what the Webbs called a " revolutionary transformation of the social and political standing of the official representatives of the trade union world " ; this being an essential element in the " recognition " of the union apparatus as " part of the social machinery of the State."[1] The reason for this was simple. " If organised Labour had been against the war it is safe to say that the national effort could not have been maintained "[2] ; and without the fullest collaboration of the union leaders and the machine they controlled, the working class could not be harnessed to the war chariot of imperialism. That collaboration could not be secured by the old-fashioned co-operation of the unions with the employers ; it required a direct and organised relation between the unions and the central organ of class rule, the State ; a relation which it was hoped to consolidate by drawing the union leaders into the State machine.

This vital change was the result of the abandonment by the union leaders, in common with their Labour Party colleagues and the majority of the old Socialist

[1] Webb, *op. cit.*, p. 635.
[2] *Ibid.*, p. 692.

69

International, of their repeated pre-war pledges to
prevent war or to end it by revolutionary means if it
did break out. The stages of that abandonment were
interesting. On August 1st Arthur Henderson and
Keir Hardie, as international representatives of the
British movement, issued a manifesto condemning
the " infamy " of war on the side of " Russian
despotism " and concluding " Workers, stand together
therefore for peace! Combine and conquer the
militarist enemy and the self-seeking imperialists,
to-day once and for all. . . . Down with class rule!
Down with the rule of brute force! Down with war!
Up with the peaceful rule of the people! " These
sentiments were repeated next day in a resolution
adopted by a united anti-war demonstration in
Trafalgar Square addressed by leading trade unionists
like Henderson and Will Thorne, by George Lansbury,
Hardie and others. On August 4th Britain declared
war on Germany. Three days later the Parliamentary
Labour Party decided to make no pronouncement on
the vote for war credits and Henderson was elected
leader in place of Ramsay MacDonald, who resigned.
A week after that the postponement " for a short
time " of the annual T.U.C. was announced ; the
postponement turned out to be cancellation. Before
the end of August an " industrial truce " was declared
by a conference of the T.U.C. Parliamentary Committee, the Labour Party Executive and the Management Committee of the General Federation of Trade
Unions. At the beginning of September the T.U.C.
Committee issued a manifesto to all trade unionists
commending the Labour Party's decision to participate in an " all-Party " recruiting campaign, and
declaring that " upon the result of the struggle in
which this country is now engaged rest the preserva-
tion and maintenance of free and unfettered demo-

cratic government." On October 15th the T.U.C.
joined with Labour M.P.s and other leaders to issue a
definitive statement of views on the war; "the
victory of Germany would mean the death of democracy in Europe," it was asserted.

" Business as usual " was the complacent slogan of
the opening months of the war ; but it soon appeared
that business was very much not as usual. Dislocation
of industry, the urgent demand for munitions (which
led to wholesale attacks on existing standards and
what an official historian has called " something little
short of a debauch of long hours "), and a steeply
rising cost of living, produced a wave of unrest and a
number of local unofficial strikes. While industrial
disputes had dwindled to twenty by the end of August
1914, they rose to seventy-four in March 1915. Most
important was the strike of engineers on the Clyde in
February, led by a " Central Withdrawal of Labour
Committee " appointed by the men in the shops ;
significant also was a strike at the great Elswick works
of Armstrong Whitworths against the putting of
unskilled men to skilled work. Accordingly the
Government summoned the principal union leaders
to a conference at the Treasury in February 1915. By
the agreement there concluded, to which the miners
refused to be party, " the trade union lamb has lain
down with the capitalist lion "[1] and the process began
which, statutorily confirmed by the Munitions of War
Acts (1915-17), was to produce " virtually ' industrial
conscription '." [2] The right to strike was abandoned
" for the duration," its place being taken by Government arbitration ; all trade union rules and conditions were suspended ; " dilution " of labour on the
most massive scale was initiated ; the introduction of

[1] *The Herald*, July 17th, 1915.
[2] Webb, *op. cit.*, p. 639.

" leaving certificates " practically tied the worker to his job.

To induce the union leaders thus to surrender every hard-earned standard, and to disarm completely into the bargain, the Government gave three pledges. The first was that the suspended union conditions should be restored in full after the war ; the second was that the removal of all restrictions should in no way redound to the private profit of the employers ; the third was that a minimum wage for war work should be ensured, together with the payment of wages to " dilutees " identical with those previously paid to skilled men on the same job. Every one of these pledges was dishonoured. Trade union conditions were not restored ; all that the Government did in 1919 was to enable workers to take legal action against employers who failed to restore them, such restoration to be obligatory for only one year. A " munitions levy " imposed in 1916 to check profits was abolished within a year in favour of the farcical Excess Profits Duty ; so that the war produced " the most amazing profits that this country has ever witnessed. . . . Above £4,000,000,000 of profits made owing to the war and during the war and in excess of the profits made before the war."[1] There were no identical wages for " dilutees," notably the women, and unending disputation and shuffling about the enforcement of any minimum wage. To sum it up :

The trade unionists, in fact, who had at the outset of the war patriotically refrained from bargaining as to the price of their aid, were, on the whole, " done " at its close. Though here and there particular sections had received exceptionally high earnings in the time of stress, the rates of wages, taking industry as a whole, did not, as the Government returns prove, rise either

[1] Lord Buckmaster in the House of Lords, February 18th, 1919.

so quickly or so high as the cost of living ; so that, whilst many persons suffered great hardship, the great majority of wage-earners found the product in commodities of their rates of pay in 1919 less rather than more than it was in 1913.[1]

Of special interest was the position in the aircraft industry, then in its infancy but already of prime military importance. The official union history subsequently revealed " how the Government was prepared even to jeopardise the winning of the war in its anxiety to propitiate the employers who were profiteering at the expense of the aircraft workers." [2] Events also showed how Government-employer " intolerable sweating " could be beaten, given strong workshop organisation and a willingness on the part of the unions themselves to unite and fight. As the newest of the war industries aircraft manufacture was then in a chaotic state ; in London, for instance, twenty-three factories paid eleven distinct and different district rates, usually below the normal rate for the class of work. Men were drawn to aircraft from many woodworking trades, covered by a dozen different unions. All the unions were represented, however, in a London District Aircraft Workers' Committee, set up in 1914 ; but two years' agitation brought no improvement and it required the handing in of strike notices[3] by 90 per cent. of the London men to secure even a limited wage concession. No general minimum rate was conceded, and this was taken up as a national issue by the National Woodworkers' Aircraft Committee which the unions united to form. In addition the Committee fought against the efforts of the employers, fully backed by the Government, to

[1] Webb, op. cit., pp. 643-4.
[2] S. Higenbottam, Our Society's History (official history of the Amalgamated Society of Woodworkers : Manchester, 1939), p. 212.
[3] Actually collective application for " leaving certificates."

generalise piecework which, the men contended, " involves danger to lives by hasty and often culpable workmanship." The Government replied :

That is our responsibility and not your responsibility. The lives of the pilots are the business of the Government, and if the Government come to the conclusion that they can afford to take risks in order to get better production, you must leave that to the wisdom of the Government.

Mr. Winston Churchill was Minister of Munitions at that time and particularly insisted on the piecework system, against which a ballot of the aircraft workers showed a huge majority. The Minister eventually agreed, in November 1917, to concede the minimum wage and other points ; but weeks passed and the necessary ministerial Order to enforce the agreement was never issued. When the chairman of the Employers' Federation coolly told the unions that " the Ministry agreeing to sign an agreement, when all is said and done, does not have the slightest effect and weight with us," arrangements were made in February 1918 for a national aircraft strike. At once the National Committee were summoned to the Ministerial presence ; let the official history finish the tale :

Churchill was supported by an imposing array of naval and military chiefs, and did his best to intimidate the Aircraft Committee by citing the various Acts which gave him power to deal with leaders who caused a national stoppage. . . . The threat to refuse to allow the strike to be called was met by the information that it had *already* been arranged and that all aircraft woodworkers in the United Kingdom would cease work on February 9th *unless* an order was issued by the Government that the employers must observe the terms of the National Agreement. This put Churchill in a quandary ; he might arrest the members of the Committee but he could not prevent over 60,000 men walking away from their work. Finally he capitulated on the evening of February 8th, 1918.[1]

The aircraft position was unusual in its combination of shop organisation with union leadership. The general feature of 1914-18 was the development of shop leadership in place of the disarmed union machine. In engineering the shop stewards, already existing as card inspectors and reporters to their union district committees, were transformed into workshop representatives and leaders. This was the more marked when, as it frequently happened, the stewards no longer functioned as official union appointees but as the unofficial delegates of all the workers in their shop, irrespective of union membership. Here was the organisation " at the point of production " which was the workers' answer to collaboration with the State machine.

Of this development the Clyde strike in 1915 was an early and significant symptom. It arose out of a dispute that was maturing before the war. In June 1914 the Glasgow District Committee of the Amalgamated Society of Engineers, faced with the anomaly that their rate was markedly less than that in other districts, had decided on an application for a 2d. an hour increase. When this came to be made, at the turn of the year, the employers, after an exasperating delay, would not concede more than ½d. At this point the men in the shops took things into their own hands ; led by their stewards, engineers in fifteen establishments, including the large armament firms, ceased overtime on all war contracts. This step was strongly opposed by the A.S.E. Executive, who on February 12th joined with the employers in recommending the men to accept a ¾d. an hour increase, provocatively

[1] Higenbottam, *op. cit.*, pp. 211-12.

delaying the necessary ballot till March 9th. This was the last straw. Shop after shop came out on strike, the shop stewards gathering to form the Central Withdrawal of Labour Committee mentioned above.

This Committee bluntly claimed exclusive rights of negotiation and settlement, on the grounds (i) that the union officials were not, owing to Government pressure, free agents, and (ii) that it was the only fully representative body—-i.e. representing all the unions concerned—acting on the men's behalf. The A.S.E. ballot, which rejected the employers' offer by 8,927 votes to 829, implicitly confirmed these claims ; and the Committee showed its strength by holding the men out till March 4th, three days after the expiry of a Government ultimatum threatening compulsory arbitration. An immediate increase of 1d. an hour, with corresponding percentage increases in piece rates, was won.

The next movement of magnitude was the strike of South Wales miners in July 1915. The M.F.G.B. had refused to be parties to the Treasury Agreement and the Welsh valleys, as we have seen, had pioneered in militant organisation in the pits. There had long been dissatisfaction with the five-year agreement of 1910, now aggravated by the brazen way in which the coalowners " persistently endeavoured to make the war redound to their own advantage "[1] ; and the demands of the South Wales Miners' Federation for a new agreement with wage increases and other concessions were first insolently waved aside. Then the Government intervened, through Mr. (later Lord) Runciman, President of the Board of Trade ; his handling of the position " practically invited a strike,"[2] on which the Federation decided by a

[1] *Labour Year Book*, 1916, p. 79.   [2] *Ibid.*, p. 78.

majority of 42,850. Hastily the Government " proclaimed " the South Wales coalfield under the punitive provisions of the Munitions Act. But 200,000 miners were not to be deterred by this threat or the wild campaign of vilification which instantly opened up throughout the entire capitalist press. They struck as one man and in less than a week the Government turned about, overrode the coalowners and conceded the main points at issue.

It was the Clyde strike, however, that marked the emergence of the shop stewards as the core of an entirely new form of workshop organisation. Out of the strike there arose the Clyde Workers' Committee, pledged to resist the Munitions Act, support of which by the union officials it stigmatised as " an act of treachery to the working class," and further proclaiming as its objects :

> to obtain an ever-increasing control over workshop conditions, to regulate the terms upon which workers shall be employed, and to organise the workers upon a class basis and to maintain the class struggle until the overthrow of the wages system, the freedom of the workers and the establishment of industrial democracy have been attained.

Workers' Committees on the Clyde model were established in other centres (London, Sheffield, etc.) and in 1916 the National Shop Stewards' and Workers' Committee Movement was formed. The unit of organisation was the Shop Committee, composed of the stewards elected in the particular shop or department ; representatives of the various shop committees formed the Works or Plant Committee ; these in turn sent their representatives to constitute the Local or District Committees, which together elected the National Administrative Council of the movement.

It was prescribed that stewards and all officers of the
movement should be elected for six months, though
eligible for re-election, and that frequent shop meetings
should be held. Two weekly papers were established
as shop stewards' organs, *The Worker* in Glasgow and
Solidarity in London.

While the shop stewards' movement adhered to the
above-quoted revolutionary objects it did not achieve
clarity on the central problem of leadership. The
Syndicalist antipathy to " leaders " and " politics "
was still strongly marked. The National Movement's
constitution laid it down that " no committee shall
have executive power, all questions of policy and
action being referred back to the rank and file."
Several leading shop stewards, especially on the Clyde,
came from the Socialist Labour Party, a strait sect
which on principle forbade its members to accept any
union office. Uncomprehending hostility to the
conception of a revolutionary working-class political
party was ideally expressed on a later occasion by
Jack Tanner (now president of the Amalgamated
Engineering Union) when, as shop stewards' delegate
to the Second Congress of the Communist International
in Moscow in 1920, he was gently but firmly taken to
task on this very subject by Lenin himself in an historic
debate.[1]

The Clyde Workers' Committee, of which William
Gallacher was chairman, enjoyed the political guidance
of John McLean, famous agitator and educator,
outstanding revolutionary Socialist and proponent
of the Bolshevik policy of revolutionary struggle
against the war and for the overthrow of the capitalist
régime. By the wide scope of its activities it built a
position of unparalleled influence, so that when Mr.
Lloyd George as Prime Minister visited Glasgow, with

[1] See *Lenin on Britain*, pp. 263-4.

Mr. Arthur Henderson in tow, he was compelled to approach the Committee to organise a meeting of shop stewards ; and then had to endure the chagrin of being shouted down. The Committee was associated with the big rent strikes which were virtually a popular uprising, and organised efficient protection for meetings and demonstrations against " patriotic " hooligans. Nor was it weakened by persecution, such as met it after its conduct of a strike at Parkhead Forge in 1916, supported by sympathetic strikes at three other large works, over the rights of shop stewards to carry out their representative duties. A number of stewards, leading members of the Committee, were arbitrarily deported from Clydeside ; among them were David Kirkwood, M.P., and the late Arthur McManus, first chairman of the Communist Party. Others were arrested and imprisoned, Gallacher getting twelve months and John McLean three years' penal servitude.

When 1917 brought the Russian Revolution the repercussions were widespread. It was the War's peak year for strikes in engineering, over 300,000 workers being involved and the " days lost " totalling nearly 2½ million. Not just shop stewards on the spot, but their new national movement, stood decisively in the lead. There were strikes at Barrow and on the Tyne in March, and an important Coventry strike in November. Biggest of all were the May strikes, which swept the Clyde, Sheffield, London and other munition centres like a tidal wave in protest against the extension of dilution and the operation of the Munitions Act ; the strikers defied a peremptory Government order to resume work and eight leaders of the Shop Stewards Movement were arrested ; but a settlement was speedily reached on terms agreeable to the men and the arrested leaders were released.

The Government had been driven to face the fact that the policy of coercion was breaking down. Up to July 1916 over 1,000 workers were convicted under the Munitions Act for strike activities ; but strikes continued and grew bigger. So general was the unrest that a Commission of Inquiry was now appointed and its investigations put on record something of the harassing conditions of the working class.[1]

The overthrow of the " gendarme of Europe " and the maturing of proletarian revolution in the former land of the Tsars had an immense political effect among the British working class and specifically among the militant trade unionists and shop stewards. This was shown at the Leeds Convention in June 1917, which met with the aim of setting up Workers' and Soldiers' Councils on the model of the Russian Soviets. Of the 1,150 delegates from all sections of the movement that attended, the largest single group was 371 from trade unions and Workers' Committees. William Gallacher, speaking as a Clyde shop steward delegate, was widely applauded when he appealed for a revolutionary struggle against the war ; and among other trade union speeches there was a fervid offering from a rising young leader of the Dockers' Union—Ernest Bevin. That the Convention was never followed through was no fault of the masses but of the un-militant leadership of the I.L.P., who were in effective control of it and proved unwilling to force the pace. In the same way it was not the rank and file who were responsible for the manœuvring and intrigue connected with the proposal, endorsed by the Petrograd Soviet, for an international Socialist peace conference at Stockholm ; they believed that it offered a hope of peace and therefore supported it, though it too came

[1] Maurice Dobb, *Trade Union Experience and Policy*, 1914-18, pp. 20-1.

to nothing and had as its main by-product the resignation of Mr. Henderson from the Coalition Cabinet.[1]

There were plenty of other signs of the times in that crucial year. Not least among these were the proposals of a Committee headed by Mr. J. H. Whitley, Speaker of the House of Commons, for the establishment of Joint Industrial Councils, bringing together employers and employed on a national, district and works basis ; a scheme with what we would now call a distinctly " corporative " flavour ; it was to leave its principal mark only in the Whitley Councils in the Civil Service. This Committee functioned under the Ministry of Reconstruction, set up to perform the diversional task of elaborately blueprinting that " new world after the war " which, of course, never materialised. The Whitley scheme, particularly the proposal for joint works councils, was evidently inspired by the desire to draw the teeth of the shop stewards as a militant force ;[2] and the same desire was clearly present in the minds of the engineering employers when they conceded recognition of shop stewards by agreement with a number of the engineering unions in December 1917, for the agreement specified that " shop stewards shall be subject to the control of the trade union " and declared that " recognition of shop stewards is accorded in order that a further safeguard may be provided against disputes."

It was in the course of 1917 also that the constitu-

[1] Trade union leaders in the Cabinet were Mr. Arthur Henderson (Ironfounders), Mr. G. N. Barnes (Engineers) and Mr. John Hodge (Iron and Steel Trades).

[2] The point is openly made by an official who was in charge of dilution on the Clyde and elsewhere and a leading labour adviser of the War Cabinet, Sir Lynden Macassey, in his *Labour Policy False and True*, pp. 266-9.

tion of the Triple Alliance was formally ratified. An Act was passed somewhat modifying the existing statutory restrictions on union amalgamation ; while, by an ingenious scheme which by-passed the stringent requirements of the law, the Iron and Steel Trades Confederation was established. Finally, at the end of the year the T.U.C. and the Labour Party jointly approved a Memorandum on War Aims. The terms proposed were publicly accepted by the Prime Minister and were shortly made the basis of President Wilson's famous Fourteen Points. With this result :

> Profound was the disappointment, and bitter the resentment, of the greater part of the organised Labour Movement of Great Britain when it was revealed how seriously the diplomatists at the Paris Conference had departed from these terms in the Treaty of Peace which was imposed on the Central Empires.[1]

During the last desperate year of war the Shop Stewards' Movement grew and strengthened. Its power was seen in the threat of a political strike on the Clyde if the most extreme stage of the conscription " comb-out " were not abandoned, and in the successful Coventry strike against a tryout of a new labour regimentation scheme (the " embargo " on change of employer by skilled munition workers). It was the shop stewards, too, who held aloft the banner of solidarity with the Russian Revolution after November 1917, in face of the unparalleled onslaught made by the ruling class and official Labour alike on the new Power of the Soviets.

At the same time union membership greatly increased, the T.U.C. grouping over $4\frac{1}{2}$ millions in 1918 against less than $2\frac{1}{4}$ millions in 1913 ; while the big employers had already united to form the Federation of British Industries, later to hand over dealings with

[1] Webb, op. cit., pp. 695-6.

labour questions to a further new body, the National Confederation of Employers' Organisations. Monopoly made giant strides, war-time State control paving the way for an unprecedented growth of over-capitalised trusts and combines, notably in the heavy industries (iron and steel, engineering and shipbuilding, and to a less degree coal), chemicals, power supply, transport of all kinds, and banking.

In August 1918 the police strike, out of which the Government hastened to bluff its way, came as a threat from an unexpected quarter. It coincided with a strike of transport workers demanding equal pay for women on men's work. Next month there was a cotton spinners' strike and an unofficial railway stoppage, affecting particularly South Wales ; the last was the work of militant rank-and-file organisation, functioning through the semi-official district councils of the National Union of Railwaymen. Great excitement was caused by the direct action taken by the electricians when the Albert Hall was refused for a militant demonstration ; they removed all the fuses and the authorities had to climb down.

By the time the Armistice came the tide of unrest was flowing fast and deep. In the key industries of engineering, shipbuilding and mining the number of workers striking was less than 1917, but the number of separate strikes was far greater, in each case being a record for the war years ; and it was in the last three months of the war that the curve of struggle was rising most steeply.[1]

[1] Wal Hannington, *Industrial History in Wartime*, pp. 64-5.

Chapter 7 : The Post-War Crisis (1919-24)

With the ending of the four years' agony of war the "revolutionary outburst" that was threatening in 1914 now appeared likely to materialise in a far more acute form. Capitalism in Britain, as throughout Europe, was in the throes of mortal crisis ; following Russia, the tide of revolution was fast rising where Hohenzollern and Habsburg had held sway. The vastly augmented army of trade unionists[1] echoed the sentiments of the emergency conference of the Labour Party which, three days after the Armistice, dragged the Labour ministers out of the Coalition Government and recorded its " protest against any patching up of the old economic order." And, though the Government of Mr. Keynes' " hard-faced men who look as if they had done very well out of the war " was victorious in the Khaki Election of 1918, the opening days of the New Year boded ill for the triumphant profiteers.

The first action was fought on Clydeside at the turn of January-February 1919. It was the famous Forty-Hour strike, when engineers, shipyard and other workers united under the leadership of the Clyde Workers' Committee and the shop stewards in a struggle to shorten their working week which everyone sensed was no ordinary strike. The authorities frankly

[1] The T.U.C. rose in 1920 to $6\frac{1}{2}$ millions : the total membership of trade unions in that year was $8\frac{1}{2}$ millions.

feared a rising. Fresh troops were rushed to the scene
immediately after the " Battle of George Square,"
when a big strike demonstration, violently attacked
by the police, had fought back with sensational effect.
But as William Gallacher, one of the strike's principal
leaders, has since written, the preoccupation of the
shop stewards' movement with industrial organisation
alone, and their contempt for " politics," meant that
" we were carrying on a strike when we ought to have
been making a revolution." [1] The strike was isolated
by the national officials of the unions concerned (who
also disciplined their local officials for supporting the
movement) and ended in a fortnight.

Meantime the miners had prepared for battle. In
January the M.F.G.B. resolved to demand a 30 per cent.
wage increase, a six-hour working day, and nationalisation of the mines with a measure of workers' control.
By 615,164 votes to 105,082 a ballot of all the coalfields favoured strike action to secure these demands.
Thus the Government—whose war-time control of
the mines continued—found itself facing a miners'
strike with exhausted coal stocks. Since the miners
were in consultation with their railway and transport
friends of the Triple Alliance, who had themselves
tabled demands, it also faced the prospect of a general
strike with revolutionary potentialities. Mr. Lloyd
George bluffed brilliantly. He offered the miners a
Royal Commission, pledging the Government to accept
its recommendations, and on the other hand threatened
that a strike would be suppressed by armed force.
The M.F.G.B. leaders, particularly President Robert
Smillie, recoiled from the threat—though in the
circumstances of the time it was an absurdly empty
one[2]—and persuaded the Federation conference by

[1] Wm. Gallacher, *Revolt on the Clyde*, p. 221.
[2] Hutt, *Post-War History of the British Working Class*, pp. 21-2.

a narrow majority to accept the Prime Minister's offer.

The Commission, presided over by Mr. Justice (later Lord) Sankey, afforded the opportunity for a detailed and documented exposure of coal capitalism, created a great sensation, and by a majority recommended nationalisation ; but the Government having, by this means and with a National Industrial Conference as a further safety-valve, tided over the moment of gravest crisis, coolly went back on its written pledge and refused to implement the Commission's recommendations. Indeed, they went further and allowed a piece of bureaucratic stupidity to provoke a stormy strike in the Yorkshire coalfield (July-August 1919).

During the summer the general industrial outlook continued thunderous, the largest movement being that of the Lancashire cotton operatives, 300,000 of whom struck in June for a 48-hour week and a 30 per cent. wage increase, which they successfully achieved. A second police strike, in July, was ruthlessly smashed, amid considerable tension. The next conflict to shake the entire nation, however, was that of the railwaymen in the autumn. It came at the end of many months of negotiations which the Government had deliberately dragged out and bore all the marks of a provocation intended to force the men into an unsuccessful struggle and thus create a breach in the trade union front. Mr. Lloyd George's denunciation of the strike as an " anarchist conspiracy," the violence of the Government-inspired Press barrage, the plan to starve the railwaymen and their families through discriminatory rationing, the sinister instructions to local authorities to enrol a " Citizen Guard," had a smell of civil war about them. Yet in one week the railwaymen won a resounding victory ; there

were to be no wage-cuts, as threatened, existing rates
were stabilised and the lowest grade secured an
advance.

The reasons for this signal success were noteworthy.
First, there was 100 per cent. unity among the railwaymen themselves ; the locomotive men were not
bribed into blacklegging by the separate concession of
their own demands. Second, the railwaymen had
willing and powerful allies—in the Co-operative Movement, which granted large credits for strike pay, and
in the Triple Alliance, whose leaders had difficulty in
" restraining their own members from impetuous
action in support of the railwaymen," [1] while London
newspaper printers threatened direct action unless
the strikers' case was fairly presented. Third, the
aggressive and expert publicity conducted by the
Labour Research Department, at the request of the
N.U.R., was something never known in a major strike
before (or since).[2]

Working-class opinion was profoundly stirred by
this sensational repulse of a frontal attack with all the
forces of the State ; and it was only the conservative
influence of Mr. J. H. Thomas and his colleagues which
prevented the strike from spreading and becoming the
starting point of a general forward movement. Subsequent gains were registered by other sections ; thus
the dockers in the spring of 1920 won wage increases
from the inquiry headed by Lord Shaw, at which Mr.
Ernest Bevin's advocacy won him the title of the
" Dockers' K.C." The miners, however, got no
further, though their case was remitted to the T.U.C.,
discussed at the Congress in September 1919 and at
two further special Congresses. A " Mines for the
Nation " propaganda campaign had not moved the
Government ; and, after a proposal for a general

[1] Webb, op. cit., p. 543.　　　[2] Hutt, op. cit., pp. 25-9.

strike had been negatived by four to one, the issue was quietly dropped. In October 1920 the M.F.G.B. conducted a brief and inconclusive national strike for wage increases (the so-called *datum line* strike), significant because the Triple Alliance failed in its first actual test. Appealed to by the miners, the railway and transport union leaders fought shy of any sympathetic action, though their members favoured it (as a ballot of the railwaymen showed). This sign of weakness encouraged the Government to rush into law the notorious Emergency Powers Act, giving English naturalisation to that alien device the " state of siege."

Well might the Government clutch at new and exceptional powers ; for they had just had a startling demonstration of the political power of the trade union movement. It was in August 1920 that the long-continued British intervention against Socialist Russia threatened to become open war in support of the invading Poles and was finally stopped by the establishment of Councils of Action and the threat of an instant general strike. This historic achievement was the climax of a long campaign against intervention in which, among the unions, the Miners' Federation had played a leading part, and in which Mr. Herbert Morrison (for example) had told the 1919 Labour Party Conference :

> They had got to realise that the present war against Russia on the part of this country, France and the other Imperialist Powers, was not war against Bolshevism or against Lenin, but against the international organisation of Socialism. It was a war against the organisation of the trade union movement itself, and as such should be resisted with the full political and industrial power of the whole trade union movement.

When the Poles, with British and French backing,

made their unprovoked assault in the spring of 1920
it was the London dockers who electrified the whole
movement by striking the *Jolly George*, one of many
freighters who were loading munitions for Poland.[1]
The *Jolly George* men had the support of the Dockers'
Union, which at its national conference a week later
decided, after a speech by Mr. Bevin exposing capitalist war intrigues, to put a general ban on the loading
of munitions for use against Russia. In the first week
of August came the threat of open war. Countrywide
demonstrations of protest, organised by local Labour
Parties and Trades Councils at the request of Labour
Party headquarters, broke all records. Unity proved
itself to be indeed strength ; and between the trade
unions and the Labour Party, and between every
shade of opinion and every organisation in the movement, there was unity in those days.

On August 13th a delegate conference, called jointly
by the T.U.C. and the Labour Party, met in London
and endorsed with unanimity and enthusiasm the
decision to establish a Council of Action to stop the
war by " any and every form of withdrawal of labour."
Mr. Bevin told the delegates that " this question you
are called upon to decide to-day—the willingness to
take any action to win world peace—transcends any
claim in connection with wages or hours of labour."
Mr. A. G. Cameron (Woodworkers), then Labour
Party chairman, perhaps answering Mr. J. H. Thomas'
claim that the decision " means a challenge to the
whole Constitution of the country," declared that
" Constitutionalism can only exist as long as it does
not outrage the conscience of the community." If
the Council had to act, he concluded, and

if the powers that be endeavour to interfere too much,

[1] The full story is told by Harry Pollitt, *Serving My Time*,
pp. 111-21.

we may be compelled to do things that will cause them to abdicate, and to tell them that if they cannot run the country in a peaceful and humane manner without interfering with the lives of other nations, we will be compelled, even against all Constitutions, to chance whether we cannot do something to take the country into our own hands for our own people.

Those were indeed days when the battles fought by the trade union movement were of unexampled scope ; and it became clear that, like an army in the field, the Army of Labour could not win victories by sectional and isolated actions ; it must have a General Staff. To this end discussion was directed, immediately after and arising out of the railway strike, and a detailed report presented to the special Trades Union Congress which met in December 1919. The result of this was the transformation of the existing Parliamentary Committee of the T.U.C., which had never been a genuine executive body, into the General Council, mandated by its Standing Orders to " promote common action by the trade union movement on general questions." Unfortunately the Council was left without the power to enforce decisions on the unions ; so the old sectionalism remained intact, and it could later be fairly said[1] that the General Councillors were " still in spirit representatives of their trades."

Warning of this possibility had come clearly from the Left at the beginning ; thus a Communist appeal to the delegates at the Cardiff T.U.C. in 1921 (when the General Council was first elected) suggested that the talk about a General Staff of Labour might amount to no more than " a new alliance of old leaders, who have already shown how incapable they are of really leading the workers against the Bastilles of capitalism.

[1] By Mr. Frank Hodges at the Southport T.U.C. (1922).

They will leave the old sectionalism of Labour intact, and this means the same old chaos and confusion hidden under a new and high-sounding name." It was urged that the T.U.C. should turn itself into a real Congress of Labour, based not on the unions alone but on a whole series of shop and works committees, grouped around the local Trades Councils.

Side by side with these developments there took place a series of amalgamations which transformed trade unionism. This was most marked in the field of transport and general labour. The grouping of the numerous unions of dockers and other transport workers in the Transport Workers' Federation gave place in 1921 to their fusion in the Transport and General Workers' Union. An ingenious structure—combining a high degree of centralisation with a double division of its members, vertically by industrial groups and horizontally by areas—enabled this powerful body to be substántially dominated by its forceful general secretary, Mr. Ernest Bevin. It subsequently absorbed the Workers' Union and became the largest single union in the country, concerned in scores of industries and sharing the general labour field with the National Union of General and Municipal Workers. The latter, lineal descendant of the Gasworkers' Union of 1889, drew into one the previously separate general labour unions. Between the two of them the T.G.W.U. and the N.U.G.M.W., with their vast card votes, were more and more to dominate the main decisions of the movement, alike at the T.U.C. and at Labour Party conferences.

Other important amalgamations took place in engineering, building, woollen textiles, iron and steel, clothing, the Civil Service (especially the Post Office) and the distributive trades. But they did not have

the same general significance nor did they thoroughly
unify their industries. Thus the expansion of the old
Amalgamated Society of Engineers into the Amalgamated Engineering Union in 1920, by the absorption
of half a dozen of the leading craft unions in the
industry, still left it honeycombed with smaller craft
societies. Building provided a similar picture, even
though the old Bricklayers and Stonemasons combined
in the Amalgamated Union of Building Trade Workers,
and the two traditional unions of carpenters and
joiners (the Amalgamated and the General Union)
formed the Amalgamated Society of Woodworkers ;
however, the National Federation of Building Trades
Operatives, founded in 1918, was to prove itself more
effective as a co-ordinating body than the federations
in other industries.

Industrial problems and policy were far from being
the only concern of the trade unions during this
period. On the political field their creation, the
Labour Party, had in 1918 for the first time assumed
the aspect of a definite party, with stated Socialist
aims and programme, opening its ranks to individual
membership and multiplying its local organisations
from under 150 in 1914 to over 2,000 in 1920. But
how were the anti-capitalist aims of the new programme, *Labour and the New Social Order*, to be
achieved ? Or were they to be achieved at all ? The
unions' aim was defined by the Webbs at this time
as " the transformation of British politics and the
supersession of the capitalist profit-maker." It seems
self-evident that such an aim must impose a policy
and outlook independent of, and fundamentally
opposed to, that of the ruling class ; not one of
dependence on, and accommodation to, the ruling
class. Yet between these two opposing policies a
battle royal developed. It began in the Labour Party,

and was fought between Mr. Ramsay MacDonald as
the leader of those favouring the policy of accommodation, and the Communists as the most uncompromising
representatives of the policy of independence and
struggle.

This was the meaning of the long and bitter fight
of MacDonaldism, and its heirs and successors in the
movement, against the Communist Party, which had
been founded in August 1920, and all who sympathised
or associated in any way with it. Details of that
significant struggle must be sought elsewhere[1] ; here
it will suffice to note that, from the foundation of the
Party in August 1920 it met with marked support
from trade union quarters in the initial stages of the
fight. Thus it was the London Trades Council and
the Miners' Federation that supported the affiliation
of the C.P. to the Labour Party when it was first discussed (in 1921), and the Glasgow Trades and Labour
Council that later intervened to bring together Communist Party representatives and the Labour Party
Executive. And, while the affiliation proposal was
rejected then and afterwards, it was noteworthy that
in 1923 the Executive had to withdraw a clause aiming
at the exclusion of Communists as trade union delegates to the Labour Party. Next year the Party
conference saw the small minority favouring Communist affiliation leap to a substantial minority on the
issue of banning Communists as Labour candidates,
while on the proposal to exclude them from individual
membership of the Party many big union votes swung
against the Executive, which only carried its point by
1,804,000 votes to 1,540,000.

It is time to turn back to the end of 1920, when the
brief post-war boom was coming to an end. Unemployment passed the million mark in February

[1] See Hutt, *op. cit.*, pp. 54-6, 71, 96-7, 119, 189-90.

1921 and the two million mark in June. The Council
of Action had earlier been asked to include the
steadily sharpening unemployment issue in its agitation, but had declared that this was not within its
mandate. There followed a series of inconclusive
inquiries and joint conferences of the Labour Party
and T.U.C. No serious effort was made to test union
opinion ; the one large union which did so, the
notably moderate Boot and Shoe Operatives, got a
declaration from its members by ballot favouring a
twenty-four hours' protest strike. This proposal the
last of the joint conferences decisively defeated,
confining itself to a general admonition to the unions
to increase their Labour Party activity. Such a
policy—or rather absence of one—turned unemployment from a potential source of strength into a source
of weakness. By the end of 1921 those unions which
paid unemployment benefit were bled white to the
tune of some £7,000,000 ; and the unemployed had
perforce organised themselves independently, establishing the National Unemployed Workers' Movement.
In 1923 the T.U.C. agreed to set up a joint advisory
council with the N.U.W.M., however, and some useful
activity, including the drafting of an Unemployed
Workers' Charter, was undertaken.

The onset of the tremendous slump of 1921 inevitably heralded a universal attack by the employers on
wages and conditions. First to meet the capitalist
offensive were the coalfields, for the double reason
that mining was the hardest-hit industry and that the
miners were the vanguard of the workers' army. The
Government worked hand in glove with the coalowners, suddenly advancing by five months the date
on which its war-time control of the mines would end.
On that date (March 31st, 1921) the miners were
locked out, having rejected the owners' smashing

demands ; these included a return from national to the old district agreements and wage-cuts so severe that they meant a return to a level below pre-war earnings (20 per cent. on the 1914 rate when the official cost-of-living index stood at 141 per cent. above 1914).

Clearly the issue involved far more than the fate of the miners. The M.F.G.B. invoked the aid of the Triple Alliance and the entire movement girded itself with enthusiasm and determination to meet what the *Daily Herald* called " a frontal attack on the whole working class by the capitalists and their Government." A general railway and transport strike was called for April 12th, and the advance response in all industrial centres was tremendous. Meantime the Government operated the new Emergency Powers Act, made an extensive display of military force and even enrolled a special corps, the Defence Force. This sabre-rattling was not surprising, since the pits had been closed down by the most complete stoppage they had ever known, even all the " safety men " being withdrawn. The M.F.G.B., too, was at the top of its strength and public opinion far from unsympathetic.

Unfortunately the enthusiasm outside found no reflection in the long and anxious colloquies of the Triple Alliance chiefs. On the very morning that the sympathetic strike was due they managed to get the miners and the Government in conference again, and the strike notices were postponed to April 15th, a Friday. By now the discussions of the Alliance leaders had become " chaotic and panicky," to quote Mr. G. D. H. Cole, one of the best-informed contemporary observers. An incident on Thursday night gave them their chance. Mr. Frank Hodges, secretary of the M.F.G.B., took it upon himself to offer a temporary " settlement " in an impromptu speech to an unofficial meeting of M.P.s, who included influential Government supporters. Next morning he was very properly disowned and reprimanded by his Executive for unauthorised personal action in a matter of such moment. Taking this as their pretext (the miners, they claimed, had thus rejected the possibility of a settlement) the Alliance leaders threw in their hand. At 3 p.m. the bald announcement was made that the strike was off. That was " Black Friday."

The effect of this last-minute call-off throughout the movement was absolutely stunning. Bitter recriminations naturally followed, with cries of " betrayal " and gibes at the " Cripple Alliance." And of the four leading personalities associated with Black Friday three subsequently crossed over to the other side—Mr. Frank Hodges (director of numerous companies), Mr. J. H. Thomas (who from the other side was constrained to go even further—out of public life), and the late Mr. Robert Williams of the Transport Workers' Federation, who after sinking into utter obscurity ended his days as a National Government propagandist. Number four was Mr. Ernest Bevin, who told the transport workers' conference in June 1921 that if he had to live Black Friday over again he would repeat his action. The collapse, he said, was due to lack of preparation and to the fact that each union was autonomous ; he claimed that " there was also weakness among their own members."[1]

No one could dispute that the degree of actual preparation had not been on a par with the spontaneous response of the mass of trade unionists ; and it was undeniable that sectionalism still prevailed. But Mr. Bevin's statement of these facts was accompanied by no acknowledgment that such matters are a responsibility of leadership ; and his allegation

[1] *Daily Herald*, June 10th, 1921.

about the membership's weakness was a very uncon-
vincing alibi. To quote Mr. G. D. H. Cole again :
during the 1919-20 upsurge, the union leaders " took
things easy, or busied themselves with small affairs,
when they should have been straining every nerve to
prepare for the coming struggle. The result was that
the slump towards the end of 1920 took them
altogether unprepared." So, in the crisis of April 1921,
" conscious of their own helplessness and lack of ideas
for dealing with the situation, and of the panic which
was laying hold of them, they attributed helplessness
and panic to the rank and file in an even higher
degree."[1]

After Black Friday there remained nothing but a
series of rearguard actions, stubbornly contested but
unable to hold the employers' attack, which was
pressed home throughout industry. The miners were
defeated by June and by the end of 1921 wage-cuts
averaging 8s. a week had been suffered by 6,000,000
workers. There was a general lockout of the cotton
trade and, in 1922, in engineering, resulting in the
employers once more securing absolute authority in
all questions of " managerial functions," and draining
dry the immense funds of the A.E.U., the union
mainly concerned, in the process. The big post-war
gains in union membership melted away. Between
1921 and 1923 affiliations to the T.U.C. dropped by
over 2,000,000, more than the increase since 1918.

By the middle of 1923, however, there were signs
of recovery. A series of strikes, many unofficial,
included builders and agricultural workers in the
Eastern Counties, seamen, boilermakers and dockers ;
the last was, significantly, not defensive but demanded

[1] Cole, " ' Black Friday ' and After " (*Labour Monthly*, July 1921,
p. 14). Mr. Cole there gave it as his view that the "mainly permanent
trade union officials " of the Transport Workers "showed up worst."

wage increases and only ceased when the T. & G.W.U.
agreed to set on foot a national wages movement.
There was more than one factor combining to make
this revived movement adopt a forward character.
The dismal sectionalism exhibited at the 1923 T.U.C.
(at Plymouth), a most petty display of inter-union
squabbling, had a big effect among active rank-and-
filers. It was followed by the experience of Mr.
MacDonald's first Labour Government, which deeply
disappointed many trade unionists, not excluding
many leaders, and contributed to the growing leftward
trend in the movement. That was hardly surprising
when the Government's main claim in regard to its
handling of strikes (to quote Mr. J. R. Clynes, one of
its Ministers), was that it " played the part of a
national Government and not a class Government."

When Mr. MacDonald and his friends took office
in January 1924 a railway strike was in progress, the
locomotivemen having rejected wage-cuts. The
A.S.L.E.F. was conducting the strike, the N.U.R.
(having accepted the cuts on behalf of its driver-
members) keeping its men at work. The division
naturally brought much bitterness ; but eventually
the locomotivemen secured some concessions, no
thanks to the Government, which had hastened to tell
the House of Commons that it " had no sympathy
with this unofficial [sic] strike." A national strike of
dockers in February was keenly and unitedly fought,
securing some wage advances ; but the Cabinet
brought extreme pressure to bear on the leaders—" I
wish it had been a Tory Government," mourned Mr.
Bevin, " we would not have been frightened by their
threats," while Mr. Ben Tillett said that he had never
heard from Tory or Liberal Ministers " the same
menacing tones or the same expressions of fear." But
among the several disputes of that year, which

included unofficial strikes in the shipyards and the
railway shops, and a national builders' lockout, the
most significant was the London traffic strike in
March. The tramwaymen struck for higher wages ;
the busmen joined them and the Tube men were
considering sympathetic action. There was a clear
strikebreaking ring about Mr. MacDonald's announcement that " the major services must be maintained,
and the Government . . . must give protection to
those engaged in legal occupations." That these were
no idle words was seen in the Government's invoking
of the Emergency Powers Act and proclamation of a
State of Emergency ; only the simultaneous end of
the strike prevented the operation of the dictatorial
measures thus prescribed.

It was important at this stage that the leftward-
moving elements secured a centre in the National
Minority Movement, launched at a conference in
London in August 1924 with the veteran Tom Mann
as its president and Harry Pollitt (Boilermakers)—
who was gaining wide repute as a T.U.C. and Labour
Party conference delegate and was a leading member
of the Communist Party—as secretary.[1] This Movement had first taken root in the coalfields, where
important districts (notably South Wales and Fife)
had recorded support for the Red International of

[1] Pollitt stated the Minority Movement's aims in these terms :
" We are not out to disrupt the unions, or to encourage any new
unions. Our sole object is to unite the workers in the factories by the
formation of factory committees ; to work for the formation of one
union for each industry ; to strengthen the local Trades Councils
so that they shall be representative of every phase of the working-
class movement, with its roots firmly embedded in the factories of
each locality. We stand for the creation of a real General Council
that shall have the power to direct, unite and co-ordinate all the
struggles and activities of the trade unions, and so make it possible
to end the present chaos and go forward in a united attack in order
to secure, not only our immediate demands, but to win complete
workers' control of industry."

Labour Unions when it was founded at Moscow in the summer of 1921. A Miners' Minority Movement had developed during 1923, and was the backbone of the campaign which secured the election of the militant A. J. Cook as secretary of the M.F.G.B. upon the enforced resignation of Mr. Hodges.

On the eve of the Labour Government's defeat in the " Zinoviev Letter " election—the biggest electoral fraud in our history, for whose effectiveness Mr. MacDonald bore the main share of responsibility— there were sufficient signs of the influence being gained by the new trends. At the Hull T.U.C. in September 1924 the atmosphere was vastly different from the Plymouth Congress the previous year. Congress adopted an Industrial Workers' Charter, gave the General Council certain new powers of intervening in disputes, endorsed by a vote of nearly two to one the principle of organisation by industry, and instructed the General Council to draft a scheme for linking the unions in " a united front . . . for improving the standards of life of the workers." The Council was likewise instructed " to call a special Congress to decide on industrial action immediately there is danger of war."

The Hull Congress made news, also, in being the first to receive a delegation from the Soviet trade unions ; and it was decided to reciprocate by the dispatch of a T.U.C. delegation to the U.S.S.R. To the problem of international trade union unity attention was similarly paid. In June of that year, at the Vienna Congress of the International Federation of Trade Unions, the British delegates had succeeded in keeping the door open for negotiations with the Soviet trade unions when the Social-Democratic majority wished to shut it tight. Of this endeavour the Hull

T.U.C. approved ; and unanimous agreement was accorded to the statement of the president, the late Mr. A. A. Purcell, that the General Council should be empowered " to take all possible steps . . . in bringing together the different elements of the Labour movement in Europe."

Chapter 8 : The General Strike and After
(1925-9)

During 1925 it was made clear, first, that the new leftward trend in the unions was gaining ground at a rapid pace, and, second, that even more than before the coalfields were to be the cockpit of a key struggle. The urge for trade union unity, national and international, which found expression at the Hull T.U.C., developed most dramatically in the international sphere. On the General Council a " left " group developed, headed by the late Mr. A. A. Purcell and Mr. George Hicks (Building Trade Workers) ; under their influence the Council took the lead in a prolonged campaign to induce the Amsterdam diehards at least to meet the Moscow International and discuss the possibilities of unity. In this matter a friendly understanding with the Soviet trade unions was initiated when the T.U.C. delegation visited the U.S.S.R. at the end of 1924, and an Anglo-Russian Joint Advisory Council later set up. These activities, and especially the notable Report of the delegation (recording how " in Russia the workers are the ruling class "), brought down upon the General Council the most incredible explosion of spleen, calumny and misrepresentation from the united forces of Continental Social-Democracy and the British ruling class. The late Mr. Fred Bramley, then general secretary of the T.U.C., summed up the Amsterdam attitude in a memorable passage :

> It appears to me you can discuss any other subject under the sun without getting into that panicky state of trembling fear and excitement and almost savage ferocity which you get into when you are discussing Russian affairs. . . . You can discuss the activities of capitalist Governments, and their destruction of the trade union movement in one country after another without this unnecessary epidemic of excitement ; but when you begin to discuss Russia, you begin to suffer from some malignant disease. . . . Get rid of the panicky fear that seems to invade and dominate your minds in dealing with Russia.[1]

But the I.F.T.U. leaders never budged, and in the event the General Council did not take the promised further step of itself calling an international unity conference.

As for the coal industry, its economic situation was so serious that it was described as " heading for irretrievable disaster." The temporary fillip afforded in 1923-4 by the French occupation of the Ruhr had passed and the owners now came forward with new demands for drastic wage-cuts, the abolition of the principle of a minimum wage and a complete reversion to district agreements. Nor were the miners the only objects of attack. British capitalism faced a desperate struggle to patch up its economy and re-establish its world position. Prime Minister Baldwin put it bluntly when he said " all the workers of this country have got to take reductions in wages to help put industry on its feet."[2]

The M.F.G.B. rejected the owners' demands and received the " complete support " of the T.U.C.

[1] Speech at the I.F.T.U. General Council meeting, Amsterdam, February 5th-7th, 1925.
[2] *Daily Herald*, July 31st. 1925.

General Council, which appointed a Special Committee
to co-operate with the miners in concerting resistance.
The Committee, assured of support by the executives
of the railway and transport unions, drew up plans
for an embargo on all coal transport in the event of
a miners' lockout. Detailed instructions were thereupon issued to all the unions concerned, and given
" unanimous and enthusiastic approval " by a special
conference of trade union executives which met on
July 30th, the day before the owners' notices were due
to expire. The Government, unprepared for such a
development, beat a hasty retreat. Eating its own
words, it announced a nine months' subsidy to enable
a Royal Commission to make a detailed inquiry. The
owners withdrew their notices and the day passed into
history as Red Friday.

This defeat for the Government was naturally an
" immense stimulus to every trade unionist," as the
General Council declared, adding the vital rider that
vigilance and " devising ways and means " to meet
a further attack was essential. That view was
universally held. " This is the first round," Mr. A. J.
Cook summed it up, " Let us prepare for the final
struggle." Behind this " unstable truce," said the
Communists, " the capitalist class will prepare for a
crushing attack upon the workers," and if the workers
" do not make effective counter-preparations then
they are doomed to shattering defeat." On the
Government side preparations were immediate and
thorough. Mr. Winston Churchill (Chancellor of the
Exchequer), now as before the Cabinet's most open
class warrior, made it plain that he and his colleagues
on Red Friday had merely decided " to postpone the
crisis " with a view to " coping effectually with it
when the time comes." The Government was as good
as Mr. Churchill's word. Official support was given

to the Organisation for the Maintenance of Supplies, a volunteer strike-breaking organisation. Blackleg " shock troops " were given technical training. An entire dictatorial apparatus, placing all power in the hands of ten ministerial Commissioners, was erected. Like an army going over the top, it was arranged that this machine should operate instantly on the receipt of an " action " signal from Whitehall.

Astonishing though it must seem, no counter-preparations at all were undertaken on the trade union side. Despite the initial warnings, there gained currency what the principal orthodox historian of the General Strike, Professor Crook, has called a " studied attitude of unpreparedness " which " had results upon the Labour forces in the actual struggle that were nothing short of disastrous." " Even if the experience of the long organisation of the Belgian Labour Party for its general strike in 1913 had not been utilised by the British leaders [he concludes], common sense should have dictated some modicum of preparation."[1]

For this surprising lapse the reason lay in the relation of forces within the leadership. That the spirit of the movement itself was fighting fit, the Scarborough T.U.C. spectacularly demonstrated in September 1925. It was indeed a demonstrative Congress, from the loudly acclaimed presidential address in which Mr. A. B. Swales (A.E.U.) plumped for " a militant and progressive policy, consistently and steadily pursued," to the smashing vote of 3,082,000 to 79,000 in favour of revolutionary opposition to British imperialism. Decisively Congress declared that the aim of the unions was to struggle " in conjunction with the Party of the workers . . . for the overthrow of capitalism," pledged itself " to

[1] Wilfrid H. Crook, *The General Strike*, p. 369.

develop and strengthen workshop organisation,"
endorsed the General Council's international unity
campaign, and condemned the Dawes Plan for the
more efficient squeezing of the German people
(principal product of Mr. MacDonald's Government).
But when it came to deeds rather than words the
picture was not so rosy. The affiliation of the Trades
Councils to Congress was ruled out of order, the key
issue of the General Council's powers was shelved
again, and two of the men of Black Friday were
elected to the General Council. They were Mr. J. H.
Thomas and Mr. Ernest Bevin ; the latter, with his
hold on his powerful union consolidated, now for the
first time moving into T.U.C. leadership. To reinforce
them there came, with the untimely death of Mr. Fred
Bramley shortly after Scarborough, the accession to
the General Council secretaryship of the assistant
secretary, Mr. W. M. Citrine (as he then was), a dark
horse who rapidly proved himself of a very different
colour from his sturdily independent predecessor.

The balance of forces on the General Council had
thus been sharply redressed in favour of the Right,
hamstringing (as it turned out) the fair-weather
" lefts " of the Purcell-Hicks group. The following
month, also, Mr. Thomas and Mr. Bevin associated
with Mr. MacDonald in making the Liverpool conference of the Labour Party a counter-demonstration to
Scarborough. The fight against the Communists was
now carried into the unions, which were urged to
refrain from electing Communist delegates to the
Labour Party. In place of the " new social order " of
1918 the Party programme was watered down to " a
co-ordinated policy of National Reconstruction and
Reform." As chairman the late Mr. C. T. Cramp (Mr.
Thomas' associate in the leadership of the N.U.R.)
proclaimed that " we transcend the conflict of

classes." It was all an unmistakable signal. Within
a fortnight the Government swooped upon the Communist apostles of preparedness, and twelve C.P. leaders
were gaoled after the biggest State trial since Chartist
days. At the beginning of November the efforts of
the now thoroughly uneasy Miners' Federation to
form an Industrial Alliance of key unions and thus
prepare for The Day were wrecked by the withdrawal
of Mr. Thomas's N.U.R.[1]

During these months the Royal Commission on the
coal industry, headed by Sir Herbert (later Lord)
Samuel, was at work, treading well-worn paths, and
producing in March 1926 a Report which was vague in
its references to State intervention for the reorganising
of coal capitalism, but precise in its assertions that the
miners should accept longer hours or lower wages.
The effect of the Samuel Report was to divide the
movement, at least at the top. The General Council
were henceforth essentially persuaded that the
miners should accept wage reductions on condition
that the industry was " reorganised," and felt that
the M.F.G.B. line " not a penny off the pay, not a
second on the day " was (as they later cynically
averred) " a mere slogan." Undeterred by signs of
weakening on the Council's part the miners' delegate
conference on April 10th stood firm ; they had had
evidence that masses of trade unionists did not share
the General Council's defeatist view when the Minority
Movement broke records at a Conference of Action it
held towards the end of March, attended by 883
delegates representing close on 1,000,000 trade
unionists. The coalowners immediately disclosed
their hand, announcing their intention to proceed
with negotiations on a district basis only, and posting
lockout notices for April 20th, demanding wage

[1] Hutt, *op. cit.*, pp. 121-2.

reductions so sweeping that even their president, Mr.
Evan Williams, admitted the resulting wage would
be " miserable."

The owners' bellicosity hardened the General
Council's attitude again in support of the miners. On
April 27th it decided for the first time to draft plans
for the large-scale action that circumstances might
impose. Executives of unions affiliated to the T.U.C.
were summoned to confer in London two days later.
But the opening statement of that conference showed
that the General Council were still bemused by the
Samuel Report—Chairman Arthur Pugh urged that
the owners and the miners should have started
negotiations with the Report as a basis—even while
they repeated their assurances of apparently unqualified support for the miners. This contradiction
was not openly resolved and was to prove fatal.
Indeed it is more than doubtful whether the General
Council would have launched the mighty movement
that it did, if the Government had not forced the
pace. The intricate and abortive negotiations which
occupied the night of April 29th, and the following
day and night till after 11 o'clock, made it clear that
the Government, all its preparations completed, stood
solid with the coalowners, was seeking to manipulate
the Press against the miners, and in all respects was
determined on provoking a conflict.

It was nearing midnight when this news was con-
veyed to an angry and excited conference by the
General Council's negotiators (the so-called Industrial
Committee, of which Mr. Thomas was a leading
member). The Executives dispersed till the morning
bearing with them a memorandum which was in fact
the General Strike order. On reassembly the vote was
taken. The strike order was dramatically endorsed
by unions representing over 3,600,000 members

against a handful representing less than 50,000. It was announced that the trades specified would strike as from midnight on Monday, May 3rd. Upstanding, the conference sang the " Red Flag " and dispersed to May Day demonstrations exalted by the call to arms.

The strike order specified a call-out in two " grades " or " lines." The first line comprised transport (all forms), printing (including the newspapers), " productive industries " (itemised as iron and steel, metal and heavy chemicals), building (with the exception of housing and hospitals). Leading the second line was engineering and shipbuilding. The maintenance of food and health services was to be undertaken by the unions. The individual unions concerned were asked to " place their powers in the hands of the General Council," but the actual calling out on strike was left to them (and as they numbered eighty-two a great deal of sectional confusion resulted). Finally, the General Council directed that " in the event of any action being taken and trade union agreements being placed in jeopardy, it be definitely agreed that there will be no general resumption of work until those agreements are fully recognised."

In the excitement of the moment few appreciated that the fatal contradiction already mentioned still subsisted. And now the General Council, having assumed direction of the entire struggle, considered that it was empowered to settle on the miners' behalf even if that involved wage reductions. The M.F.G.B., on the other hand, held that their only authorisation to the General Council was to act for them on the basis of the repeated declarations of solidarity in resisting any reduction whatever in their living standards. They certainly protested vehemently against the Industrial Committee's reopening of negotiations with the Government within a few hours of the strike decision and the dispersal of the Miners' Executive to their districts. Those negotiations, whose complicated course occupied the entire week-end, boiled down to the old point—acceptance of the Samuel Report, implying wage reductions. Eventually agreement appeared to have been reached on this, and it only remained for the General Council to confront the M.F.G.B. Executive, hastily recalled by telegram, with a *fait accompli.*

At this stage a violent change was effected by the sudden strike of printing staffs at the *Daily Mail*, with the Natsopa men in the lead, as a result of a blood-and-thunder anti-union leading article. Mr. Baldwin instantly told the General Council negotiators that the Government regarded this as an " overt act " of war, and demanded the unconditional withdrawal of the General Strike notices if negotiations were to continue. He thereupon retired to bed, and when the General Council dispatched a repudiation of the *Daily Mail* men to Downing Street the door was (literally) shut in their face. Thus at last " the T.U.C. stood as a combatant in a war which had been forced upon it and which it feared to win." [1] And which it feared even more that the strikers, the working class, might win in a revolutionary fashion, as subsequent statements by Mr. Bevin, Mr. Thomas, Mr. Charles Dukes (General Workers) made clear.[2]

That it had a defeatist General Staff hardly entered the minds of the millions-strong army which went over the top with incomparable *élan* at midnight on Monday, May 3rd. Next day the T.U.C. communiqué said : " We have from all over the country reports that have surpassed all our expectations. Not only

[1] Kingsley Martin, *The British Public and the General Strike*, p. 58.
[2] Hutt, *op. cit.*, pp. 134-5.

the railwaymen and transport men, but all other trades
came out in a manner we did not expect immediately.
The difficulty of the General Council has been to keep
men in what we might call the second line of defence
rather than call them out." Nor in the apocalyptic
Nine Days that followed was there ever any appreciable weakening of the strike ; the Government
propaganda was entirely at variance with its own
confidential reports.   Indeed, as the second week
opened the strike was developing and deepening, so
far as the masses were concerned. The local Councils
of Action had consolidated, mass picketing, defence
corps, local propaganda through a myriad of dupli-
cated bulletins, were well in their stride. Despite the
General Council's anxious protestations that the strike
was only an industrial dispute (" We beg Mr. Baldwin
to believe that ") it was obviously assuming an ever
sharper political character.

From the start the General Council remained on
the defensive, allowing the opposing forces to take
every initiative. It did not produce its own organ,
the *British Worker*, until the Government had
established the official *British Gazette*[1] with Mr.
Churchill—the Cabinet's real War Lord in this
struggle—as super-editor of a sheet summed up in
its description of the strikers as " the enemy " ; and
the *British Worker* was kept in leading-strings by a
General Council censorship as timorous as it was
strict. Never was there any carrying of the war into
the enemy's camp ; the lessons of the 1919 railway
strike publicity appeared completely forgotten. Yet
the Government's provocative actions—the array of
military force, the suppression of conciliatory moves

[1] With vital aid from Lord Beaverbrook who, since the Government could not obtain a single blackleg linotype operator, loaned
one of the mechanical chiefs of the *Express*.

on its own side, the playing up of Sir John Simon's laughably bad legal threats, the orgy of police batoning, wholesale arrests and gaolings on the flimsiest pretexts—were enough to show that its position was far from being as strong as its propaganda ceaselessly and loudly pretended.

By the end of the first week, in fact, the General Council's attention was concentrated, not on leading the strike, but on negotiations to end it. " It seemed," wrote Mr. A. J. Cook, " that the only desire of some leaders was to call off the General Strike at any cost, without any guarantees for the workers, miners or others." That is exactly what happened ; except that it was not some leaders, but the whole General Council, including the Purcell-Hicks " lefts." The thing was done on the basis of a Memorandum prepared by Sir Herbert Samuel, rehashing his Commission's Report. This, though Sir Herbert made it clear that he could give no assurances on the Government's behalf, the General Council unanimously endorsed, and, without having received any guarantees of any kind decided, against the declared opposition of the M.F.G.B., to terminate the strike.

On Wednesday morning, May 12th, the Council accordingly waited on the Prime Minister and, in a humiliating scene, announced their unconditional capitulation. Such was their pitiable confusion that the " second line " had been called out, according to plan, only a few hours before ; such their wishful thinking that some among them actually sent " victory " circulars to their members ; such their sense of guilt that the *British Worker* utterly suppressed the M.F.G.B. repudiation of the call-off and even sought to suggest that the miners were in agreement with the Council. Immediately the employers struck, as the Government intended they should do,

" determined if possible to impose non-unionism, reduced wages or servile conditions."[1] But the strikers remained solid ; and the soldiers' battle of Thursday, May 13th, magnificently saved the surrender from becoming a debacle, even though the new agreements were very unfavourable and opened the door to much victimisation.

The Nine Days, and even more the days of the rear-guard action that followed them, had made the working class feel its own power, had taught what unity and a fighting spirit could do, had " proved conclusively," as Mr. A. J. Cook wrote, " that the Labour movement has the men and women that are capable in an emergency of providing the means of carrying on the country." It taught the leaders something too ; but that was summed up in Mr. C. T. Cramp's public ejaculation " Never Again! " No doubt they felt that in those days of May they had gazed too closely at what the late Mr. Arthur Henderson subsequently called the " terrible prospect " of a collapse of the present social and political order. Not for nothing had they passed the historic turning-point of 1914, that fusion of the trade unions with the State machine which has been described in an earlier chapter. Henceforth they were not to stray from the path of accommodation to, and collaboration with, the régime of monopoly capital.

It took some time for this policy in its new form to come to fruition. The General Strike was over by the middle of May, but the miners remained stubbornly in the field till December, even at the very end reject-ing surrender, which now involved the loss of the seven-hour day as well as wage cuts, by 480,000 votes to 313,000. Their ranks had been thinned by breakaways, notably in the Midlands, where Mr. G. A. Spencer,

[1] *The Scottish Worker*, May 14th, 1926.

leader of the Notts Miners' Association, formed a
" Non-Political " union with the support of the
coalowners that was to bedevil those coalfields for
years. The T.U.C. General Council and their colleagues
on the Labour Party Executive damped down the
still universal solidarity with the miners that was
expressed in the widespread union demand for a levy
on all trade unionists and an embargo on coal imports.
Danger in this respect·was also avoided by the postponement of the Conference of Executives to discuss
the General Strike (promised for the end of June), and
the singular banning of the subject at the Bournemouth T.U.C. in September. When the Conference
finally met, in January 1927, it turned out according
to plan—a formal inquest which returned the required
verdict.

Given this outcome of the General Strike it was not
surprising that the Government was able to press
through, against only a platform campaign from the
General Council, its central legal attack on trade
unionism. In 1927 the Trade Disputes and Trade
Unions Act (the " Blacklegs' Charter ") was placed
on the Statute Book. Not only general strikes but
sympathetic strikes, even when purely industrial in
aim, were made illegal. A clause without precedent
suggested that it might be a criminal offence for persons not actually in employment to refuse to accept
employment on an employer's terms. Anyone leading
or participating in an " illegal " strike was liable to
fine or imprisonment (up to two years, on indictment),
while union funds were made liable for civil damages,
thus removing the immunity conferred by the Act of
1906. Mass picketing was forbidden and ordinary
picketing hamstrung by a blanket definition of
" intimidation." Civil Service unions were forbidden
to affiliate to the T.U.C. or the Labour Party. Trade

unionists who blacklegged were protected against any
disciplinary action by their unions. A blow was struck
at the unions' political activity by changing the
existing legal arrangements regarding political levies.
Instead of objectors to the political levy having to
" contract-out," its supporters now had to " contract-
in." The Act was appropriately summed up as " the
most reactionary sample of British labour legislation
placed on the statute book since the evil Combination
Laws of 1799-1800 . . . a crudely framed piece of
restrictive class legislation."[1]

Little over a month after the enactment of this law
for the disarming of the trade union movement, the
presidential address to the Edinburgh T.U.C. offered
to co-operate with the employers " in a common
endeavour to improve the efficiency of industry and
to raise the workers' standard of life." It was pronounced by Mr. George Hicks, former leading figure of
the General Council " lefts." In November this
invitation was taken up by a group of twenty leading
industrialists headed by the late Lord Melchett (then
Sir Alfred Mond), founder of the mammoth Imperial
Chemical Industries combine. In January 1928 the
first joint meeting between this group and the
General Council took place. " Mondism " was born,
its lone opponent on the General Council being Mr.
A. J. Cook.

Reporting to the Swansea T.U.C. in September
1928 the General Council outlined three possible
policies for trade unionism. The policy of militant
working-class struggle it dismissed as " futile, certain
to fail, and sure to lead to bloodshed and misery."
The orthodox policy of letting the employers run
industry while the unions fought for their members'
rights and interests was disposed of as " inconsistent

Wilfrid H. Crook, *op. cit.*, pp. 481, 484.

with the modern demand for a completely altered status of the workers in industry." Policy number three (approved) was " for the trade union movement to say boldly that not only is it concerned with the prosperity of industry, but that it is going to have a voice in the way industry is carried on . . . the unions can use their power to promote and guide the scientific reorganisation of industry." What that approved policy meant had been suggested in the first joint report of the General Council and the Mond group. This declared that the tendency to rationalisation and trustification " should be welcomed and encouraged." It proposed the establishment of a National Industrial Council, representing the General Council and the employers (through their National Confederation and the Federation of British Industries), and under which a system of compulsory conciliation was to be operated. In return the employers conceded a species of union recognition which looked like the universalising of the ingenious system of disguised company unionism devised by the late Mr. Havelock Wilson to the greater profit of the shipowners and the easier exploitation of the seamen. Involving, as Mr. E. Shinwell, M.P., put it, the " blunt bargain " whereby " the trade union keeps the men in order ; the employer in return agrees to employ union men only."

It soon transpired that the policy of peace with the employers meant war within the unions. There was a substantial body of union opinion opposed to Mondism, rallying 768,000 votes at the Swansea T.U.C. against a majority of 2,920,000 ; and the General Council did not appear to have very convincing arguments to offer, Mr. Bevin booming at the anti-Mondists at the Belfast T.U.C. in 1929 that he " objected to the inferiority complex." Strong arm methods were

therefore resorted to. Already in 1926 the Bournemouth Congress had carried the General Council's
appeal to Trades Councils not to affiliate to the
Minority Movement ; the Council's spokesman, Mr.
A. Conley (Garment Workers) naïvely remarking
that " if the Council had agreed to this affiliation,
within a short time the Minority Movement would
become the majority."[1] The National Union of
General and Municipal Workers led the way in
reviving the old employers' weapon of the " document " to exclude Communists or Minority Movement
supporters from office. Their example was in varying
degree followed by the Railwaymen, Transport
Workers, Shop Assistants, Natsopa, Electrical Trades,
Boot and Shoe Operatives, Bakers, Painters and
Boilermakers (the last aimed directly at Harry
Pollitt). Most sensational of all was the splitting of
the Scottish Miners' Union in 1927-8 by the old
officials, when duly and constitutionally voted out by
their members in favour of Communists and men of
the left[2] ; the chaos thus induced eventually compelled the militants to establish for a time a new
union, the United Mineworkers of Scotland.

The meaning of Mondism was not long in making
itself clear. Throughout industry conditions worsened,
with extensive speeding-up, breaking of piece-rates,
violating of agreements. The railwaymen suffered a
wage-cut and the misery in the coalfields was intense,
the average miners' wage being only 30 per cent. over
1914 level, with the cost-of-living index 67 per cent.
over 1914. Union membership shrank, T.U.C. affiliations declining by half a million between 1926-8. But
with the opening months of 1929 a new tide of revolt

[1] *Daily Herald*, September 8th, 1926.
[2] Details of these remarkable proceedings are given in Hutt, *op.
cit.*, pp. 183-7.

was beginning to rise, seen in keenly-fought local
strikes typified by the ten weeks' struggle of the girls
at the Rego clothing factory in London for union
recognition, and the fifteen weeks' fight of the 3,000
miners at Dawdon (Durham) against a heavy wage-
cut.

CHAPTER 9 : THE ROAD TO CATASTROPHE (1930-9)

MONDISM, it has to be emphasised, was not the personal and temporary deviation of union leaders on the rebound from the General Strike. It was the expression of a consistent and continuous policy ; the dominant policy of the movement's top leadership throughout the final pre-war decade, as in the years immediately preceding. The specific proposals and character of Mondism have been touched on in the previous chapter. Here it may be well to analyse in more detail the essential nature of the policy, since that will provide a key to the period now to be reviewed. For this it is only necessary to refer to what we may call Sir Walter Citrine's introduction to Mondism, written at the close of 1927, before the conversations of the General Council with Lord Melchett's group had actually begun.[1]

This programmatic statement outlined, almost in the same words, subsequent General Council pronouncements ; for example, in the description of the three alternative policies facing trade unionism and in the development of the old Whitley proposals for a National Industrial Council and joint councils in each industry. Getting down to bedrock, the statement stressed that a turning-point had been reached, and

[1] W. M. Citrine, article in *Manchester Guardian* Industrial Relations Supplement, November 30th, 1927 ; quoted in W. Milne-Bailey, *Trade Union Documents*, pp. 431-8.

that " the next stage in the evolution of trade
unionism " connoted two things. First, any policy
of struggle against, or opposition to, large-scale
modern capitalism must be rejected (" the approach
to a new industrial order is not by way of a social
explosion ; " the aim should be " an effective rela-
tionship which will ensure greater stability and
harmony in industry "). Second, trade unions as the
monopolists of labour (" trade unionism . . . has
established a virtually unchallenged control of the
organised power of the workers ") must enter into
partnership with the monopolists of capital, the aim
being " a concerted effort to raise industry to its
highest efficiency." Making Mr. Bevin's thunderings
against " inferiority complex " sound most para-
doxical,[1] it was plainly suggested that in this partnership the unions would play the junior rôle ; all they
hoped for was " a larger share of control in directing
industrial changes," while for their members they
would only ask " an equitable share in the gains
resulting from increased productivity."

An old fallacy was re-furbished in the suggestion
that increased production was the gateway to working-
class prosperity (" promoting the largest possible
output so as to provide a rising standard of life and
continuously improving conditions of employment ").
Rationalisation of industry was viewed not as a
process of intensification of labour through speed-up,
mechanisation, etc., but as " a more efficient, econo-
mical and humane system of production." While
Taylorism, for instance, might produce an " inevitable
psychological reaction " if " autocratically introduced
without consultation " with the union officials, all
would be well given the desired partnership of the
organised employers and the union apparatus. Then

[1] See p. 116 above.

there would be " numerous possibilities of mutual agreement . . . in the application of the principles of scientific management." At the same time, the unions " will not be afraid to face " the " reciprocal responsibility " of such alleged restrictions on production as " ca' canny," demarcation disputes, existing union rules and customs ; and, in conclusion, the old objections to profit-sharing and employee-shareholding schemes might disappear if they were operated " on a collectivist basis with the union acting as steward and trustee."

In so propounding the complete integration of the union machine with that of capitalist industry in the interests of " highest efficiency " and " gains from increased productivity," Sir Walter Citrine was no isolated extremist. The policy he enunciated so clearly was acceptable to the majority of the T.U.C. General Council, first and foremost to their leading member, Mr. Ernest Bevin, autocrat of the Transport and General Workers' Union. And in operating along these lines leaders were able to take advantage of the marked change in the composition of the T.U.C. which became evident during the 1930's ; the affiliated membership of the miners, engineers, textile workers (for instance) had greatly declined, while the T. & G.W.U. was now the biggest single union, with the other big general union, the National Union of General and Municipal Workers, third in the Congress list.[1] The block vote of these two unions gave the Citrine policy massive backing. Nor was this limited to Mondism as an economic policy ; both unions

[1] Memberships were : T. & G.W.U. 523,000, N.U.G.M.W. 340,000, Mineworkers' Federation 518,000, National Union of Railwaymen 338,000, Amalgamated Engineering Union 250,000 (figures for 1936). The war has brought new changes, e.g., the Amalgamated Engineering Union's near-million membership is not so far behind that of the T. & G.W.U.

mentioned had a high proportion of members "contracting-in" to the Labour Party (T. & G.W.U. 301,000, N.U.G.M.W. 242,000); thus there was vote-fodder for the projection of Mondism on to the wider plane of politics which became a feature of the period.[1]

This feature was the accompaniment and sequel to the final playing-out of the tragi-comical farce of MacDonaldism in the Second Labour Government. The Labour Party won the General Election of 1929 —or rather the Conservatives lost it—on the crest of a wave of working-class resentment against the Baldwin Government, legacy of the General Strike, the crushing of the miners and the passing of the punitive Trade Union Act. But it was soon seen that the new Government represented a retrogression even on its predecessor of 1924. It " cringed before the rich man's frown " and showed not the slightest desire to protect the standards of those whom Mr. MacDonald pleasantly called the " eazy-oozy asses." Election pledges were not honoured ; the seven-hour day was not restored to the miners, who instead were driven to strike in Scotland, and were locked out in South Wales, through disputes provoked by the Government's prescription of an hours' spreadover ; the Trade Union Act was not repealed, the Government prevaricating so shamelessly that Mr. Bevin was driven to protest. In a series of big textile disputes the Government intervened with arbitration or court of inquiry proceedings which awarded wage

---

[1] Of this an important example was the transfer of the *Daily Herald* in 1930 to the millionaire newspaper concern of Odhams Press, giving them a majority share control (51 per cent), while retaining the joint T.U.C. and Labour Party representation on the *Herald* board, Mr. Bevin being the principal figure and the leading defender of Lord Southwood's daily in face of the criticism which was voiced at later Trades Union Congresses.

cuts; this occurred in the cotton spinning lockout of
1929 and the woollen lockout of 1930, the latter case
being rendered more scandalous by the police violence
employed in the West Riding during a dogged two
months' fight.   In 1931 the Lancashire weavers were
locked out to enforce the masters' more-looms-per-
weaver demand.   Though their leaders were uncertain,
the weavers stood solid and won ; one of the delegation which the locked-out weavers dispatched to
London to voice their case put it bluntly, " Lancashire
weavers," he[1] said, " were having to fight, not merely
the employers, but their own Central Committee and
the Labour Government itself."   With the surging
flood of unemployment that followed the onset of the
world economic crisis the Government proved itself
totally incapable of dealing, save by proposing " econo-
mies " at the expense of the unemployed and the
working class in general.

Meantime the General Council had continued its
Mondist explorations, though the full organisational
plans were not then realised.   The Federation of
British Industries and the National Confederation of
Employers' Organisations conferred with the General
Council to examine methods of co-operation, but the
proposed National Industrial Council did not materialise.   However, the F.B.I. and the General Council
prepared a joint memorandum for the Imperial
Conference of 1930, a significant document which
broke with the traditional policy of free trade, urging
tariffs and an Empire economic bloc.   The open
imperialism of this memorandum was reflected in its
narrow endorsement at the Nottingham T.U.C. (by
1,878,000 votes to 1,401,000) after a debate in which
Mr. Bevin's key speech in favour was noteworthy for

[1] Mr. Zeph Hutchinson, secretary of the Bacup Weavers' Association.

its anti-Soviet passages.[1] Next year the character of the T.U.C.'s new associates was illuminated in a vehement attack made by the National Confederation on unemployment insurance.

Contrasting with this attitude at the top were signs of militant tendencies at the bottom. Thus 2,000 delegates attended a conference organised by the Manchester Trades Council in May 1931, resolving to demand a 40-hour week and pledging resistance to all wage-cuts and attacks on social services. The previous month a Convention met in London to endorse the Workers' Charter launched by the Minority Movement (a simple programme embodying demands for increased unemployment benefit, extended social services, a 7-hour day and a minimum wage of £3 a week) ; here, however, the drive against the militants in the unions left its mark, for of the near 800 delegates little more than one-sixth were representative trade unionists.

These symptoms in no way deterred the General Council. Nor was it turned from its path by the crash of the Labour Government in August 1931 and the defection of MacDonald, Thomas and Snowden to the new Tory-dominated "National" Government. There was, indeed, a radical contradiction in the protests at this inevitable end of MacDonaldism that arose among the union High Command ; for, as Mr. Ellis Smith (Patternmakers, now M.P. for Stoke) pointedly asked the Bristol T.U.C. in September 1931, how could they " condemn MacDonald, Snowden and Thomas for collaborating with opposed political parties when the General Council did the same thing

---

[1] Mr. Bevin attacked what he called Soviet " dumping," declared (quite contrary to commercial experience) that Russian trade " is very often only 10 per cent. orders and 90 per cent. propaganda," and averred that the Soviet " Empire " had an " attitude to subject races very much the same " as that of other Empires.

in the industrial field " ? Or was there really such a contradiction ? It did not appear that there was an objection in principle to the kind of coalition that the MacDonaldites had entered. That same Congress heard, without critical reaction, the late Mr. Arthur Henderson declare that he " would have preferred that the idea of a National Government had been seriously considered and approached in a proper way, and that the Labour movement should have been consulted, preferably at a specially convened Labour conference." And while the movement as a whole admirably withstood the shock of the defection, its " break with MacDonaldism," as Mr. G. D. H. Cole wrote at the time, " was far more instinctive than rational."[1] Nor did the leadership ever seek to make that break " rational " (that is, conscious, reasoned) ; instead, as suggested above, they projected the Mondist policy on to the political plane and thereby constituted themselves the heirs, administrators and assigns of MacDonaldism. The new feature was that henceforth the central political direction of the movement was in the hands, not of the Labour Party leaders who remained, but of the small group at the head of the T.U.C. General Council.

While the " National " Government in its several modifications pursued from 1931 onwards the path of reaction at home and abroad, sapping popular liberties and standards of life on the one hand and making war inevitable on the other, there was henceforth at no point a concerted and united resistance to it from the Labour leadership. With the single exception of cotton, there were to be no more large-scale official strikes or co-ordinated forward movements. The initial fight against the " economy " cuts, the pro-

---

[1] Cole, *Short History of the British Working-Class Movement* (1932 edition), Foreword, p. x.

longed struggle of the unemployed against the slashing
of benefits and the Means Test, remained a soldiers'
war. Where the struggle was not spontaneous (as was
the mutiny of the Atlantic Fleet at Invergordon) it
was aided and directed by the officially outlawed
Communists or their friends on the left. The incessant
unemployed demonstrations, Hunger Marches, battles
with the police of those days, were led by the National
Unemployed Workers' Movement.

The unemployed issue showed how the Mondist
politicians were carrying on the MacDonaldite tradition of disruption and heresy-hunting. In the first
year of reaction after the General Strike the General
Council had terminated its relations with the N.U.W.M.;
in 1932, at the height of the unemployed agitation, it
went further and urged Trades Councils to set up their
own local unemployed associations. The several
National Hunger Marches were ostracised, though rank-
and-file union support could not be stayed ; the
March of 1932, for instance, was welcomed by a crowd
of 100,000 in Hyde Park and on the following Sunday
drew 150,000 to Trafalgar Square.[1] But unemployed
deputations to the T.U.C., which were annually
organised by the N.U.W.M., were always refused

---

[1] Still wider was the response of Trades Councils and union
branches to the March of 1934, which climaxed in a Congress of
Unity and Action where the 1,500 delegates included representatives
of 245 branches of 50 different unions (including 81 delegates from
43 branches of Mr. Bevin's union). The public interest aroused was
intense and the Government was shortly compelled to restore the
1931 cuts in unemployed benefit. The March of 1936 surpassed even
this record, for it got Mr. Attlee, leader of the Labour Party, and
Wal Hannington on to the same platform. In its annual report for
1936 the London Trades Council observed that " the most significant
feature of the march was the support given by people of all classes,
creeds and politics . . . this wave of sympathy should serve as an
impetus to the Labour movement to seek ways and means of har-
nessing the great forces of public opinion in the fight " against the
Means Test, the March's particular object.

admission (refusals backed with unceremonious displays of force by the local constabulary, horse and foot), even though there was a wide feeling in Congress that they should be heard. Nor was the political character of the refusal disguised. Thus Secretary Citrine declared at Newcastle (1932) that the N.U.W.M. was " a subsidiary of the Communist Party," aiming " to hold up the General Council to ridicule and contumely,"[1] and at Brighton (1933) proclaimed his objection to " allowing people to advocate a united front by a backdoor method."

The political leadership assumed by the union High Command, with Mr. Bevin as Commander-in-Chief and Sir Walter Citrine as Chief of Staff, was inspired by the same outlook as their industrial leadership. No opposition to, but full collaboration with, the governing class. This appeared clearly over the basic political issues that came to occupy the attention of the trade union movement, summed up in the twin menace of Fascism and War, which assumed its most urgent aspect with the placing in power of Hitler and the Nazi Party in Germany in 1933.

There was no lack of evidence of the potential strength that the union leaders could command if they desired to make a firm stand. On the industrial front unrest and militancy were marked. The preceding conflicts in Lancashire were entirely eclipsed by the weavers' strike in the summer of 1932, whose stormy battles to pull out the " knobsticks," and mass marches

[1] Typifying the contrary view was Mr. Dawson (Textile Workers), who said that he was no Communist, but " a loyal officer of the trade union movement who has stood four-square on all occasions with the movement." He urged that Congress should not " waste time as to who is behind this unemployed organisation." " Do not," he begged, "be sidetracked by Mr. Citrine's reference. . . . What he has said may be correct. I do not challenge it at all, but as men and women facing this problem, we ought to be able to co-operate with either angels from heaven or fiends from hell."

from town to town to close down all mills, recalled the insurrectionary General Strike of 1842 ; despite police violence and repeated "intimidation" gaolings under the 1927 Act, the weavers fought on to the end of September, when the final enforcement of wage-cuts and the more-looms system left the cotton industry seething. In London that same summer the busmen successfully checked a severe attack on wages and conditions, which their union (the T. & G.W.U.) was prepared to accept, by organising the London Busmen's Rank-and-File Movement, embracing a majority of the bus branches ; next January this Movement led an unofficial strike—jointly condemned by the union executive and the employers—against speed-up, and concessions were gained. On the anti-fascist front a newly vigilant public opinion (reflected in the establishment of the Council of Civil Liberties) was aroused by sinister Government measures like the Incitement to Disaffection Act, while provocative demonstrations by the Mosleyites at Olympia and in Hyde Park were met by impressive counter-demonstrations—which the General Council ineffectively sought to boycott.

Unhappily these factors do not appear to have been taken into account ; nor was heed paid to the lessons of disunity, passivity and capitulation suggested by the collapse of German Social-Democracy. In March 1933 the T.U.C. General Council and the Labour Party Executive rejected joint action proposed by the Communist Party and the I.L.P. and instead the National Council of Labour issued a manifesto entitled *Democracy versus Dictatorship*. This document linked together the dictatorship of Fascism and the dictatorship of the working class (called " reaction on the ' Left ' "), described the Labour Party as " the spearhead of political power against dictators, Fascist

or Communist," and told the workers that their
" historic task today is to uphold the principles of
Social-Democracy." The mischievous bracketing of
the Soviets and Fascism was repeated at the
Brighton T.U.C. in September 1933, when Sir
Walter Citrine spoke to a General Council statement
on Fascism—a helpless review which presented Fascism
as an automatic and inevitable product of deepening
crisis and growing unemployment. " In Great Britain,
just as in Germany," said Sir Walter, " we have a
serious unemployment problem. If unemployment
gets more desperate neither myself nor any member of
the General Council will be prepared to answer for the
consequences." Referring to the collapse of the
German leaders, Sir Walter limited himself to the
pious ejaculation : " I hope to God we are never put
into a similar position."

The development of policy on war was even more
singular. That the movement was of one mind in its
uncompromising opposition to war was made clear at
the autumn conferences in 1933. At the Hastings
Conference of the Labour Party a resolution, accepted
by the Executive, was carried unanimously and with
acclamation pledging the Party " to take no part in
war and to resist it with the whole force of the Labour
movement . . . including a General Strike." At the
Brighton T.U.C. similar sentiments were voiced in a
resolution moved by the A.S.L.E. & F., and the whole
matter was referred to the General Council to report
further to a special congress or specially summoned
conference of union executives. Then things began to
happen. No special conference was held. A joint committee appointed by the National Council of Labour
occupied some months in discussions from which
there " emerged the fact that it would be impossible
to lay down a definite line of action for all future

emergencies." Sir Walter Citrine announced the sensational discovery that a General Strike against war would be illegal (a truism that had been fully appreciated in the Hastings debate). Arguments redolent of Mr. Bevin's views were propounded ; such as that the sole responsibility of resistance to war should not rest upon the unions, and that there could be no refusal to handle munitions since that would also lead to a General Strike.

In June 1934 these signs of a turnabout came to a head in a statement by the National Council prescribing the " duty of supporting our Government unflinchingly " in the event of war, qualified as military " support of the League in restraining an aggressor nation." The qualification was only the sugar on the pill ; opposition to war had been switched to support for war. Mr. Rowlands (Painters) summed up the feelings of many when he told the following T.U.C., at Weymouth, that " the Labour leaders in 1914 waited until war broke out before going over to the support of their Government. In this report they were going over before the war started." Nevertheless the T.U.C. endorsed the new policy, as did the Labour Party at Southport, Mr. Bevin oddly averring that " what they did was to keep the weapon of the General Strike " (this was the last that was heard of it).

Parallel with all this, however, rank-and-file activity continued unabated. There was a series of strikes at large factories in the high-speed and little unionised " new " industries, together with wage movements among the railwaymen, engineers and miners ; in the South Wales coalfield the structure of the S.W.M.F. was refashioned and democratised, under militant leadership summed up in the presidency of Arthur Horner, and its greatly shrunk membership rapidly increased again. The position was recognised by Mr. A. Conley (Garment Workers) in his presidential address to the Weymouth T.U.C. Noting that " piecemeal wage movements are on foot," he urged that " these sporadic and unco-ordinated movements should be linked together in a disciplined and ordered effort to carry the unions forward as a united body." The point was not taken. Indeed Weymouth drew the complacent City comment that " the trade union wing of the Labour Party is not really interested . . . in destroying the so-called capitalist system."[1] Nor, to turn the phrase around, was the Labour Party wing of the trade unions.   The Southport conference adopted a new programme, *For Socialism and Peace*, in place of the MacDonaldite *Labour and the Nation* ; it was described by the Socialist League opposition as " not a plan for Socialism, but a repetition of the 1929 attempt to work within declining capitalism " ; indeed as " a form of organisation leading to the Corporate State."

The year 1935 marked a turning point. It began with the most striking demonstration since 1920 that a united working-class defence could defeat a Government attack, no matter how inflated the Parliamentary majority. The occasion was the scheduled operation on January 7th of Part II of the new Unemployment Act, which stiffened the Means Test and was accompanied by relief scales inflicting heavy cuts.   South Wales and Sheffield were the main centres of the storm that arose. The South Wales Miners' Federation Executive took the initiative in calling an all-in conference of trade union and all working-class organisations, irrespective of political colour ;   around the united front thus established the mass of the population gathered and on February 3rd astonishing demonstrations up and down the mining valleys rallied no

[1] *The Economist*, September 8th, 1934.

less than 300,000 persons. Unemployment Assistance
Board premises were stormed and wrecked. The ruling
class were flung into what Premier Baldwin called a
" curious state of hysteria and panic "; and the
Government hastily cancelled the cuts.

How did the movement's High Command react in
this situation when, as *The Times* put it, " the spirit
of 1926, which produced the General Strike, is showing
itself again " ?   Appeals from the left for unity were
rejected, as before, by the General Council and the
Labour Party Executive. When the united movement
was under way the National Council of Labour issued
an " Appeal to the National Conscience," urging " all
leaders of public opinion . . . in no partisan spirit " to
concern themselves with the " lamentable state of
affairs." To appeals from their constituents on the
scene of action the General Council returned super-
cilious and hostile answers.[1] Yet the general upward
swing brought by this victory of unity was soon shown
in leaping Labour by-election votes, in numerous local
strike successes and in a national forward move by the

[1] In a letter to the General Council the Abertillery Trades Council
alleged that the T.U.C. " never gave a lead to the workers to fight
and resist this attack. . . . Take our local position ; before the Council
took an official part in this present movement, 7,000 employed and
unemployed demonstrated to the U.A.B. on this matter. The
N.U.W.M. initiated this movement and it gained mass support.
Then the Council associated itself with the united front, which
embraced all organisations, including ministers of the church and
shopkeepers. This movement has extended right throughout the
country. . . . We call upon the T.U.C. to get on with the fight. . . .
All we ask for is action." To this the organising department of the
General Council retorted that " it appears that your Council feel that
the action taken by a few Communists in South Wales is of more
importance than the deputation to the Minister of Labour and the
debates in the House of Commons—a point of view with which I can
only express surprise. . . . The fact that your Council are connected
with the united front will be reported to the appropriate committee
of the General Council at their next meeting." (Quoted in Wal
Hannington, *Unemployed Struggles*, 1919-36, p. 311.)

miners ; the M.F.G.B. decided to campaign for a wage increase and a national agreement, securing a majority of 93 per cent. for strike action, and national attention was centred on the successful " stay-down " strike at Nine Mile Point in Monmouthshire.

It is a matter of history that the General Council, far from developing the successful action against the Unemployment Act into a counter-attack all along the line, turned its fire still more keenly against unity. In March it adopted two circulars (Nos. 16 and 17, generally referred to simply as the " Black Circular "), ordering Trades Councils to ban delegates who were Communists or had any associations with Communists, and requesting unions to modify their rules so as to exclude Communists from any office.[1] Wide exception was taken to this and the M.F.G.B., the three railway unions, the Transport Workers, Woodworkers, Engineers, Distributive Workers, Painters, Electrical Trades, with many smaller societies, went on record against the " Black Circular." At the Margate T.U.C. in- September 1935 the disruptive recommendation was only endorsed (by 1,869,000 votes to 1,274,000)

[1] Answering the conventional charge of " disruption," the Communists later declared that there was " one piece of disruption to which we plead guilty. We have disrupted non-political unionism for ever." J. R. Campbell said : " For eight years after 1926, the dominant right wing leadership in the mining industry refused to tackle non-political unionism either in South Wales or in Notts. It was only when Communist leadership began to dominate in the anthracite coalfield, only when that Communist leadership attacked the non-political union at the Emlyn Colliery, only on the basis of that success that the South Wales miners were encouraged, again under Communist influence, to go forward to attack Taff Merthyr and to storm the citadel of non-political unionism in South Wales, Bedwas itself. Without the victories in South Wales, the M.F.G.B. would never have supported Harworth when Harworth, again under Communist leadership, came out in the fight against non-political unionism." (*Report of the Fourteenth Congress of the C.P.G.B.* 1937, p. 112.)

after a reported last-minute swing-over of the Transport Workers' vote. The other side of the medal was seen in the acceptance of honours, amid a flood of protests ; most notable being the star and purple ribbon of Knight Commander of the Most Excellent Order of the British Empire conferred on Mr. Walter M. Citrine. It was a " generous admission," purred the *Daily Telegraph*, " that those also serve who oppose the Government of the day." And the year was rounded off by the first striking demonstration of what the new war policy of the movement meant in practice. Entirely uncritical support was accorded to the Government over the Abyssinia-Sanctions crisis, Premier Baldwin's most successful confidence trick ; used to hamstring the opposition at the General Election that November, after which the Prime Minister unsealed his lips to announce that the real business—general rearmament—would forthwith begin.

Rearmament introduced a " boom " period—unemployment fell in 1937 to the " low " level of 1½ millions from its 1932 height of 2¾ millions—which threw a most significant light on the working out in practice of the industrial policy of the General Council leadership. The bounding output for which Sir Walter Citrine had yearned in his 1927 statement was certainly being achieved ; but it was equally certainly not providing any " rising standard of life and continuously improving conditions of employment." One index of productivity showed a rise of 20 per cent. in the five years from 1932 to 1937.[1] But net real wages were static or declining while relatively to the total wealth produced wages fell enormously. During the " boom " years from 1935-7 wages rose on the average

[1] Jurgen Kuczynski, *The Condition of the Workers in Great Britain, Germany and the Soviet Union*, 1932-38, p. 59.

by 7·6 per cent., but the cost of living rose by 8·2 per cent. and industrial profits rose by 25 per cent. In 1937 itself profits rose by 17 per cent. to a new high record while a wage increase of 4 per cent. was more than offset by a cost of living rise of 6 per cent.[1] The worsening of the position of the working class relative to that of the wealthy could be expressed in index form thus : taking 1932 as 100 that relative position in 1937 had declined to 84.[2]

The 1927 Citrine statement had referred in passing to the necessity for " adequate wages " ; the policy of Sir Walter and his colleagues produced nothing but wages of the most sensational inadequacy. To compare, say, even the wage-rates of 1920 with those of 1934 was startling enough. The average fall was nearly 40 per cent., but for skilled workers in basic industries much higher (e.g. miners 58 per cent., iron and steel workers 57½ per cent., textile workers nearly 50 per cent.). In terms of money it could be calculated that in 1936 weekly wages of skilled men averaged £3 to £8 10s., or unskilled men somewhat over £2 to £2 10s., of women 27s. to 28s.[3]

What standard of life did these figures represent ? One so low that " even on the intolerable Bowley standard an appallingly high proportion of the total working-class population has been found to be below the ' poverty line ' in recent social surveys "—for example in Merseyside, Southampton, London.[4] If the Rowntree " human needs " standard, which was low enough in all conscience, were taken instead of Professor Bowley's " bare subsistence " standard the proportion leapt so that in London one-third of the

[1] *The Economist*, May 14th, 1938.
[2] Jurgen Kuczynski, *op. cit.*, p. 43.
[3] G. D. H. and M. I. Cole, *The Condition of Britain*, pp. 244, 249-52.
[4] *Ibid.*, pp. 260-1.

households were below or near the poverty line, and another third not very much above it. Applying the Rowntree standard to separate industries it could be demonstrated that in mining 80 per cent. of the workers were below the poverty line, in public utility services 57 per cent., in building 50 per cent., in textiles 46 per cent.[1] In broad terms of public health the meaning of all this was authoritatively revealed by leading nutrition experts like Sir John Orr and the late Dr. M'Gonigle ; their researches disclosed that no less than one-half the entire population were below a satisfactory nutritional level—in other words that number of people just could not afford to buy enough of the right foods to maintain them in full health.

In the light of this situation the complete failure to take advantage of the boom was the more noteworthy. So respectable an authority as Mr. G. D. H. Cole wrote :

> Now, assuredly, is the time both for the organised workers to win advances by militant action and for the movement to bring effectively within its ranks the mass of unorganised workers in the rapidly-developing new industries and services. But the old leaders only found, in the recent boom, a new excuse for inaction. Every sign of trade union militancy can now be attributed to the machinations of a handful of Communists, who have somehow found the art of being in a hundred places at once, and in whom it is regarded as a crime to induce non-unionists to join a trade union, or to suggest to the workers that they had better act promptly, while profits are high, instead of staying quiet until the precarious chance passes away.[2]

This unshakable passivity and inactivity of the top leadership had an inevitable result ; the crop of unofficial strikes grew luxuriant. Many key aircraft

[1] Jurgen Kuczynski, *op cit.*, p. 26.
[2] G. D. H. Cole and others, *British Trade Unionism Today*, p. 540.

concerns were affected by strikes, frequently for the recognition of shop stewards, whose valiant efforts on the job were making this speedily expanding industry a stronghold of trade unionism, and who shortly came together to establish an Aircraft Shop Stewards' National Council, forerunner of similar organisation in other industries. The miners' fight against " non-political " unionism was mirrored in bitter strikes at Taff Merthyr in South Wales and Harworth in Nottinghamshire, where the Trade Union Act and the new Public Order Act were used to gaol many of the most active people. In the end the " non-pols " went down for the count and the Spencer Union in Notts reunited with the *bona fide* Notts Miners' Association.[1] There was unrest among railwaymen, postal workers, busmen ; the strike of the London busmen during the Coronation celebrations in 1937 produced some sensations—not least the farce of the union executive keeping the tramwaymen at work—and led to a temporary purge of militants in the T. & G.W.U., with the consequent formation, against the strong opposition of the Communists and their supporters, of a breakaway union. Of prime importance was the movement among engineer apprentices, which produced a strike of 13,000 lads on the Clyde in April 1937 and nearly 20,000 in Lancashire and the Midlands in September ; at a national apprentices' conference in Manchester 84,000 lads from near a score of different centres were represented and made a call for national strike action to enforce their demands for wage increases, proper training and so on ; for the first time the employers were induced to recognise the right of the A.E.U. to negotiate on behalf of the apprentices.

Passivity also made itself evident in regard to the

[1] See footnote to p. 133 above.

basic problem of organisation confronting the trade
union movement—namely, of building itself strongly
in those newer, mass-production industries which
remained almost entirely unorganised. The magnitude of the problem could be gauged from these few
examples ; in the miscellaneous metal trades only
5 per cent. were organised ; in food, drink and
tobacco the same ; in automobiles 15 per cent. ; in
the distributive trades 11 per cent. ; and the mass of
workers here concerned was some four million.
Clearly the solution to this problem was not to be
found in traditional and sporadic campaigns of leaflet
distribution. It required, as the Communists pointed
out, " that the trade union leaders stop fighting their
own militants and start mobilising the working-class
to storm the Bastille of unorganised labour," by a
sustained national campaign for wage increases, the
forty-hour week, new industrial legislation, by co-
ordinated union action and the building of trade
union unity ; with attention to the special problems
of female labour and youth.[1]   To remain in complacent contemplation of the gradual turn in the tide
of union membership that began in 1935 was to toy
with the problem ; and just as it was only by " mass-
movements from below that trade unionism has won
its present degree of power and recognition," so it
appeared that now " a new mass-movement of the
same character " was needed.[2]

From the facts already set forth it will be apparent
that any such revivifying forward movement in trade
unionism must inevitably conflict, and sharply, with
the dominant leadership. The point was confirmed by

[1] *Report of the Fourteenth Congress of the C.P.G.B.*, 1937, pp. 96-116.
[2] Cole, *op. cit.*, pp. 525-6, 534. The T.U.C. in 1935 reported an
increase of 94,000 in affiliated membership (the first increase since
1930). Later increases were 225,000 (1936), nearly 400,000 (1937),
452,000 (1938), 208,000 (1939), 198,000 (1940), 212,000 (1941).

the further development of official policy on the wider
political issues. Here the manner in which the con-
trollers of the trade union machine swung their weight
behind the policies of the governing class was truly
phenomenal.

Endorsement of rearmament was put over at the
1937 conferences, after a period of confusion the
previous year. Though the official statement, *International Policy and Defence*, in form adumbrated a
foreign policy of collective security, it was sufficiently
clear that the heart of the matter was support of
rearmament under the reactionary " appeasing "
government of the late Mr. Neville Chamberlain.
" Rearmament cannot await the advent of a Labour
Government," said Sir Walter Citrine at the Norwich
T.U.C., while the Executive spokesman at the
Bournemouth Labour Party conference, Mr. James
Walker (Iron and Steel Trades), delivered what the
Manchester Guardian called " the first big Labour
conference speech for a generation that has struck the
patriotic note."

When Fascism struck in Spain, the Chamberlain
Government sided with General Franco (and his Nazi
and Italian backers) through the foul farce of " non-
intervention." Though the movement, and democratic opinion in general, was more aroused and
enthused by the Spanish struggle than it had been
since the days of the Council of Action, Mr. Bevin
and Sir Walter Citrine were outstanding in their
efforts to keep it a " quiescent partner " in the
Government's " hellish duplicity."[1] And this, by the
most incredible manipulations of the issue, they con-
trived to do during the supremely critical opening

[1] To apply a phrase of Mr. John Hill, the veteran ex-secretary of
the Boilermakers and sometime member of the General Council.
(*Daily Herald*, January 8th, 1937.)

period of the Spanish War. Their performance at the Plymouth T.U.C. in 1936 won the approving comment from Sir Samuel Hoare at the Conservative Party conference that " the wise attitude adopted by the Trades Union Congress over the Spanish crisis shows that in the ranks of Labour there is a solid force of patriotic responsibility." And even when this dis-astrous policy was later reversed, no aid-for-Spain campaign was ever officially conducted on the scale that the occasion demanded.[1]

When the Fascist offensive switched eastward with the rape of Austria in March 1938, the leadership again enabled Mr. Chamberlain to get away with it. There was a first-class political crisis and the Government tottered ; but the National Council of Labour never gave the lead that could have pushed it over. Instead the Council lamely announced that it would await the Prime Minister's declaration of policy. Next day the General Council of the T.U.C. were summoned to Downing Street, and listened obediently to Mr. Chamberlain's appeal for the " goodwill and help " of Labour. The arch-appeaser had been saved, and was able to proceed to his final triumph of Munich and the destruction of democracy's last bastion in Central Europe ; for the later declarations of solidarity with the Czechoslovak Republic, endorsed at the Blackpool T.U.C. in September 1938, remained verbal declara-tions. Indeed it was at that Congress that Sir Walter Citrine gave one of the most astonishing performances in defence of the General Council's policy of pro-Chamberlain passivity. The then critical position of the Spanish Republic had inspired a general desire for effective solidarity action, and an organised embargo

---

[1] A detailed documentation of this disastrous attitude to the Spanish War may be found in Hutt, *Post-War History*, Chap. XI.

on exports to Franco Spain was suggested. Sir
Walter, however, indicated that such action would be
a breach of the Trade Union Act and would involve
the confiscation of union funds; alternatively that
such action was impossible because the T. & G.W.U.
(meaning, of course, Mr. Bevin) was against it. Comment is superfluous on this rehash of Sir Walter's
1934 arguments against action to stop war, referred
to above.[1]

Nor was there any foundation for the interpretation
that the General Council leadership, in their unconditional support for the Government, were merely
expressing the view of their affiliated unions. This was
seen when the key union for war production, the
A.E.U., met Ministers in 1938 to discuss industrial
policy, dilution, etc., in the light of rearmament. The
line taken by the engineers was the opposite of that
taken by the General Council; they raised inconvenient " political " questions at the outset (arms for
Spain, the Government's encouragement of Fascist
Powers). Similarly when the General Council early in
1939 responded without question to the Government's
approaches for collaboration in national service
schemes, it was repudiated by important bodies
like the Distributive Workers and the Shop
Assistants.

In general during these fateful pre-war years the
leadership of Mr. Bevin and Sir Walter Citrine was
employed to paralyse effective opposition to the

[1] On the same occasion Sir Walter advanced the argument against
the wide demand for State control of the so-profitable arms industries
that this would involve State control of labour. The monstrous
fantasy of this " argument " was to be sufficiently demonstrated
with the wartime State control, and conscription, of labour—supported by Sir Walter and expounded by his leading colleague, the
Rt. Hon. Ernest Bevin, M.P., Minister of Labour and National
Service.

monstrous regiment of Chamberlain by its refusal of any working-class, or general popular and democratic, unity. Communist affiliation to the Labour Party was rejected in 1935-6 with an exhumation of the " Moscow gold " and " violence " bogey, as employed by Mr. MacDonald in 1920-5. The unity campaign launched in 1937 by the Communists, Socialist League and I.L.P., on a programme little different from the Short Programme adopted by the Labour Party, was damned by Mr. Bevin in an engaging comparison of Sir Stafford Cripps with Mosley. The campaigns for a popular front (the *Reynolds News* United Peace Alliance call in 1938; the Cripps Memorandum and Petition in 1939) were crushed to the cry of " Pure Socialism," " Socialism or Surrender." The first pamphlet issued by the Cripps Petition Committee answered :

> As the Dictators press their claims for colonies the imperialist ruling classes may have to fight . . . not for democracy but for empire, and they will go into battle stripped of their strategical assets and without the allies they have betrayed. In that desperate struggle would the Labour Party, for the sake of Socialism, refuse its political collaboration ? The chances are that it would again join a National Coalition, this time under Tory leadership. Out of that, with our civil liberties suspended and victory both distant and doubtful, what would emerge is more probably Fascism than Socialism.

That point did not carry at the Labour Party conference in Southport over Whitsun 1939. " We are nearer to power than ever before," cried Mr. Bevin, leading the big battalions to overwhelm this lawyer who then wanted to fight and defeat Chamberlain ; and with that cry coupled a remarkable intervention pleading for a pooling of the world's colonial resources in order to give Germany, Japan and Italy their place ;

a new line in " appeasement." The conference concluded with a " Soldiers! To your places " call by Mr. Greenwood. The phrase was more literally apposite than its author may have realised. Trade unionists had attended their last pre-war conference.

CHAPTER 10 : TRADE UNIONS AND THE WAR (1939-42)

Two years before war broke out the official trade
union line had already been adumbrated, in words
echoing the Webbs' comments on 1914.[1] At the
Norwich T.U.C. in 1937 Sir Walter Citrine said : " I
do not believe any Government could wage war of any
kind without the backing of the Labour movement."
Mr. Ernest Bevin declared that the T.U.C., by which
he obviously meant the oligarchic machine of Transport House, had " now virtually become an integral
part of the State." With the September days of
1939 the full significance of these observations became
evident.

From the start the General Council insisted that
they be consulted by the Government on all relevant
matters, and this was conceded alike by Mr. Chamberlain and Mr. Churchill. Trades Union Congress
representatives were placed on the whole war-time
range of governmental committees, dealing with
supply, fuel, food, propaganda (information) and so
on.

" Integral " collaboration with the State was paralleled by collaboration with the masters of the State,
organised Big Business. In October 1939 a Joint
Advisory Council was established, giving equal
representation to the British Employers' Confederation
and the T.U.C. General Council, and having the

[1] See p. 69 above.

Minister of Labour as chairman. The following May a similar but more select body, the Joint Consultative Committee, took the place for practical purposes of the full Council.

A natural accompaniment of this dual collaboration was the so-called political and industrial " truce," which might more appropriately be described as an attempted demobilisation of the movement. Union branch life and activity slumped during the first year of war.

When the T.U.C. met at Bridlington in September 1939, on the day after the declaration of war, it received from the General Council no objective analysis of the war, its cause and character, no lines of policy for protecting the economic and social interests of the working class. Next year the Congress met at Southport ; the aerial *blitzkrieg* had begun and there was general criticism from the floor on the urgent theme of A.R.P. ; but Sir Walter Citrine replied by repeating the official shibboleths then current, e.g. that there was now no time to dig deep shelters. Symptomatic of Southport, too, was the remission of resolutions on such subjects as the restoration of trade union conditions and the capital levy, the " previous questioning " of a resolution demanding the removal of Municheers from the Government, and the rejection of an N.U.R. resolution requiring, in the interests of union democracy, that voting divisions in the General Council should be recorded.

The war naturally brought great changes in political and class relationships. Defence Regulations 18B (power to imprison without trial and without charge) and 2D (power to suppress newspapers without stating a case and with no appeal) typified the new dictatorial powers of the Executive. The domination of all the State industrial controls by big business

representatives made the " war Socialism " of which
some ignorantly spoke no more than " the bastard
Socialism of the vested interests," as Sir Arthur Salter
put it.   There was outrageous profiteering and mismanagement.   As for the condition of the working
class, authoritative surveys showed how the first year
of war brought a sharp decline ; in the large London
borough of Islington, for instance, it was found that
six out of seven families were driven below their
peace-time standards, while in a munitions centre like
Coventry barely one-half of the families had increased
their incomes, with 20 per cent. of the remainder
falling even below the pre-war level.[1]

Some wage increases were grudgingly conceded in
the early part of 1940, notably to the miners, engineers
and railwaymen ; but they did not average more than
half the amounts reasonably demanded. The Joint
Advisory Council above-mentioned prepared memor-
anda on the evils of " excessive wages," though no
agreed policy was reached ; and when compulsory
arbitration was introduced, with the forbidding of
strikes, in July 1940, under Order 1305, the National
Tribunal soon showed itself a most parsimonious body
(e.g. the engineers, applying for 10s. a week, were
awarded 3s. 6d.).

Within the trade union movement the leaders'
policy inevitably involved them in still more extreme
attacks on all militancy or opposition, first and foremost on the Communists. During the first year of the
war the General Council brought under fire a score of
Trades Councils.[2] The National Council of Labour

[1] *Economic Journal*, July 1940.
[2] Critical working-class sentiments had been voiced, for example,
by the Trades Councils of Glasgow (which created a stir by convoking
a wide anti-war conference) and Cardiff (which called for a campaign
to overthrow the Chamberlain " Government of the ruling class of
bankers and capitalists, opposed to the interests of the workers").

played a leading part in the wild anti-Soviet campaign over the war in Finland ; its representatives sat in committee with the friends of Franco. Leaders of the T.U.C. were in the forefront of the attack on the *Daily Worker* ; first through the libel action brought by Sir Walter Citrine and others, and then, with the judgment gained as a basis, taking the unprecedented step of excluding *Worker* reporters from the 1940 Congress.[1]

A different picture was presented by the rank-and-file. In the first three months of war there were forty local and factory strikes ; and in 1940, while the number of days lost in industrial disputes was a low record, the total number of disputes was the third highest for ten years—strikes were small and short, in fact, but there were a lot of them. From many union branches came sharp protests at the Finnish war's anti-Soviet orgy ; as later came a mounting wave of protest at the suppression of the *Daily Worker*. On the political side it was significant that of the 200 resolutions on the agenda for the Bournemouth Labour Party Conference at Whitsun 1940, there were fifty on the political truce, the vast majority demanding its end ; discussion was shelved on the pretext of the entry of the Labour leaders into Mr. Churchill's Government on the eve of the conference.

Steadily the factory basis of the forward movement became more evident and important. The first national

[1] The suppression in January 1941 underlined the protest of delegate W. Smart (Building Trade Workers), who said that " the action of the General Council . . . constitutes not only a vicious attack on the freedom of the press, but the signal for further attacks by the Government against the working class, its press and its organisations. . . . Congress is being asked, through the General Council, to become the instrument of the Government whereby Mr. Morrison can achieve what Sir John Anderson failed to accomplish, namely, an attack upon a working-class newspaper."

shop stewards' conference met at Birmingham in April 1940. Over 217,000 workers in the engineering and allied trades were represented by 282 delegates from 107 factories. It was decided to move for the establishment of a co-ordinated national shop stewards' movement, and a lengthy resolution outlined an agreed policy, including the achievement of 100 per cent. trade unionism among all workers (including women), increased wages, better workshop conditions, defence of democracy within the unions.[1]

Union and factory representation was a feature of the People's Convention which gathered in London in January 1941. Among the two-thousand odd delegates there were 665 from 497 union organisations and 471 from 239 factories, who endorsed the Convention's eight-point programme for a People's Government, aiming at the democratic defence of the people against Fascism both at home and abroad—in the closest unity with the Soviet Union—at the raising of living standards, and the safeguarding and extension of trade union and all democratic rights. Evidence of widening support for such a policy was clearly provided some months later by the National Committee of the A.E.U. After a long and impassioned debate the engineers' grand council went on record in favour of the Convention programme by 29 votes to 21. The news made a sensation in the papers of June 21st, 1941.

Next day came the treacherous Nazi assault on the Soviet Union. That night Mr. Churchill made his " historic utterance " (Stalin) pledging Britain's full support to the U.S.S.R. At the very moment when the Men of Munich witnessed the sensational achievement

---

[1] The full text of the resolution will be found in Wal Hannington, *Industrial History in Wartime*, pp. 113-19.   The conference was the origin of the Engineering and Allied Trades Shop Stewards' National Council.

of the grand aim of their appeasement policy—a
Hitlerite anti-Soviet war—they had to endure the
supreme chagrin of seeing Britain on the Soviet side.
The war had not, as they hoped, been " switched " ;
it had been transformed.   And this marked a historic
and complete turning point for the trade union
movement as for everything and everybody else.
It was evident that the full alliance established
between Britain and the U.S.S.R. with the agreement
of July 12th required a parallel trade union bond, for
the new situation confronted the unions with new
tasks, new duties. The T.U.C. General Council took
the initiative in proposing the establishment of an
Anglo-Soviet Trade Union Committee. This proposal
was endorsed with acclamation at the Edinburgh
Congress in September and the first meeting of the
Committee was held in Moscow the following month,
the T.U.C. delegation being headed by Chairman
Frank Wolstencroft (Woodworkers) and Secretary
Sir Walter Citrine. The Moscow meeting made
its mark by concluding the following unanimous
agreement :

1. To unite the British and Soviet trade unions in the
organisation of mutual aid in the war against Hitlerite
Germany.

2. To render all possible assistance to the Governments of the U.S.S.R. and Great Britain in their common
war for the defeat of Hitlerite Germany.

3. To strengthen the industrial effort of both countries
with a view to the maximum increase in the output of
tanks, aircraft, guns, shells and other munitions.

4. To support the cause of maximum assistance in
arms to the Soviet Union on the part of Great Britain.

5. To make use of all means of propaganda such as

the Press, radio, cinema, workers' meetings, etc., in the struggle against Hitlerism.

6. To render all possible assistance to the peoples of the countries occupied by Hitler Germany who are fighting for liberation from the Hitlerite yoke, for their independence and for the re-establishment of their democratic liberties.

7. To organise mutual aid and exchange of information between the trade unions of the U.S.S.R. and Great Britain.

8. To strengthen personal contact between the representatives of the trade union movement of the U.S.S.R. and Great Britain.

This historic agreement, duly ratified by the General Council of the T.U.C. and the Presidium of the Central Council of Trade Unions of the U.S.S.R., did not meet with the instant follow-up on the British side which many anticipated. The next step in carrying it forward was not taken until the arrival here, at the turn of the year, of a delegation of Soviet trade unionists headed by N. M. Shvernik and the late K. I. Nikolayeva, joint secretaries of the A.U.C.C.T.U. It can safely be said that Shvernik and his colleagues gave the British movement a striking fraternal demonstration of the nature of real trade union leadership in an anti-Fascist war of the present kind. Speaking to the T.U.C. General Council on January 2nd, 1942, Shvernik laid the first emphasis on British-Soviet trade union unity and friendship, " which must be daily reinforced." He went on to stress that the entire union machine and movement " must be brought into full action," especially in organising the workers to carry out every war measure.

At the same time there was the " fundamental and dominant problem " of increasing the output of armaments, which meant so organising that every individual worker could and would increase his or her productivity of labour.

The Soviet delegation made a tour of the country which rapidly turned into a triumphal progress. They visited some sixty war factories, mines and shipyards ; there they were greeted by the workers, as well as at the mass meetings they addressed in the principal industrial centres, with unrestrained enthusiasm. In a considered summing-up of their visit, Shvernik paid tribute to the " splendid morale " of British working men and women, particularly valuable because British war industry needed to increase the tempo of its work. In tackling speedily this last problem the delegation pointed especially to industry's " very considerable unutilised reserves " ; if any factory wanted to discover where its unused reserves lay, and what to do about them, all that was necessary was " to have a talk with the working men and women."

Since June 22nd, indeed, the working men and women themselves had been talking plenty. Talking —and acting. Long before that day of great change there had been a mounting wave of revelations of the waste, mismanagement and chaos in too many factories ; trade union inquiries, shop stewards' meetings and deputations to ministers, had made these a matter of common knowledge. What now happened—something without precedent, something truly new—was the putting forward by the workers of *positive* proposals for maximising output in place of the previous essentially *negative* exposures. And here again it was the rank and file and the N.C.O.s of the factory front, the workers on the job and their shop stewards, who took the lead.

A foremost part was played by the Engineering and Allied Trades Shop Stewards' National Council and its organ the *New Propellor*. This body organised an all-London production conference on August 23rd, 1941, and followed it up with a national conference on October 19th. No one who attended this remarkable gathering in the Stoll Theatre, London, would deny, I think, that it was the most striking, indeed sensational, working-class and trade union assembly of the war.[1] From some 300 factories, works and yards in the key war industries there came 1,237 delegates representing half a million builders and repairers of ships, makers of tanks and planes and guns and shells. Compared with the shop stewards' first national conference in the spring of 1940 there were over four times as many delegates, three times as many factories and well over twice the number of workers represented. The quality of the representation was likewise rémarkable. Responsible delegates were here speaking in the name of workers at great munition plants whose names are household words—Vickers-Armstrong, John Brown, Humber-Hillman, Fairfields, Cammell Laird, Thorneycroft, Harland & Wolff, Metropolitan-Vickers, Bristol and Gloucester Aircraft, de Havillands, Napiers.

Perhaps the biggest thing about the conference of October 19th was that it did not abstract the problem of production from the whole problem of total war. Its essential slogan could be expressed as " work and fight "—the emphasis being equal. *Fight* : the conference gave its loudest applause to the demand for the opening of a Western Front. *Work* : the conference acclaimed the detailed proposals placed before it for increasing production by scrapping traditional methods, craft exclusiveness and demarcation, by training women to do the most skilled jobs (and also training them in trade union organisation). At the

[1] The reader may be referred to my report of the conference, " Production—Key to Victory," in the *Labour Monthly*, November 1941.

heart of the matter lay the proposal for the formation of Joint Production Committees in every factory, with full facilities for shop steward participation. The industrial potentialities awaiting this new approach, with its unleashing of the mighty force of the workers' own initiative, were suggested at the conference. Delegate after delegate told, Stakhanov-like, of a trebling of output of a gun part here, of a schedule reduced from 40 to 12 hours there, of a special job for the U.S.S.R. completed in two days instead of seven.

In the ensuing months the shop stewards manfully played their part in carrying out the line of this conference. Joint Production Committees multiplied. In February 1942 it was announced that the Government proposed to institute such committees in all its Ordnance Factories, while the Minister of Labour initiated discussions with the employers and the Trades Union Congress for the establishment of production committees in all undertakings scheduled under the Essential Work Order. Eventually a National Advisory Committee of representatives of the engineering trade unions and of the Trades Union Congress General Council was set up to co-ordinate the work of the Production Committees in engineering, the first industry affected.

Joint District Committees in the various areas received nominations from the workers at the factories for seats on the Production Committees and co-operated with the employers in supervising the ballot vote.[1]

[1] The Amalgamated Engineering Union, the Confederation of Shipbuilding and Engineering Trade Unions, representing some forty separate organisations, the National Union of Foundry Workers, and the Association of Engineering and Shipbuilding Draughtsmen, were the unions concerned. In 1944 there were 82 of these Joint District Committees, while Joint Production Committees totalled 4,500, of which 1,600 were in establishments employing less than 150.

Thus in this year of great change, 1941-42, the trade unions, and every single trade unionist, faced a vital task in the great drive for production and in rallying every worker to the arduous but exhilarating effort of total war in a just cause.

As an essential means to this end, however, there remained the problem of unity ; and unfortunately, the leading group of the T.U.C. General Council continued to harden their hearts in regard to the acid test of unity with the Communists. On July 81st, 1941, the General Council joined with the Labour Party Executive to state that, though new proposals of common action between them and the Communist Party had been made, "they see nothing in the situation which would justify such collaboration." In September, at the Edinburgh T.U.C., President George Gibson emphasised, while welcoming the U.S.S.R. as an ally, that the C.P. was still beyond the pale—" the astonishing gyrations of these people have placed them in the lowest category in the esteem of the British working class." [1] In December Transport House was able to record a victorious end to a prolonged campaign, in the final pushing through the country's premier Trades Council, London, of the red-baiting " Black Circular " of 1935.

Yet Sir Walter Citrine and his colleagues made some significant moves with the times. Of that the Edinburgh Congress was eloquent. Reference has already been made to the General Council's proposal for Anglo-Soviet trade union unity and its important results. On the basic question of wages there was no more of the earlier talk of the " dangers " of " excessive wages." Sir Walter himself exploded the myth of war

[1] It would have been hard for Mr. Gibson to account for the Communist Party increasing its membership from 19,000 odd in November 1941 to 53,000 in May 1942.

workers' wealth by citing the simple fact that as against a 30 per cent. rise in the cost of living the rise in wages was only 20 per cent. ; and Congress endorsed the General Council's refusal to accept a flat wage stabilisation policy.

But still more remarkable at Edinburgh was the growing differentiation among the Big Five unions who effectively dominate Congress. On two issues the great general labour unions (Transport Workers, General and Municipal Workers) were isolated and only just scraped through on a card vote. Thus a motion by the National Union of Public Employees requiring the General Council to examine trade union organisation to see whether industrial unionism would not be more effective was only defeated by 2,548,000 votes to 2,384,000. A proposal for the re-admission of the Chemical Workers' Union (to which the T. & G.W.U. and the N.U.G.M.W. are particularly hostile) was only defeated by 2,404,000 votes to 2,333,000. Such close card votes on controversial questions were a record.

In individual unions, too, new trends were to be discerned, new forces rising to leadership. It was scarcely an accident that the A.E.U. should in this respect be once again marching in the van ; that the " proud mechanics " of old should have voted for the admission of women (shades of the founding fathers of 1851!), and that they should have elected such noted militants as Joe Scott and Wal Hannington as Executive Councilman and National Organiser respectively. Nor was it an accident that the differentiation noted above should be sharply paralleled in the campaign for the lifting of the ban on the *Daily Worker*. By the spring of 1942 there were thirty national unions affiliated to the T.U.C. on record against the monstrous maintenance of that ban. They represented a membership of nearly 2,300,000 and included a majority of the Big Five; namely the A.E.U., Mineworkers' Federation and N.U.R. In the light of this it appeared strange that the General Council should publicly announce that it could not associate itself with the demand for raising the ban. It looked still stranger after the debate at the Labour Party Conference in May, with its striking defeat of the platform by 1,244,000 votes to 1,231,000 in favour of the *Worker*. Trade unionists did not rally, literally in millions, to demand the *Daily Worker* back as a *party* political issue, but simply because they regarded it as an earnest for the fullest mobilisation of the working class of Britain for total war and speedy victory.

On the eve of the 1942 T.U.C. at Blackpool, the *Daily Worker* ban was at last lifted, for it had become evident that the Congress vote on this issue would be overwhelming. The paper re-started with a mass basis that it had never known before, rapidly achieved its permitted maximum of 100,000 copies a day (initial orders received were in excess of half a million) and made itself an important and respected force in the factories and specifically in the trade union and labour movement. Of the growth of the *Worker's* trade union backing at the highest level it must suffice here to note the association of the hitherto hostile Transport and General Workers' Union with others of the Big Five in its support; this was in 1944, over the notorious war correspondent ban.[1]

The Blackpool Congress itself showed that the

---

[1] The 1944 T.U.C. unanimously endorsed a resolution of protest from the National Union of Journalists against this ban, and subsequently dispatched a deputation, headed by Sir Walter Citrine, to the Prime Minister. The Cabinet's rejection of that deputation's plea caused the N.U.J. annual delegate meeting (Easter 1945) to decide on launching a national protest campaign.

signs of change and development visible at Edinburgh were no passing feature. The decisive issues of the war were the decisive issues of the Congress. Thus there was universal agreement on the need for the opening of a Second Front on the continent of Europe ; though the official resolution emasculated the demand by leaving time and place " to the competent authorities." An A.E.U. amendment, calling for an immediate opening, secured 1,526,000 votes against 3,584,000. On questions of production a series of positive resolutions were carried—demanding the inclusion of workers' representatives on boards of management, central planning of scientific research, and the making compulsory of Joint Production Committees with obligatory representation of technical and administrative staffs.

There was a remarkably keen and searching debate on education. Despite the bogey of the Catholic vote, said to be an important factor in certain unions, Congress decisively defeated the religious sectarians in their plea for exceptional treatment, rejecting the whole principle of separate Church schools.

But it was in relation to the problem of unity in its various aspects that Blackpool most clearly exemplified the continuing forward pressure in the movement. Though the General Council successfully resisted a resolution from the N.U.R. requiring it to examine union structure and recommend any changes necessary in the interests of closer unity, this rallied over 2,000,000 votes. In the international field there were notable expressions of dissatisfaction at what were described as the " one-sided " negotiations carried out by Sir Walter Citrine with the diehard chiefs of the American Federation of Labour, and the cold-shouldering of the progressive Congress of Industrial Organisations ; a resolution was carried urging the

General Council to develop the wartime relationships between all trade unions of the United Nations as a basis for a world-wide International Federation after the war.   Most significant of all was the breach in that citadel of reaction, the " Black Circular."   Moved by the A.E.U., a resolution for the withdrawal of the circular was defeated by the very narrow margin of 2,550,000 votes to 2,151,000 ; of eight speakers only one, the General Council spokesman, favoured its continuance.

CHAPTER 11 : TOWARDS VICTORY AND PEACE
(1943-5)

WE have outlined the great changes in process in the trade union movement during the year and a half from the U.S.S.R.'s entry into the war up to the end of 1942. With 1943, while the current tasks of war continued to dominate the trade union scene, it was possible to see emerging something of the character of the forthcoming tasks of peace ; to a proper consideration of these new tasks, to the determination of the movement's rôle and policy in relation to the fundamental problems of the post-war period, trade union thought began to address itself. This development was a natural accompaniment of a year that began with the turning-point triumph of Stalingrad and ended with the Churchill-Stalin-Roosevelt conference and policy declaration at Teheran.

British trade unionism faced this situation conscious that it was stronger than ever before in its history, and that its strength was growing greater from day to day. By 1944 the record membership of 1920 had already been substantially exceeded, T.U.C. affiliations nearing the 7,000,000 mark.[1] Problems of organisation that had baffled a generation of trade unionists were now being solved. At long last the miners achieved the historic step of transforming their Federation of autonomous district unions into a

[1] The leading unions reached seven-figure memberships ; thus the Transport and General Workers recorded 1,122,480 members at the end of 1943, and the A.E.U., with 923,000, opened its million-member drive in the summer of 1944.

single National Union of Mineworkers, operating as from January 1st, 1945 ; the ballot vote of 430,630 to 39,464 in favour showed how false were the fears of those who held that district parochialism was still strong in the coalfields.   From the traditional discord of the railways, new and striking harmony emerged. The three unions, the National Union of Railwaymen, the Associated Society of Locomotive Engineers and Firemen, and the Railway Clerks, in 1943 set up a permanent joint committee, agreeing that they should consult together on all wage claims and co-ordinate their general policy.   The terms of the long-discussed amalgamation of the Distributive Workers and the Shop Assistants were finally agreed and the Union of Shop, Distributive and Allied Workers later (1950) rated a membership of over 340,000.

The trade union movement maintained its firm attitude on wages policy, and wages movements were keenly pressed.   There were significant achieve-ments, such as the £5 national minimum for miners (underground workers) with important overtime con-cessions, and the £3 5s. minimum for agricultural workers.   In this connection the rapid spread of Joint Industrial Councils, notably in lower-paid indus-tries, was of importance ; since 1940 forty new Councils had been set up, the outstanding instance being retail distribution.   Reference should also be made to Mr. Bevin's Wages Councils Act, which affected some 15½ million workers ; the Wages Councils were joint bodies like Trade Boards (which they replaced) but with much wider powers, in effect imposing a " fair wages clause " over the whole of industry and encouraging collective bargaining where it is weakest.[1]

[1] The Act and its background is analysed in *Labour Research*, February 1945, pp. 24-5.

Both Trades Union Congresses of this period—
Southport, 1943, and Blackpool, 1944—clearly illus-
trated the trends in the movement's development as
victory and peace approached. New forces were seen
at both emerging into Congress leadership. The
domination of the great general secretaries and of the
General Council ceased to be marked. Younger and
fresher elements in union executive and district positions, more closely reflecting the moods and will of
the rank-and-file, came to the fore in debate.

Of special significance was the prominent and constructive part played by the delegates of the rapidly
growing professional workers' unions—the Association of Scientific Workers, Bank Officers' Guild, Guild
of Insurance Officials, Association of Engineering and
Shipbuilding Draughtsmen. It was from these quarters that there came, for example, a resolution for the
legal recognition of trade unions, carried at Southport
against General Council objections, and the successful
reference back (at Blackpool) of the General Council's
veiled approval of a peculiar body calling itself the
World Trade Alliance, which united certain prominent
union leaders and prominent industrialists.

Eloquent of the sturdy independence of the movement was the opposition at both Congresses to the
Government's obstinate refusal to amend the " vin-
dictive, iniquitous and unjust " Trade Disputes Act
of 1927,[1] whose complete repeal was urged as a
General Election aim, while at Blackpool anger
at the anti-strike Defence Regulation 1AA was
expressed in a vote of 2,802,000 against 3,686,000

[1] The main issue here was the desire for the repeal of Clause 5 of
the Act, barring the affiliation of civil service unions to the T.U.C.
The General Council itself sharply raised the question in 1943 by
provisionally accepting an application from the Union of Post
Office Workers.

for the General Council's support of the **Regu-lation**.[1]

Southport was a Congress which marked exceptionally important advances. The prolonged controversy over the Chemical Workers' Union was finally settled by 3,258,000 votes to 2,451,000 in favour of its re-affiliation. And the General Council itself came forward to propose the withdrawal of the " Black Circular " ; the fact that it did so with protestation of its continued belief in Communist " disruption " and declared that it would not hesitate to ask Congress to reimpose the ban if it thought this necessary, in no way detracted from the significance of the decision, which was unanimously endorsed. The mind of the delegates was suitably expressed by speakers from the Shop Assistants and Locomotive-men, who sharply warned against the real danger of disruption, namely the heresy-hunting attitude that had initiated the Circular eight years before.

Southport's scrapping of the " Black Circular " involved much more than the specific question of the right of union branches to send Communists as delegates to Trades Councils[2] ; it was a decisive gain on a matter of fundamental principle—precisely that acid test of unity referred to in the preceding chapter. There still remained, however, the wider political aspects of unity, the whole question of the unity of the

[1] Blackpool also showed Congress' independence when it unanimously adhered to a resolution of the previous year to admit only N.U.J. journalists to its press table. The ensuing " boycott " of Congress by the Press Lords in the name of " freedom of the press " made a great passing stir, but was effectively turned (for instance in the scathing statement at the T.U.C. by Sir Walter Citrine, as he then was) to their disadvantage.

[2] It is of interest to note that in 1941-2, after the final forcing of the " Black Circular " on the London Trades Council, its affiliated membership rose by only 16,000 odd ; in 1943-4, after the withdrawal of the Circular, it rose by over 170,000.

entire working-class movement politically and its rôle
as the leader of the united progressive forces of the
nation. Here 1944 brought signs of serious developments in union opinion. Thus in March the A.E.U.
Executive Council (with the later endorsement of the
National Committee) urged the Labour Party Executive to convene an all-in conference to formulate a
common policy for the working-class movement in
readiness for the General Election. A proposal made
by the Communist Party to the Labour Party to open
discussions with a view to ensuring the return of a
Labour and progressive majority received the support
of a number of national unions and was endorsed in
an appeal signed by 131 national executive members
of unions affiliated to the Labour Party.[1]

On the three main policy questions of Germany and
the peace settlement, trade union structure and post-
war reconstruction, the T.U.C.s of 1943 and 1944
were directly linked. Mandated by Southport to
prepare interim reports on the last two heads, the
General Council presented documents of the first
importance at Blackpool (it was symptomatic that
the 1943 request for inquiry into union structure,
carried unanimously, was on much the same lines as
those which, as we have noted, the two previous
Congresses had rejected). In regard to Germany,
while Southport sharply differentiated Congress from
Vansittartite declarations with which some leaders
sought by resolution to associate it, Blackpool even
more sharply rebuffed the " soft peace " advocates.

The Blackpool debate arose on the report of the
Anglo-Soviet Trade Union Committee, the main
points of which were later developed by the General
Council in an emergency resolution on Trade Unions
and the War. The central conclusion was that " the

[1] *Daily Worker*, October 16th, 1944.

German people cannot be absolved from all responsibility for the crimes committed during the war," that there must be reparation in kind and by labour, trial of war criminals, " a responsible share " for the trade unions in determining the terms and conditions of the peace settlement, which must be enduring as well as just, and provide for the re-birth of democratic trade unionism in Germany.   Reference back of the report was supported by some good anti-Fascist trade unionists, who were bemused by memories of the reparations tragi-comedy after the last war, in addition to the pacifist-Trotskyist element ; but after a varied and vigorous interchange of views it was overwhelmingly defeated by 5,056,000 votes to 1,850,000.

Under the title Trade Union Structure and Closer Unity the General Council presented a massive 85-section report which the Blackpool Congress unanimously adopted, unfortunately (and rather disturbingly) without discussion.   The main conclusions of this elaborate and thoughtful survey may be summarised as follows :

1. Basic alteration of trade union structure is impracticable because of the variety of interests and theories of organisation (craft, industry, etc.).

2. Amalgamation remains the most effective mode of uniting related unions, but it can only be achieved voluntarily and on a basis of mutual concessions.   It cannot be forced, nor has the T.U.C. power to do so, though the General Council has always striven to encourage amalgamation.

8. Industrial Federation may assist unity where amalgamation is not yet possible.   This may be by way of strengthening existing Federations or establishing Federations where none exist.   Industrial Federations as thus visualised would deal generally with all economic

questions, including collective bargaining and the
formulation of general policy, together with trade union
recruitment. The Federation would provide the expert
research and technical services for its constituent
unions, in order to formulate claims and rebut employers' arguments, etc.

4. At the same time the T.U.C. should develop its own
machinery in order to assist and co-ordinate the work of
the Industrial Federations. It is proposed that the
present system of T.U.C. Advisory Committees should
be extended to cover each industry, each Federation
being thus associated with its appropriate Advisory
Committee.

5. While federated unions would remain fully autonomous in respect of their normal internal administrative
functions, including general protection of members,
enforcement of agreements, collection of contributions,
educational work, etc., attention would need to be
given to the constant improvement of efficiency in
internal administration, stress being laid on trade union
technical education.

6. Inter-union competition in recruiting should be
avoided by extending the wartime practice of the
mutual recognition of cards, by transfer agreements,
the establishment of inter-union machinery to deal with
problems of co-ordination of recruiting, and the like.

In more general terms the report stressed that
changing times had rendered it impossible for unions
to be content with pre-war conceptions of organisation. Nor was it adequate to visualise the necessary
changes as a prolonged, gentle process; " for the
future, unions cannot afford to maintain the rate of
evolution of the last 20 years."

Finally, the Blackpool T.U.C. unanimously endorsed
the General Council's Interim Report on Post-War
Reconstruction. This 52-page document, easily the
most powerful and impressive policy statement to

emanate from the Labour movement in our day, clearly outlined a realistic and flexible programme for the attainment of a planned economy and full employment in post-war Britain. This it notably presented, not as a sectional trade union policy, but as one for the entire British people, the tiny minority of vested interests and monopolists excepted. To give an adequate outline of so detailed a statement is not possible here, and the reader must be referred to the Report itself, or to the summaries which appeared in the press of October 3rd, 1944.[1] The main heads of the policy, whose central conception was that of public control over, and democratisation of, the whole of economic life, were :

(a) *Public ownership* of the key industries : fuel and power, transport, iron and steel.

(b) *Public control*, through joint industrial boards, or other large-scale industries, particularly the highly monopolised ones.

(c) *A National Industrial Council* as a central co-ordinating body, with trade union representation, at the top ; the development of joint production committees (or works councils) at the bottom.

(d) *Consumer goods* : price and quality control, continuance of " utility " production, bulk purchase and distribution by Government agencies, establishment of a representative and effective Consumers' Council.

(e) *Finance and Investment* to be planned by a National Investment Board, taking account of national and social needs. Bank of England to be controlled by (as a minimum) Government appointment of its Governor ; a Co-ordinating Committee to guide the operations of the private banks.

---

[1] E.g., the *Daily Worker* of that date ; *Labour Research* also carried a useful outline (November 1944, pp. 166-9).

The concluding item of this stage of our history was, appropriately enough, the most imposing of all, a summation at the highest level of the basic issues—trade unions and the war, the peace settlement, and unity.   I refer to the World Trade Union Conference which met in London, February 6th-17th, 1945.

Originally the conference was summoned for the summer of 1944, on the initiative of the British T.U.C.   This followed a resolution passed at the Southport Congress in 1943, after the General Council had shown itself averse to a Soviet suggestion that the Anglo-Soviet Trade Union Committee should be widened to include representatives of the unions of the other United Nations.   In calling the conference the T.U.C. stressed that it would be of a consultative and exploratory character.

When the conference foregathered it was soon apparent that here was a working-class assembly without precedent, a truly world affair, representing no fewer than 60,000,000 organised workers.   Side by side with the delegations from Britain, the U.S.S.R. and the U.S.A.[1] were the representatives of France and the other liberated European countries, of China and India, of Latin America, of Australasia, of Africa and Palestine.

It was no secret that certain of the most influential elements in the British leadership were not enamoured of the conference, and did not expect or desire it to be more than a fraternal gathering without serious concrete consequences ; in the sphere of organisation they clung to the pre-war International Federation of Trade Unions, conceding that there might be some

[1] Though duly invited, the American Federation of Labour refused to attend, and President Green violently attacked the " Communistically-dominated " conference while it was in session. The U.S. were represented by the Congress of Industrial Organisations.

vague future reconstruction. But such negative and stand-pat attitudes were simply engulfed in the conference's irresistible urge to unity and positive action. Mr. George Isaacs, M.P., the British chairman, spoke the plain truth when he said in his closing address— " the conference marks a turning-point in working-class history. There have been some small discords but they are small in comparison with the great unity which the conference has manifested."

On the main issues of intensifying the allied war effort (including aid and freedom to liberated countries), the peace settlement and the treatment of Germany (including the demand for trade union representation at the San Francisco United Nations conference), and post-war reconstruction, there was a significant parallel to the coincident Crimea conference of the Big Three. At London the organised workers of the United Nations were mobilising to carry out the general line of the great alliance.

It was, indeed, only natural that there should be wholehearted unity on these issues ; the triumph of unity on the big controversial issue of a new all-inclusive International was the conference's sensational achievement. That triumph was presaged by early signs of the conference's determination and capacity to resolve sharp divergences of view. On the second day the British delegation took strong, even threatening, exception to recommendations by the Standing Orders Committee of which the chief were that ex-enemy countries (Italy, Finland, Bulgaria, Rumania) should be invited to be present and that the conference should be empowered to take a majority vote on vital issues should it so desire. But the will of the conference made itself unmistakably clear, notably through the fraternal but firm speeches of the United States, Latin American, French and

Soviet delegations, and the recommendations were endorsed.

The case for a new World Trade Union Federation, to be prepared forthwith by an appropriate organ appointed from the London conference, was put in a masterly statement by Mr. Sidney Hillman, leader of the C.I.O. delegation. Thereafter it was only a question of the character and precise terms of reference of this organ, or " continuation committee," as Mr. Hillman called it. The British delegation proposed a small committee, with restricted representation, but ultimately there was general agreement on a large and fully representative committee of fifty.

Meeting immediately after the conference, the Committee decided to re-convene the World Conference in Paris in the autumn ; and on October 3rd, 1945, the constitution was accepted by the delegates of 56 countries. The World Federation of Trade Unions, shortly to embrace 70,000,000 trade unionists in 71 countries, was born. It was the supreme achievement of all trade union history. Foremost among its aims were " the extermination of every manifestation of fascism, under whatever form it operates and by whatever name it may be known " and " to combat war and the causes of war and to work for a stable and enduring peace and to carry on a struggle against reaction and for the full exercise of the democratic rights and liberties of all peoples."[1]

[1] Betty Wallace : *World Labour Comes of Age*, pp. 156-62.

CHAPTER 12 : THE POST-WAR CRISIS (1945-51)

IN the first flush of victory in 1945 the Labour movement in general, and trade unionism in particular, was riding on the crest of the wave. To a different war a different victory ; and the movement was in an incomparably stronger and more advanced position than it had been in 1918. Mr. Churchill and the Tories sought to repeat that year's snap " Khaki Election." It recoiled fearfully on their heads. The " man who won the war " appealed to the men who won the war ; when the poll was declared on July 26th he got his answer. Not only was the Services' vote thrown overwhelmingly against the Tories (it was a soldier who gave the *Daily Worker* its eve-of-poll slogan " Vote as Red as You Can "), the spirit of militant unity in the ranks of the organised workers brought the unorganised " marginal " voter to the side of Labour as never before. From the heart of trade unionism came the demand for progressive political unity—including the Communists. At Whitsun, 1945, within a few days of Churchill's election challenge, a motion to this effect was sponsored at the Labour Party conference by Mr. Jack Tanner, president of the Amalgamated Engineering Union. Significantly, it registered the closest vote ever recorded on such an issue, Mr. Morrison's party machine only scraping through with a majority of less than 100,000 (1,814,000 to 1,219,000 on a card vote).

It was this tone in the movement that made the General Election of 1945 a landslide unheard-of since 1906—engulfing the party of privilege and pelf and giving the Labour Party for the first time an absolute majority. Communist representation rose to two, Phil Piratin (Mile End) joining William Gallacher (West Fife). With 390 seats to the Tory 211 (Liberals and Independents being reduced to a bare 10 apiece) the Third Labour Government, with Mr. Attlee as Prime Minister, had in the most decisive measure power as well as office.

A period of initiative and achievement opened. The Blackpool T.U.C. in September 1945, followed its predecessor of 1944 in the constructive working-out of policies concerning post-war industrial reconstruction, improvement of trade union organisation and the like ; it struck a healthy note by proclaiming its attitude towards the Labour Government to be one of " full support combined with fearless criticism." That same month the T.U.C. representatives played a leading part in the historic constitution of the W.F.T.U., described in the preceding chapter. There were also a number of solid practical advantages gained by the trade union movement in this initial period of the Attlee Administration. The " Blacklegs' Charter " of 1927 was repealed and the full return of the Civil Service unions to the T.U.C., added to the general buoyancy caused by the continuance of full employment, brought Congress affiliations to the new record of over 7,500,000 by 1947. Trade unionists benefited from social reforms like the National Health Service and the comprehensive National Insurance scheme.

The experience of the wide measures of nationalisation that were introduced was more mixed. Certainly there was something symbolic, and not unmoving, about that day when the blue-and-white flag of the

National Coal Board first flew from every pithead in the country ; a historic demand had at last been met —nearly 30 years late. But the Labour Government's nationalisation, beginning with the mines and extending to transport and the utilities (gas and electricity), was of the State capitalist type, paying compensation to the former owners at a rate that constituted a formidable financial burden, and establishing a cumbrous and over-centralised administrative apparatus. It created a substantial and highly paid labour market for trade union officials[1] but was very shortly seen by the mass of trade unionists to be something far other than the Socialist measure for which the movement had traditionally stood. New Board too often had too many of the aspects of old Capitalist ; even, indeed, retaining many of the former directing personnel. Complaints under this head, and demands for effective trade union participation in the direction of State industry, were to become more and more insistent.

One early consequence of Labour Government was a certain change in leading trade union personalities. Lord Citrine (as he became) resigned the T.U.C. secretaryship after eighteen years to join, first, the Coal Board and then to become head of the Electricity Board ; he was succeeded by his assistant, Mr. (now Sir) Vincent Tewson. Citrine was the outstanding thinker of reformist trade unionism and an advocate of great skill ; he was a craft unionist who had worked at his trade and risen in the usual way by election to union office. Tewson was purely a product of the trade union " Civil Service " ; he had begun as a clerk in a union office in Bradford and was never a working

---

[1] The seamier side of " jobs-for-the-boys " had its reflection at the Lynskey Tribunal (1948), when the remarkable connections of a cosmopolitan " contact man," one Sydney Stanley, with Labour Ministers and official personages were examined in detail.

trade unionist in the ordinary sense at all. In the
mammoth Transport and General Workers' Union Mr.
Ernest Bevin finally retired and Mr. Arthur Deakin,
who had been acting general secretary since 1940, was
confirmed as his successor. Again the new No. 1 was
a pale copy of the old. Mr. Bevin's bullying bombast
had a lot of cunning behind it which Mr. Deakin quite
lacked. When, after a brief flirtation with unity as
president of the W.F.T.U., he turned to become the
most frenzied of Communist-hunters, Mr. Deakin
specialised in old Red scares that were certainly not
what they used to be in Mr. Bevin's time ; some so
improbable, in fact, that they could not even rate a
serious show in the usually receptive millionaire Press.

Mr. Bevin's retirement from union office was far
from ending his significance for the trade union movement. It was precisely because he was the dominant
figure in right-wing trade unionism, the architect and
prime manipulator of the powerful Transport House
machine, that Prime Minister Attlee leaned upon him
as his principal coadjutor and appointed him to the
key post of Foreign Secretary. For Mr. Bevin, up to
his death early in 1951, personified those forces in the
reformist leadership which were able, no matter how
wide the criticisms of home policy, to harness the trade
union movement by and large to a Churchillian foreign
policy. Just like Ramsay MacDonald twenty years
before, Mr. Bevin stood for the " continuity " of
foreign policy—being pro-American, anti-Soviet and
actively hostile to the new popular movements that
were everywhere arising against the bankrupt old
order (the most monstrous single example being the
continuation of the Churchill policy of intervention to
bolster the Royalist-Fascist regime in Greece). Mr.
Bevin started off on the reactionary foot in respect of
the central problem of Germany. He took the earliest

opportunity to roar out—in one of his characteristic pieces of bellicose rhetoric—that Russia was " coming across the throat of the British Empire " (because of the proposal for a Soviet mandate in Tripolitania). He played a leading part in bringing to naught the Council of Foreign Ministers meeting in London in October, 1945.

Only the most far-sighted and militant trade unionists appreciated that the reactionary policy of Bevinism abroad could not fail to have grave effects on the home political and economic situation. Intervention in Indonesia, Greece, Palestine helped to maintain the burden of military expenditure. The ending of Lease-Lend revealed the highly critical state of Britain's economy, with an immense trade deficit ; nor did the negotiation of a U.S. loan, symptomatic of the growing American orientation for which Bevinism stood, prove more than a stop-gap, greatly reduced in value by President Truman's ending of price controls.

As 1946 wore on, the beginning of the end of the Labour Government's " honeymoon period " could be clearly seen, with all that that implied for the trade union movement. Hopes of capital reconstruction in industry and of radical advances in housing (the top priority problem on the home front) dwindled as the Government nervously avoided a showdown with the steel barons on the nationalisation of their industry —the key of keys, economically speaking. At the Brighton T.U.C. in September Mr. Attlee devoted a substantial part of his address to an attack on the Communist Party—the growth of the Party's influence in the unions had just been symbolised in the election of Arthur Horner to the secretaryship of the National Union of Mineworkers—and took the unusual step, for a guest speaker, of denouncing a motion on the Congress agenda. That motion, criticising the Government's foreign policy, was proposed by the Electrical Trades Union (Communist " dupes and fellow travellers," the Prime Minister had called them) ; it was defeated by 3,557,000 to 2,440,000 on a card vote. In October Sir Stafford Cripps reflected the growing divergence between the Cabinet and the mass of trade unionists with this revised version of the traditional Tory " Labour-is-not-fit-to-govern " sneer : " There is not as yet a very large number of workers in Britain capable of taking over large enterprises."

Nineteen forty-seven was the year of the decisive turn in the post-war situation, both nationally and internationally. The climatic accident of the freeze-up of January-March exposed not merely a fuel crisis but a general crisis of Government economic policy, which White Paper bleats against what was called " totalitarian " planning (i.e. against any serious planning at all) did nothing to solve. American policy began to force the pace on a world scale. Dollar pressure re-formed the Governments of France, Italy and Belgium, squeezing the Communist Ministers out of the post-liberation Coalitions. In June came the Marshall " Plan," welcomed and pressed on with special enthusiasm by Mr. Bevin, for the capitalist reconstruction of Western Europe as an American appanage, and in particular for the reactionary revival of Western Germany and the Ruhr industries as the keystone of the European base which Wall Street needed to carry out its plans for world domination. Of this world picture Britain was an integral part ; the immediate economic reactions in this country were sharp and roused wide concern in the trade union movement.

Thus when, in July 1947, Britain's dollar reserves began to melt away at an alarming pace, the Government's lack of any bold and positive policy—already witnessed during the freeze-up—was again made manifest. It could only retreat and cut. Sir Stafford Cripps' " austerity " plan, introduced in September, put paid to any serious capital reconstruction of industry, while prescribing substantial increases in productivity and a further extension of exports. That same month the demand for an immediate steel nationalisation Bill received an important minority vote at the Southport T.U.C., where also there were loud cheers for delegates who urged that the country should stand on its own feet, not in pawn to America, and where a more than usually reactionary speaker from the American Federation of Labour was shouted down for the spleen and violence of his anti-Soviet diatribes and his slandering of the World Federation of Trade Unions. But though the Foundry Workers rallied 2,360,000 for their steel resolution, the opposing vote of 4,857,000 showed that the Cabinet could still rely on the T.U.C.'s big battalions.

The central feature of the period that now opened was the policy of the wage-freeze, prescribed by the Government and endorsed by the right-wing majority of the trade union leadership. In February, 1948, a " Statement on Personal Incomes, Costs and Prices " was read by the Prime Minister to Parliament and issued as a White Paper ; even the T.U.C. General Council was initially shocked by " the limited and weak character of the White Paper's references to profits " ; but it eventually recommended a Conference of Trade Union Executives to accept the White Paper's policy of " general stabilisation " (i.e. wage-freezing) " on condition that the Government pursues vigorously and firmly a policy designed not only to stabilise but to reduce profits and prices." That Conference, meeting in London at the end of March, was far from a walkover for the General Council, even though its recommendations were accepted by

5,421,000 to 2,032,000. The minority was much more
substantial than had been thought likely ; and the
debating honours certainly went to its representatives.
When the issue was fought out again in detail at the
Margate T.U.C. the division was about the same—a
resolution critical of the wage-freeze being defeated
by 5,207,000 votes to 2,184,000.

From the start there was a distinct element of
humbug about the majority support for the wage-
freeze, in the sense that some of the big votes cast for
it came from unions who (like the miners) were
excepted from its operation ; there were a series of
escape clauses, allowing for wage increases where
output increased, or where wages were " below a
reasonable standard of subsistence," or where it was
necessary to attract labour to under-manned essential
industries, or where in the interests of productivity it
was essential to maintain craft differentials.

Any sort of wage-freeze could clearly not be maintained for a measurable period of time without
removing the principal militant forces in union leadership—the Communists and their sympathisers. The
call for an anti-Communist witch-hunt came first from
the political side, in the shape of a statement from
Labour Party secretary Morgan Phillips ; then, in
October, 1948, the T.U.C. General Council evoked the
spirit of the former " Black Circulars " aiming to ban
Communists from union office, and threatening local
trades councils with removal from the official T.U.C.
list (" de-registration ") unless they toed the Transport
House line. Some trades councils were de-registered
and the London Trades Council itself was (1950)
threatened, though in view of its massive support
throughout the metropolis the threat was later uncon-
ditionally withdrawn. It was significant, however,
that the new witch-hunt was proclaimed in much more

general and so to say permissive terms than the notorious Circulars 16 and 17.[1] The General Council's statement merely said, in rather lurid language, that the Council was " convinced " that trade unionists and their Executives would " give short shrift " to Communists (melodramatically described as " abject and slavish agents of forces working incessantly to intensify social misery "). This theme was duly embroidered in two pamphlets, *Defend Democracy* and *The Tactics of Disruption*, which were broadcast to all unions and trades councils.

The General Council's exhortations were endorsed by the deceptively large vote of 6,746,000 to 760,000 at the Southport T.U.C. in 1949 ; but this in no way represented trade union reaction to the witch-hunt. The principal unions refused to outlaw members for their political opinions, delegate conferences in a number of cases repudiating the witch-hunt by impressive majorities. The one outstanding, and not surprising, exception was the Transport and General Workers' Union, which employed the ancient device of the " document " to purge itself of such notable leaders as A. F. Papworth, Sam Henderson and a whole group of elected Executive members and officers. At the same time, in unions which retained normal democratic procedures, right-wing electioneering was now seriously organised and in the ensuing periodical re-election of officers (for example in the A.E.U.) some well-known Communists were narrowly defeated. But overall the witch-hunt fell markedly short of the hopes of its begetters.

The tactics of disruption thus adopted by the T.U.C. leadership at home had their natural corollary on the international field. The " cold war " launched by the Americans and their " Western Bloc " satellites

[1] See p. 133 above.

faced early debacle if the newly forged international
unity of the organised working class in the W.F.T.U.
remained unbroken. And it was the British General
Council, having disowned the American Federation
of Labour spokesman's violent attacks on the
W.F.T.U. at Southport, that now turned to follow the
disruptive line of the professional splitters of the
A.F.L., shortly to be joined by their erstwhile
opponents of the Congress of Industrial Organisations
in a new-found common fraternity as overseas labour
agents of Wall Street imperialism.

Since 1945 the A.F.L. had been spending money like
water on disruptive intrigues in Europe, successfully
engineering the so-called " Workers' Strength " breakaway from the French C.G.T. Its agents now began
to force the issue over Marshall Aid, hoping that this
would serve to split the W.F.T.U. Conferences of
union representatives from Marshall-designated countries were held in London in March and July, 1948,
under T.U.C. auspices and with A.F.L. collaboration.
A European Recovery Programme Trade Union
Advisory Committee was set up. But the W.F.T.U.
majority was not to be so easily drawn ; its Rome
Executive meeting in April-May agreed that attitude
to Marshall Aid was the individual affair of the
affiliated national centres, and unanimously adopted a
six-point scheme to avoid conflicts between national
centres and the Federation. The A.F.L. were furious
that the split had not come ; and all attention was
concentrated on the British leaders. " Once the
British T.U.C. frees itself," wrote A.F.L. chief David
Dubinsky, " from its paralysing ties with the World
Federation the E.R.P. Trade Union Advisory Committee will be able to go forward."

At the Margate T.U.C. the General Council came
down on the A.F.L. side. Mr. Deakin, President of the

W.F.T.U., who only seven weeks before had publicly denied that the Federation was " acting as a tool of Soviet imperialism,"[1] told Congress that it, was " nothing more than another platform and instrument for the furtherance of Soviet policy." Mr. Deakin was speaking on behalf of the General Council ; and after a poor debate Congress rejected a motion urging the maintenance of W.F.T.U. unity. This, though clearly no mandate of any sort, was good enough for the General Council to go forward, with its American associates, and present an ultimatum to the W.F.T.U. That body was virtually told to commit suicide (suspend activities for a year) on pain of British and American withdrawal. The ultimatum was rejected and on January 19th, 1949, the British, American and Dutch representatives walked out of the W.F.T.U. Executive meeting in Paris, taking their organisations with them. Within a few weeks Mr. Deakin was welcoming A.F.L. proposals for the establishment of a breakaway, anti-Communist International ; and in London in December, 1949, the International Confederation of Free Trade Unions duly held its founding conference.[2]

[1] " Vigorous denial that the World Federation of Trade Unions was acting as a tool of Soviet imperialism was made by Mr. Arthur Deakin at the International Transport Workers' Congress in Oslo yesterday."—*Daily Herald*, July 21st, 1948.

[2] Louis Saillant, general secretary of the W.F.T.U., later characterised the 1949 split as an event which " revealed the narrow nationalist character and discriminatory tendencies of these American and British trade union leaders who, contrary to all logic, wanted to make the international trade union movement into something which was not only limited but entirely governed by the requirements of the foreign policy of their respective Governments " (*World Trade Union Movement*, English edition, No. 20, October 20th, 1951, p. 3). In July, 1951, the W.F.T.U. Executive, meeting in Milan, addressed an appeal for joint action around the workers' immediate demands to the I.C.F.T.U. and to the International of Christian Trade Unions. The latter body replied civilly, promising to examine the proposal, the I.C.F.T.U. with polemical insults only.

Spanning the twelve months from mid-1948 to mid-1949 the rank and file's battle against the attempt to enforce an official wage-freeze from above was expressed in a general quickening of activity on all the main sectors of the industrial front, whether the issues were directly concerned with wages or not. There was widespread unrest among the railwaymen, poorest paid of the great industries ; their 1947 claim for £1 rise and hours reductions was rejected, as was their modified 1948 claim for 12s. 6d. (and, later, for a £5 minimum) ; in the summer of 1949 widespread local work-to-rule movements erupted spontaneously and so general was the discontent that at one point a delegate meeting of the N.U.R. voted 71–8 in favour of working to rule ; at the same time locomotivemen, notably throughout the north-east, staged a series of weekend strikes against the extension of lodging turns. By the autumn of 1948 the principal building unions had gone on record against any pegging of wages and were demanding a 3d. an hour increase, while during the following year opinion hardened sharply against the continuance of the new incentive bonus. So strong was feeling among the engineers over the contrast between wage anomalies and the mounting profits in their industry that a demand for an immediate strike ballot was only narrowly defeated (28–23) at the national committee of the A.E.U. in June 1948 ; there were short, sharp strikes in a number of key factories like Austin's and De Havilland's ; and in the autumn of 1949 the Confederation of Shipbuilding and Engineering Unions put forward the general claim for £1 increase. Uneasiness in the coalfields was symbolised in the strike which swept Lancashire in the first fortnight of May 1949 ; over sixty pits were closed and nearly 50,000 miners brought out over the local issue of concessionary coal.

From the standpoint of basic trade union problems, however, the most remarkable developments were those in dockland. Here the remote machine of a highly centralised trade union (the Transport and General Workers) met the remote administrative apparatus of a nationalised industry. This combination conditioned the London dock strike of June, 1948. A local dispute, pursued through the normal channels, over the rate to be paid for handling a cargo of zinc oxide, was followed by the suspension of certain of the men concerned ; the strike flared up as a spontaneous and unofficial protest against what was claimed to be the arbitrary use by the National Dock Labour Board of its disciplinary powers. Before the strike ended it had spread to Merseyside, some 30,000 dockers were affected, the Government had sent troops into the docks and had proclaimed a State of Emergency. There were strident outcries that this necessarily unofficial movement was a Communist conspiracy ; in fact the elected strike committee which conducted it, and which was the forerunner of the rank-and-file Port Workers' Committees shortly to spring up, had only five Communists out of forty-two members.

In April 1949, a brisk, brief skirmish brought 15,000 men out in the London docks over the issue of the removal from the register of a handful of aged stevedores ; but the next major battle raged from May to July—one of the most historic struggles ever waged by the dockers or any other section of British workers. The issue was not one of wages or conditions but of international working-class solidarity. Canadian seamen were on strike against wage cuts ; and Dominion shipowners, in alliance with a rival union affiliated to the American Federation of Labour, were doing their utmost to break both the strike and the Canadian Seamen's Union. When the first Canadian vessel with

a blackleg crew, the *Montreal City*, arrived in Avonmouth on May 14th the dockers refused to unload her.
A second attempt to unload brought the whole of
Avonmouth docks out. The port employers then
declared a lockout, refusing to allow any other vessels
to be handled until the *Montreal City* was unloaded.
Tugmen and lockmen joined the dockers. The
Government sent troops in, whereupon the crane-
drivers struck. Crews of some British ships in port
refused to sail because Service personnel were operating the lock gates. The smuggling of a Canadian cargo
from Avonmouth to Liverpool spread the struggle to
Merseyside, where 11,000 dockers were out by the
beginning of June. London was involved when it was
sought to unload two Canadian vessels there, and once
again the Government proclaimed a State of Emergency (on July 11th)—the net result being to increase
the number of London dockers out from 14,000 to
15,500. The struggle only ended when the C.S.U.
announced that they had secured certain terms and
themselves asked for the solidarity actions to be
called off.

Even with these multiplying signs of militancy the
General Council appeared to be in an immensely
strong position over its " restraint " policy as late as
the Bridlington T.U.C. in September 1949 (when,
incidentally, the highest-ever Congress membership of
almost 8,000,000 was reported). The Council's policy
was endorsed by 6,485,000 votes to 1,088,000. But
ten days later came the bombshell of devaluation of the
pound, which put paid to any pretence that domestic
prices could be stabilised. The General Council,
compelled to admit its concern over the price situation
as well as the cynically mounting curve of profits, still
desperately clung to the wage-freeze ; and in a
circular of November 1949, used most peremptory

expressions—unions were told that they " must pay
regard to the realities of the economic situation " and
" act loyally in conformity " with General Council
policy. The " realities of the economic situation "
were rapidly turning union opinion in a quite opposite
direction ; even the distorting mirror of the revised
official cost-of-living index reflected these realities in
the harsh form of a rise from the September 1947 base
of 100 to 113 in December 1949. When a new Conference of Executives met on January 12th, 1950, the
General Council faced a keen and critical debate and
barely won—by 4,263,000 votes to 3,606,000, a
majority of only 657,000. Over 2,000,000 of the
Council's vote came from the two great general labour
unions (T. & G.W.U. and N.U.G.M.W.), upon which
the most significant sidelight came from the miners ;
for, while a delegate conference of the N.U.M. had
endorsed the General Council policy by practically
two to one, this had been reversed by the lodge votes
in the majority of the coalfields ; and a turnover of
the N.U.M. vote at the January conference was the
result.

The Labour Government was now approaching the
constitutional limit to its term of office. Its last major
legislative act was—too late and too little—a highly
diluted and compromising measure of steel nationalisation. This became one of the issues in the General
Election of February 1950, whose result was a sharp
warning to the entire movement ; the great majority
of 1945 was swept away, the Tories made a sensational
recovery, and with only 315 seats to the Tory 299
(Liberals and Independents reduced to an aggregate
of 11) the Labour Party retained but a tenuous grip
on power. The Communist Party lost both its M.P.s.

The situation as a whole now became steadily more
tense. In the summer the American intervention in

Korea, with its subsequent involvement of Britain and other countries, flung the shadow of a third world war hideously over mankind. Now utterly in the toils of the American " Atlantic " war organisation the British Government servilely shouldered the astronomical £4,700,000,000 rearmament programme, with all the added burden it meant for the mass of the working people. Clearly the wage-freeze could no longer be maintained. In April the Scottish T.U.C. (which simultaneously testified to the strength of anti-war feeling by unanimously demanding the banning of all atomic weapons) voted for its modification by 242 to 67. In June the General Council made a final face-saving effort in a circular conceding that there must be " greater flexibility in wages movements." But in September the Brighton T.U.C. rejected this by 3,898,000 to 3,521,000 and by 3,949,000 to 3,727,000 carried a resolution (moved by the E.T.U. and seconded by the Civil Service Clerical Association) formally repudiating the wage-freeze.[1]

Outstanding among the now greatly extending wage movements were those of the engineers and the railwaymen. The engineers' £1 claim, pressed through the Confederation of Shipbuilding and Engineering Unions, came eventually before the National Arbitration Tribunal in November 1950 ; that body took the unusual step of refraining from making an award in the first place, but instead suggesting the bases of an agreement. Briefly these were an increase of 11s. to skilled workers (on time) and 8s. to unskilled ; corresponding percentages were proposed for piece-

---

[1] The Brighton Congress not only over-ruled the General Council on the central issue of the wage-freeze ; it administered an even sharper rebuff on the long-standing demand for equal pay in the Government service. A motion by the Civil Service Clerical Association, which the Council did its best to sidetrack, was carried by 4,490,000 votes to 2,367,000.

workers, but these were so unreal in relation to the general level of piece earnings that a whole series of local disputes broke out in the principal engineering centres. These mostly followed a standard pattern of banning piece-work and overtime unless local or works concessions were made to the piece-workers. In a number of cases the employers replied by lockouts but were unable to withstand the solidarity of the men and the strength of the unions ; the engineers scored local victories in large and famous works like those of Tweeddale and Smalley (Rochdale), Ambrose Shard-low (Sheffield), Fairbairn, Lawson and John Fowler (Leeds), Kearns (Manchester). Most notable success was that at Craven Bros. (Stockport), the celebrated machine tool manufacturers, who gained national notoriety in the course of a piece-work dispute, by proclaiming that they would never re-engage " active Communists " ; the Confederation declared a general boycott of the Craven works for castings, etc., and the firm gave way.

Throughout the whole of this period there was a series of factory strikes, too numerous to particularise, on the use of the traditional pretext of " redundancy " to winkle out militant shop stewards. For the most part officially recognised by the unions concerned, these strikes were also substantially successful, even though the fight was frequently prolonged. Biggest was that at Short Bros. and Harland (Belfast), the aircraft firm, which lasted for nine weeks and involved 8,000 men before ending in victory. A particular triumph was the two months' strike of 1,000 workers at Duples Motor Bodies, Hendon.

In September 1950 the Railway Executive rejected the three railwaymen's unions' claim for overall increases ranging from 7½ to 15 per cent., according to grade. In February 1951, a Court of Inquiry endorsed the Railway Executive's offer of 5 per cent. overall, with only 1s. 6d. for the lowest grade. This the N.U.R. and A.S.L.E. & F. Executives promptly rejected and widespread work-to-rule movements and depot strikes of locomen followed. The N.U.R. turned down a request from the Minister of Labour that it should advise its members not to work to rule. The Railway Executive thereupon made a slightly improved offer, but the unions stood firm and negotiations broke down. Chaos was now spreading fast on the railways and the Executive hastily offered a still further improvement—this time to a $7\frac{1}{2}$ per cent. overall increase, with 6s. 6d. to the lowest paid, bringing them over the £5 minimum. This the unions accepted, together with a separate agreement to co-operate in increasing efficiency. But by the summer of 1951 this modest achievement had been outdated by the soaring cost of living and the three unions submitted a new claim for a 10 per cent. overall increase ; in November they were awarded, and accepted, 8 per cent.

Apart from partial strikes in Scotland and South Wales there was no major movement among the miners during this period. Two increases brought the minimum rates to £6 7s. and £5 10s., for underground and surface workers respectively, though this did not meet the demands of the low-paid day-wage men. A second week's holiday with pay was conceded and the five-day week nominally retained, though (contrary to substantial feeling in the coalfields) the N.U.M. Executive agreed to the re-introduction of voluntary Saturday or overtime working. In December, 1951, a new increase to £7 0s. 6d. and £6 1s. 6d. was conceded.

Among miscellaneous movements most interesting was the unusual phenomenon of a London compositors' wage dispute—in effect a lockout—which paralysed the printing trade of the metropolis in the autumn of 1950 ; it was pointedly asked why the penal clauses of Arbitration Order 1305 were not invoked against the master printers. Nationally the printing unions concluded a new type of agreement, to be copied in other industries, combining wage increases with a cost of living sliding scale (1s. a point up or down according to the movement of the official index over the September 1950 level of 114 ; with the index at 124 in the summer of 1951 this meant a weekly bonus of 10s.).

Beyond question, after the defeat of the wage-freeze, the most dramatic contemporary triumph of trade unionism was the smashing of Order 1305. During 1950-51 this strike-banning regulation was used, in the most blatant fashion since its inception, as a weapon of legal intimidation against strikers in key industries. The gasworks maintenance engineers in London, who had been demanding an extra 4½d. an hour, were conceded only 1½d. The men at Beckton struck in mid-September 1950, and within a few days were followed by their colleagues at thirteen other metropolitan gasworks, involving in all some 1,500 key men. The entire trade union movement was shaken when ten of the leading strikers were prosecuted at Bow Street under the Conspiracy and Protection of Property Act, 1875, and under Order 1305 ; they were sentenced to one month's imprisonment, varied on appeal to a fine of £50 each. The strike ended on an agreement of no victimisation and negotiations for bonus payments ; but the main effect was the launching, after a mass protest meeting in Hyde Park and a successful *ad hoc* conference—attended by 389 delegates representing 194,000 London trade unionists—of a Joint Trade Union Defence Committee to conduct a nation-wide campaign for the ending of Order 1305.

This campaign was beginning to gather way when Order 1305 made a still more sensational appearance, to its own final undoing. There was continuing unrest in the docks over the failure to attain the Dockers' Charter (accepted by the unions in 1945)—a minimum wage of 25s. a day, a fortnight's holiday and pensions for aged dockers. In February 1951 a national docks delegate conference accepted a wage increase of 2s., making the minimum 21s. a day ; the voting was 46 to 23, but there were so many abstentions that the dockers claimed that this was not a true majority decision. The very next day a protest strike began on Merseyside and spread to Manchester ; in London only a handful of men came out. Suddenly, on February 9th, seven leading London and Merseyside members of the unofficial Port Workers' Committee were arrested and charged with conspiracy to contravene Order 1305. Immediately thousands of London dockers struck, and the strikes were repeated, involving up to 9,000 men, every time the seven appeared in court, both at Bow Street in March and at their Old Bailey trial in April. The prosecution was conducted by the Attorney-General, Sir Hartley Shawcross, in person ; the spectacle of a Labour administration challenging the right to strike by way of a criminal case recalling the bad old days of judicial persecution of trade unionism really sealed the fate of Order 1305. An imposing demonstration of dockers outside the Old Bailey itself—with its accompaniment of police charges and arrests—was paralleled by a display of traditional British independence on the part of the jury. On one major count they returned a verdict of Not Guilty, the deeply chagrined Sir Hartley had no alternative but to drop the remaining charges, and the seven were discharged. Amid scenes of high carnival in dockland Ted Dickens, Harry

Constable, Albert Timothy, Bob Crosbie, Bill Johnson, Joe Harrison and Joe Cowley entered into trade union history as the men who killed Order 1305. In August 1951 the Minister of Labour announced the withdrawal of Order 1305 and the introduction of a new Industrial Disputes Order which substituted voluntary for compulsory arbitration ; though the new Order provided certain definitions and exclusions (e.g. of strikes against victimisation) which might presage future dissension, 1305's over-riding ban on strikes —and lockouts—was annulled.[1]

By the beginning of 1951 it had already been possible to see that the extending and intensifying wage struggles, the fight against 1305, the widening trend to criticism and opposition on basic policy issues, particularly the crucial questions of foreign policy, required a clear and precise platform. That was provided in February when the Communist Party issued *The British Road to Socialism*, its positive policy document drafted in terms of the concrete national conditions of Britain and Britain's position in the world. By the summer *The British Road* had sold over 200,000 copies, the widest distribution of any basic political document of the kind since the war—and largely to the organised active rank and file of the movement.

The signs of change were evident at the Scottish

---

[1] A fortnight's strike of 440 shop assistants in South Wales in September for union recognition and the negotiation of wage increases by collective agreement was completely successful. They were employed by George Masons, one of the subsidiaries of the International Tea Co. ; assistants in London and Birmingham subsidiaries, involving in all 1,400 food shops, had decided to strike in sympathy when the employers agreed to a settlement with the Union of Shop, Distributive and Allied Workers. A later highly significant movement was the demonstrative " sit-down " by the firemen in pursuance of the Fire Brigades Union demand for pay increases equal to those granted to the police.

T.U.C. that Easter. A substantial minority was mustered against rearmament (which was nevertheless endorsed by two to one) and the right-wing leadership shaken by the passage of resolutions supporting all current wage demands, opposing Britain's dependence on the U.S., and calling for trade and friendship with the Eastern countries. Next month came a further sign—that the revolt and crisis of policy in the movement was forcing a reflection, even though a somewhat perverse and confused one, in the top political leadership. The resignation of Mr. Aneurin Bevan and Mr. Harold Wilson from the Cabinet, and the subsequent appearance under the ægis of themselves and their Parliamentary associates of the critical policy statement *One Way Only*, amply testified to this.

During the summer two of the T.U.C.'s Big Five, the A.E.U. and the N.U.R., lined up with the militant-led E.T.U. and the Foundry Workers, both pioneers of the fight for a new deal in foreign affairs ; this brought important new reinforcements to the policy of a Five Power Peace Pact, opposition to German and Japanese rearmament, the inclusion of People's China in the United Nations, peace in Korea (with the withdrawal of foreign troops), independence of America. Symptoms of acute disquiet were even manifest in the highly purged atmosphere of the conferences of the two big Communist-banning general unions. That bastion of extreme right-wing policy, the National Union of General and Municipal Workers, heard one of its leaders, Mr. G. Davison, call on the Government to be more independent in international affairs ; while he criticised the Soviet Union, Mr. Davison also criticised " America's bellicose attitude and her vast world-wide war preparations. . . . If there was anything more blackguardly and more evil than America's expressed intention towards China, he had yet to come across it."[1]

But it was the T.U.C. at Blackpool in September which reflected the general increase in strength of the critical trend in the movement. At Brighton in 1950 the opposition card vote on foreign policy issues was under 600,000 and the General Council carried its policy—the test question being its report supporting the Korea war and damning the World Peace Movement with the utmost Red-baiting virulence—by over eleven to one. At Blackpool the opposition card vote approximated 2,000,000, ranging from 1,795,000 on the issue of East-West trade (with independence of America) to 2,608,000 on the rearming of Germany and Japan ; thus within a year the General Council's lead had shortened to an average of a little over two to one, though every attempt was made to whip up prejudice by retailing a farrago of stale American-inspired anti-Soviet and anti-Communist fabrications. It was noteworthy that the opposition spokesmen were not unevenly divided between Communists and progressive Labour men.[2] At the Scarborough conference of the Labour Party at the beginning of October the wide controversy that had been anticipated, and that had been bespoken by a highly critical agenda, was neatly shelved on the pretext that the General Election campaign was just opening ; but the trend of rank-and-file opinion was seen in the sensational return of Bevanites at the head of the constituency section of the Party Executive, with the resounding defeat of Mr. Shinwell.

[1] *Daily Worker*, June 22nd, 1951. The N.U.G.M.W. congress did not support Mr. Davison, but it unanimously carried a resolution " welcoming any negotiations " which lessened the danger of a third world war, " fervently hoping " for an early settlement of the Korea war, and a better understanding with China.

[2] *Labour Monthly*, October, 1951, pp. 467-74.

This stage of our history concludes, appropriately enough, with the General Election of October 1951. Appropriately, because this Election was above all a soldiers' battle, fought by the rank and file in the factories and the unions. Initial defeatism in the Labour ranks was dispelled by the unprecedented mobilisation of shop stewards and trade union branches, inspired and led by Communist and militant workers. The Communist Party's unity gesture of reducing its own candidatures to a token ten freed a powerful contingent of the best commandos of the working-class army to battle with their Labour Party comrades-in-arms against the Tory onslaught. Thus, despite the heavy handicap of the Labour Government's record, the advancing catastrophe induced by rearmament, and the total failure of the Labour leadership to offer any positive policy, the Tory hopes of a decisive victory were dashed. Final result was Tory 321, Labour 296, Liberal 6, Irish Nationalist 2. The Bevanite candidates did notably well, all holding marginal seats with increased votes. Mr. Churchill's final overall majority was only 17, and on a minority vote; the Labour vote, an all-time record, was 13,952,105, the Tory total 13,718,069.

At its first meeting after the formation of the Churchill Government, the T.U.C. General Council went out of its way to issue a statement on its attitude to the Government, indicating that other things being equal it hoped to maintain " amicable relations " with the Tory Ministers. A few days later Mr. Tom Williamson, N.U.G.M.W. general secretary and right-wing General Council leader, made a remarkable declaration at a conference called by the British Employers' Confederation and attended by the new Minister of Labour and American E.C.A. representatives. Mr. Williamson stressed " the need for a realistic appreciation on the part of both trade unions and managements of the gravity of Britain's national economic position." He went on :

The immediate problem was not so much the improve-ment of our standard of living as the maintenance of the standard which we had achieved. The most ingenious plan for division of the cake would not make it any larger. " We are face to face with the stark fact that we must explore every possible avenue to increase produc-tion, or accept the inevitable consequence of a decline in our standard of living and the weakening of our national prestige." Much of the difficulty regarding the introduction of new techniques had arisen because the unions " have not had men capable of fully understand-ing what was being done or what was going on."[1]

But these signs of a new model Mondism were sharply offset in other directions. An appeal by Harry Pollitt for the recall of the Labour Party conference to hammer out a new policy struck an immediate chord. Thus a resolution to this effect was signed by all fifty delegates, representing forty branches, at a private conference of the A.E.U. in Sheffield addressed by Mr. Harold Wilson, Mr. Bevan's chief aide. General rank-and-file repudiation of the General Council's " amicable " line was pioneered by engineers' and miners' branches and areas and by key trades councils like London.

Eloquent of rising militancy was the countrywide campaign organised in the first fortnight of November by the Confederation of Shipbuilding and Engineering Unions and its thirty-eight constituents to express the determination of 3,000,000 metal workers to win their £1 a week wage increase demand. There were remark-able turnouts in Glasgow, Birmingham (delegates

---

[1] *The Observer*, November 4th, 1951.

representing 250,000), Tyneside (representing 70,000), Merseyside (representing 50,000), Sheffield (representing 60,000), Belfast and Manchester—a torchlight rally in the last-named city being described as the most impressive demonstration there since 1926. In South Wales the miners elected an outstanding Communist, Mr. Will Paynter, as their new president by 41,927 votes to 34,002 for an orthodox Labour man. And an important member of the General Council, Mr. J. B. Figgins, N.U.R. general secretary, wrote in his union journal—on the eve of his departure for the Soviet Union at the head of a railwaymen's delegation—that " British Labour must appreciate the full significance of the present period, and the urgency of their taking vigorous action by a radical change of policy and its exposition to the people, if the interests of the British people, not merely the workers, are to be protected."[1]

As the Labour movement entered the 'fifties the unions, and above all the union branches, remained its heart and core. To them fell the primary responsibility of carrying forward the struggle, not only on wages and hours and the organising of the unorganised, but also forging, in alliance with the Communists, the resolute class political leadership that the hour demanded. The cost of living index (1947—100) had risen to 130. The Tories, their class bloated with an unparalleled surfeit of profits (rising by 13 per cent from 1948 to 1950 to reach a total of £2,147,000,000), were speaking of " great and grave cuts " ahead. And it was evident that to defend the workers' standards also meant fighting for a reduction in the crushing burden of rearmament, that is to say meant fighting for peace.

[1] *Railway Review*, November 2nd, 1951.

CHAPTER 13 : THE TORY DECADE
(1951–61)

DURING ten years of Tory Party rule, undisturbed by the shadow-boxing of the right-wing Labour leadership at the General Elections of 1955 and 1959,[1] the basic issues outlined at the close of the last chapter have confronted the organised working class in even sharper fashion. The trade union movement is operating in circumstances where ruling-class policy is not just the same, but much more so. " Restrain " wages, push up prices, let rents and profits skyrocket, cut-and-squeeze on social and health services—to document this fully would require not a chapter, but a book of its own. At the same time the concentration of capital has been proceeding at a pace and to an extent never before known in this country. " Take-over " is now a daily word. As 1961 closed the Tory *Observer* could suavely announce that a score of mammoth concerns had qualified for its " Hundred Million Club," i.e. companies whose *net* assets each exceed £100,000,000 Total annual profits rose to £3,608,000,000 in 1960.

The exploitation of the working class has increased through increased productivity, a lengthened working week (through chronic overtime), and the growing threat of redundancy (due partly to the spread of

[1] General Election results (with the aggregate vote in parentheses) were: 1955, Tory 345 (13,266,526), Labour 277 (12,405,246), Liberal 6 (722,395) ; 1959, Tory 365 (13,743,152), Labour 258 (12,216,166), Liberal 6 (1,640,761).

automation). This has to be related to the background, at home, of a comparatively stagnant economy, the rate of increase of British production lagging far behind that of its principal capitalist competitors, notably West Germany. Abroad, there is the America-N.A.T.O.-directed cold war and trade-hampering international tension, with the West German-dominated Common Market as an essential political as well as economic part of the picture. Overall, and as the final appalling pay-off of the impoverishing burden of rearmament, hangs the megaton menace of nuclear war; peace is now the most crucial of all issues.

In these complex and critical conditions British trade unionism has not weakened. Numerically it ends the decade still stronger, T.U.C. affiliations. having increased from 7,827,000 to 8,300,000. Militant outlook and activity has likewise grown, while the progressive forces have made breaches in the central bastions of the right wing which can no longer be closed. The fight goes on ; the right-wing leadership can carry the day on this issue or that ; but their old absolute domination is over, as the survey below of the latest major conferences shows.

The story of industrial struggles in the last ten years is a rich and varied one. Space compels a concentration on the highlights only. This particularly applies to the many significant individual factory disputes of the period, which begins in 1952 with a strike against redundancy at Smiths, the well-known instrument makers, and ends in the autumn of 1961 with a long drawn-out strike and lockout over redundancy at the Rootes Group's British Light Steel Pressings, Acton. The B.L.S.P. dispute was noteworthy for differences in union attitude; while some declared it official, the A.E.U. in particular did not, its leadership even going to the ignominious lengths of threatening shop stewards with expulsion. Very different was the strike of bricklayers at the Steel Company of Wales (September–October 1961) against worsened conditions. This was an official A.U.B.T.W. strike. The bricklayers had behind them complete solidarity both inside the giant Port Talbot works and outside (the South Wales area of the N.U.M.). Attempts to organise black-legging, and later the sensational closedown of the works, the biggest steel plant in Europe, both failed the employers, who had to capitulate.

This brings us to the moral which has been signally driven home by the whole of this period ; namely, that an official lead for action will always win a remarkable response. Nowhere has this been more marked than in the key fields of industry covered by the Confederation of Shipbuilding and Engineering Unions. Two examples must suffice. *First* was the Midlands car industry crisis of the summer of 1956. For some months there had been concern over redundancies at the Standard and other plants ; then in June came a British Motor Corporation bombshell— the sack for 6,000 workers. After a somewhat confused strike reaction at Austins, the union executives concerned met and decided on a general B.M.C. strike for mid-July. What won the day was not only this united and decisive call, but the universal solidarity it evoked. The two general unions stood firm beside their craft brethren ; the railway and transport unions unitedly proclaimed their intention to " black " the B.M.C. *Second* was the Confederation movement of the spring of 1957, when the employers rejected a 10 per cent. wage increase claim. The shipyards came out to a man, 200,000-strong, on March 16th. A week later nearly a million engineers stopped at the Confederation's call in ten main centres, to be followed in a

THE TORY DECADE 199

further week by half-a-million in the London region.
The Midlands were called to strike on April 6th, the
last wave and probably the most decisive. That the
strike was called off before that date, on the offer of a
Court of Inquiry (which awarded considerably less
than the initial demand) did not make the most
massive engineering movement for more than a
generation any the less meaningful.[1]

Among other features of the engineering scene not
least were the two successful apprentice strikes of
1952 and 1960, led by the Clydeside lads with great
vim and vigour, and winning appreciable increases.
The policy-making of the rank-and-file governing
body of the million-strong A.E.U., the National
Committee, has continued to be progressive and
militant. On redundancy (its resolution of 1957 on
the right to work), on pay demands, the 40-hour week,
extra holidays with pay, its line has been consistent.
The problem for the A.E.U. has come to be the
pronounced divergence between its forward-looking
National Committee and its now heavily right-wing
Executive Council, dominated by the president, Mr.
William Carron, a Catholic anti-Communist witch-
hunter of the most unbridled sort who took over in
1956.

Turning now to major struggles in other industries
we may note two striking instances of those being
conducted in isolation, the T.U.C. General Council
failing to organise solidarity action. Thus in the
summer of 1958 the 53,000 London busmen struck
after the Industrial Court has rejected their wage
claim. It was an important matter of principle; but
the General Council's " leadership " consisted in

[1] The Confederation decision was due to the casting of the
dominating A.E.U. vote, by President W. Carron, in favour of the
call-off.

advising the T. & G.W.U. not to extend the strike and in organising loans from other unions to assist the payment of strike benefit.   A year later the print unions took the field in the biggest national movement of their industry's history, closing down the general trade and the provincial Press.   That their demand for wage increases and more particularly the 40-hour week far transcended the boundaries of print was immediately recognised by the British Employers' Confederation in a bellicose statement throwing the whole weight of the employing class behind the master printers and the newspaper proprietors.   But the General Council lagged even in its verbal response to this employers' challenge ; its main efforts were directed to the opening of negotiations for a settlement.

In the two principal nationalised spheres of mining and railways the unions face the grim consequences of capitalist decay.   Ruthless cut-and-close surgery is the prescription of British Transport Commission chief Dr. Beeching (I.C.I. tycoon brought in at the unprecedented salary of £24,000 a year) and National Coal Board chief Lord Robens (right-wing Labour politician : £10,000 a year, plus : motto " strikes are out of date "). The unions have to meet these threats while wrestling with the chronic problems of low pay on the railways and of daywagemen and surface workers in the mines.   The traditional divergences between the three railway unions have yet to be finally overcome, as exemplified in the A.S.L.E. & F.'s separate strike, over differentials, in the summer of 1955.   Yet the railways also gave an outstanding example of the way in which a resolute stand can bring results ; in February 1960, pursuing a rejected pay claim, the N.U.R. executive put in strike notices and refused to budge, despite a united chorus of denunciation from Tory Minister and right-wing Labour leaders ; it won important concessions.[1]

During the entire period the coalfields have been prolific of local struggles—strikes by pits or groups of pits (notably in Yorkshire) over piece-rates, or the protest strike by 40,000 South Wales men in 1952 against the first round of Tory social service cuts. But the over-riding concern of the N.U.M. has been with the continual cuts in production and manpower (the maximum programme is now 200 million tons a year, instead of the planned 240–250 million), the mass pit closures of 1959 and 1961–2 in Scotland and South Wales (including modern " show " pits like Glenochil in Clackmannan), the refusal of a national fuel policy (the oil monopolists are doing too well) and the attempt to negate nationalisation and resume cut-throat coalfield competition by the policy of " decentralisation." While the majority of the N.U.M. leadership has remained right wing, and the miners have not consistently played the advanced role in the general movement that they once did, nevertheless Communists have notably retained the members' confidence in leading elective positions. When Mr. Arthur Horner retired from the general secretaryship in 1959 he was succeeded by Mr. Will Paynter, who polled 249,638 votes to 197,334 for Mr. Sid Ford (who later became N.U.M. president). When Mr. Abe Moffat, famed president of the Scottish miners, retired in 1961 his brother Alex had an easy victory for the

[1] Of other transport struggles, including many at the docks, one of the outstanding, both in scope and militancy, was the dockers' strike of 1954 against compulsory overtime—hailed as a " Red plot " by Mr. Arthur Deakin. Significant, too, was the seamen's strike of 1960, which pinpointed the lack of democracy in the National Union of Seamen ; it was led by the National Seamen's Reform Movement whose chairman, Mr. Patrick Neary and two of his colleagues were later (December 1961) expelled from the N.U.S.

vacant chair, as did another Communist, Mr. Michael McGahey, for the vice-presidency.

Grievances on the job, coupled with the elephantine slowness of much negotiating procedure and the inertia of right-wing leadership, produced a steady crop of " unofficial " strikes throughout our period. The usual engines of propaganda were set in motion to create the maximum prejudice against these strikes (the Press borrowed the term " wildcat " from the Americans) and against their leaders, the shop stewards. This was naturally much encouraged by the employers, who sought every opportunity to rid themselves of militant shop stewards and as a result had many anti-victimisation strikes on their hands. Of these the most celebrated was the 1957 strike at Briggs Bodies, the Ford subsidiary, in defence of steward Mr. John McLoughlin ; the day was only lost because the A.E.U. executive accepted a Court of Inquiry, under lawyer Lord Cameron, which found for Fords. The steward-hunt was continued next year by a Court of Inquiry, under Professor Jack, into a B.O.A.C. strike; the Jack Report made much stir with its diatribes against shop stewards. But the prize contribution came from Mr. Carron, who in his presidential address to the A.E.U. National Committee in 1960 described militant shop stewards as " werewolves who are rushing madly towards industrial ruin and howling delightedly at the foam upon their muzzles, which they accept as the guiding light."[1] This Carronade may be contrasted with the findings of the T.U.C. who, that same year, after circulating a detailed

[1] The riposte of the National Committee was to carry resolutions on nuclear disarmament and nationalisation in the teeth of Mr. Carron and the executive ; to record a substantial minority for an unprecedented proposal not to print the president's address ; and to vote a salary increase to district officials, with nothing for the president and his national colleagues.

questionnaire to affiliated unions on strikes and shop
stewards, reported that trade unionism was deeply
indebted to its 200,000 shop stewards, who " settle
thousands of problems quickly and suitably. Most of
them do very well . . . They work loyally under
difficulties and with personal sacrifice."[1]

Turning now to the policy battles at the movement's
top level, the annual Trades Union Congresses, it can
be said that up to the mid-'fifties, though the right-
wing General Council was still able to carry the day,
the opposition vote grew steadily. From an average
around 2 million in 1952 it had become $3\frac{1}{2}$ million in
1955. This was the case with the E.T.U.'s repeated
motions against any wage-freeze, for instance, and
with the opposition to rearmament, especially German
rearmament. The big turn came at the Brighton
T.U.C. in 1956. By then the General Council had lost
two of its leading hatchet men ; steel leader Mr.
Lincoln Evans had taken a knighthood and the vice-
chairmanship of the Steel Board (at £5,000 a year)
and Mr. Arthur Deakin had died. With the progressive
Mr. Frank Cousins replacing the arch-reactionary Mr.
Deakin as head of the T. & G.W.U., that mammoth
union, breaking the traditional right-wing front of the
two big general unions, entered the lists against wage
restraint ; and even the N.U.G.M.W. backed a critical
E.T.U. motion on automation. In the teeth of the
General Council a 40-hour week resolution was carried.
Ruefully *The Times* wrote that the T.U.C. was " once
again an opposition body."

The following year, at Blackpool, the militant trend
reached the point where the right wing feared to press
any major issue to a card vote. The T. & G.W.U.
walked away with its motion on the wages issue,
while the E.T.U. motion urging a European collective

[1] *T.U.C. Report* 1960, p. 128.

security system with Soviet participation was carried unanimously.[1] By this time the H-bomb menace was alarming and arousing opinion more and more, and the question of nuclear disarmament became the central one.   In 1959 the T. & G.W.U. adopted a nuclear disarmament resolution which rejected the official Labour policy (Mr. Gaitskell's " non-nuclear club ") and proposed a series of anti-nuclear steps that a British Labour Government should take unilaterally.   More sensational was the carrying of a " unilateralist " resolution at the N.U.G.M.W. conference by 150 votes to 126 ; a horrified Sir Thomas Williamson (as he had become) had to take the unprecented step of summoning a recall conference to get this vote rescinded.

At the 1959 T.U.C. Mr. Cousins gathered a respectable minority for the T. & G.W.U. motion ; significantly, Congress carried a Draughtsmen's resolution opposing U.S. missile bases in Britain and—overwhelmingly, by nearly four to one—a Vehicle Builders' resolution opposing the nuclear arming of West Germany and urging a peaceful settlement of the Berlin question. The 1959 presidential address of Mr. Robert Willis, general secretary of the London Typographical Society and for many years the print unions' representative on the General Council, was so outstanding that it requires a reference. To the evident discomfort of his council colleagues he forthrightly outlined the fundamental problems of structure, organisation and inter-relation facing all unions today ; to solve these

[1] The 1957 T.U.C. said good-bye, in private session, to its nominal joint control, with Odhams Press, of the *Daily Herald*. The *Herald* was handed over, on a twenty-five-year licence, to the Long Acre tycoons, themselves absorbed in 1961 into Mr. Cecil King's *Daily Mirror* empire.   Thus there could no longer be any pretence that there was any Labour movement daily paper other than the *Daily Worker*.

problems, he emphasised, called for a " Socialist approach "; nothing could be achieved, he went on, without assuring peace and banishing the " menacing shadow " of the H-bomb ; prejudice should not be allowed to hamper the development of international contracts, including those with Soviet trade unions.

Reaction to the Labour Party fiasco in the 1959 General Election stiffened union opinion and at the Douglas T.U.C. in 1960 the T. & G.W.U. anti-nuclear resolution was carried by 4,356,000 votes to 3,213,000. The egregious Mr. Carron sought to offset this flat rejection of the official General Council/Labour Party defence policy by the astonishing " facing-both-ways " trick of getting the A.E.U. delegation to agree (by 17–16) to cast their vote for the official policy as well, which was thus carried by a phoney majority of 750,000. It did not, of course, take anybody in. The stage was now set for the great political breakthrough at the Scarborough conference of the Labour Party; but before discussing that event and its repercussions it is appropriate to record here that Sir Vincent Tewson retired at the Douglas T.U.C., being succeeded as general secretary by his No. 2, Mr. George Woodcock, another product of the trade union " Civil Service "; and Mr. Woodcock's first Congress, at Portsmouth in 1961, was overshadowed by the deplorable decision to expel the E.T.U.

Viewed simply as an event in trade union history the expulsion from the T.U.C. of one of the Big Seven —those unions with memberships exceeding 200,000 —was quite without precedent. From time to time there have been expulsions of minor unions for offences, more or less flagrant, against Congress rules and procedure ; here was a key union, respected for its power and its leading part in the general

206 BRITISH TRADE UNIONISM

movement, against which no such offences were
alleged. The sole motive adduced for the E.T.U's
expulsion was the charge of misconduct in its own
internal affairs.[1]

But this charge was a pretext to disrupt the long-
standing Communist and left leadership under which
the E.T.U. had gone from strength to strength. The
1960 membership, 243,000, was a fivefold increase over
the pre-war figure. A militant industrial policy, exemplified in the ably-led " guerilla " strikes of 1953–4,
brought substantial wage gains to electricians, whose
average pay is four times the pre-war level, compared
with three and a half times in industry generally. One £2
a week increase was the post-war record for any industry. In 1960 E.T.U. income exceeded expenditure
by £188,357 and the total funds were over £1,000,000.
Many new social benefits had been introduced—a
convalescent home, free holidays for aged members,
Britain's first residential trade union college. The
principal E.T.U. leaders all made their mark in trade
unionism. President Frank Foulkes was an outstanding president of the Confederation of Shipbuilding
and Engineering Unions. General secretary Walter
Stevens, until his untimely death in 1954, was in the
forefront of the progressive fight at the T.U.C. on all
major issues (the wage-freeze, for instance). His role
was later amply sustained by his successor Frank
Haxell.

A smear campaign, asserting that the E.T.U.

[1] At the Portsmouth T.U.C. Mr. Woodcock said, referring to " the
suspicion that this is a Communist witch-hunt," that " it is nothing
of the kind at all . . . I am not criticising them, nor are the General
Council, because they are Communists. We are criticising them
because they were implicated in fraud ; that is the issue, fraud not
Communism " (*T.U.C. Report* 1961, p. 302). A month later the
Blackpool Labour Party conference was officially told that the issue
(for expelling the E.T.U. from the party) was Communism not
fraud. You pays your money and you takes your choice !

leadership only maintained its position by ballot-rigging, was launched in the Press and on television in 1957. Inspired by two individuals in the union leadership who had left the Communist Party, and who exhibited the virulence often shown by such persons, its initial sponsors were television " person-alities " Messrs. Woodrow Wyatt, M.P. and John Freeman (later editor of the *New Statesman*). The name of Mr. Wyatt is indeed a programme—Labour right-wing advocate of a Liberal alliance, racehorse owner, wealthy player of the Stock market, newspaper proprietor and specialist in anti-Communism. A campaign of such dubious origin, taken up solo and chorus by all the reactionary mass media of the Establishment, only requires the comment that it was subsequently ruled in the High Court to be unsubstantiated with regard to most of the charges—prior to the election of December 1959 for the general secretaryship.[1]

Nevertheless, though that election became the central issue in what followed, a couple of years' persistent and fierce Press and television campaigning —plugging the anti-Communist line, hinting that Communists were ballot-riggers—had inevitably created, as it was intended to create, a highly pre-judicial atmosphere. That atmosphere was heightened by the intervention of the T.U.C. General Council, which as early as December 1958, opened its own correspondence-campaign ; its right-wing majority were clearly only too pleased to seize the opportunity to make difficulties for a leadership which was a challenge to them.

---

[1] Of the pre-1959 charges Mr. Justice Winn said : " My considered judgment upon all these topics is that when fully examined, as they have been in at least adequate detail, they do not amount to or establish any fraudulent practice by any of the defendants."

In December 1959, Mr. Haxell was declared re-elected general secretary ; his right-wing opponent, Mr. J. T. Byrne, with Mr. F. Chapple (one of the two Communist renegades mentioned above), brought a High Court action which was heard in the summer of 1961. Lasting forty days, with total costs approaching £100,000, this marathon case ended with Mr. Justice Winn finding Messrs. Foulkes and Haxell, with three other union officials, guilty of fraudulent conspiracy in respect of the 1959 election, and declaring Mr. Byrne general secretary of the E.T.U.

The General Council at once moved in for the kill. An unprecedented ultimatum to the E.T.U. executive " directing " them to bar from any office for five years Mr. Haxell and four other officials, and to have President Foulkes (nearing retiring age) submit himself to a ballot, quite contrary to rule, was inevitably rejected as " an unwarranted interference in the affairs of the E.T.U." So the expulsion was rushed through at the T.U.C. in September, undoubtedly with an eye to the E.T.U. executive elections that same month ; and it was not surprising that right-wing candidates won nine out of the eleven executive seats —through the whipping-up of the habitual non-voters, not through any loss of votes by the Communists and left candidates. The T.U.C. card vote of 7,320,000 to 735,000 for the expulsion did not conceal the grave concern felt by powerful union leaders. Mr. D. McGarvey, the boilermakers' president, warned that it was a " dangerous precedent." Mr. R. W. Briginshaw, Natsopa general secretary, said that it was " humbugging "—and if it " had been tested on the biblical phrase ' Let him who is without sin cast the first stone ' few would have been cast."

In a statement on the day of Mr. Justice Winn's judgment, the Communist Party made plain its opposition to any undemocratic union practices.[1] At the beginning of December 1961 the Party executive, having fully investigated the affair, issued a further and detailed statement in which it concluded that in the 1959 election there were actions at the E.T.U. head office " which amounted to distorting the real position for the scrutineers," that close questioning had not been able to pin responsibility on any individual, and that Mr. Haxell, as the chief officer concerned, must accept responsibility. Mr. Haxell thereupon proffered his resignation from the Party, which was accepted. The following may well be taken as the key passage in the December statement:

> None of the witnesses at the trial (including the ex-Communists) gave a single instance of Communist groups in the union discussing ballot-rigging or any other form of electoral sharp practice. We unreservedly condemn such malpractices, but we remind all E.T.U. members that the capitalist drive against the union was not concerned with malpractices. If malpractices had been the target, it would have found much more to attack in the electoral arrangements of right-wing unions. It was concerned to attack the E.T.U. because of its militant trade union and political policy.[2]

While the implications of the E.T.U. affair are grave enough, it can be regarded as a side-issue so far as the general development and political advance of trade unionism are concerned. That advance, as has already been noted, reached its first climax at the Scarborough conference of the Labour Party in 1960.

[1] " The Communist Party is, and has been, the most consistent opponent of all undemocratic practices . . . The Communist Party will never condone such practices which inflict damage on the trade unions and are completely against the principles of the Communist Party " (*Daily Worker*, June 30th, 1961).

[2] *Daily Worker*, December 4th, 1961.

Here was the definitive demonstration of the decisive role of the trade unions in the politics of the Labour movement. During the months preceding the conference union opinion had been clearly voiced on foreign and nuclear policy and in defence of the Socialist Clause 4 of the Labour Party constitution which, following the election, the Gaitskell faction were eager to emasculate. At Scarborough the official defence policy was rejected by 3,339,000 votes to 3,042,000 and the T. & G.W.U. anti-nuclear resolution carried by 3,282,000 votes to 3,239,000; while that last majority was a narrow one, it multiplied nearly tenfold for an A.E.U. resolution opposing missile bases and the testing and manufacture of H-bombs, which carried by 3,303,000 votes to 2,896,000. The authority of the annual conference over the Party (including its M.P.s) was proclaimed, and Clause 4 reaffirmed, though the position was confused by the parallel adoption of the Gaitskellite 12-point policy which featured the new right-wing nostrum of State shares in private industry as a substitute for Socialism.

Scarborough was a sensational policy victory for the left ; but the right wing remained in the saddle. Mr. Gaitskell made no sort of pretence that he would carry out democratic decisions. In a melodramatic speech he cried that he would " fight, fight and fight again " to overturn the central decisions on nuclear disarmament. This he and his faction, using their control of the Transport House machine, of the Parliamentary Labour Party, of certain union leaders, proceeded to do. They launched the " Campaign for Democratic Socialism " (an ironic piece of terminology ; it means something that is neither democratic nor Socialist) and were backed to the hilt by the mass media of the Establishment—press, radio and television. A manifesto backing the official policy defeated

at Scarborough was signed by twenty members of the
T.U.C. General Council, many of them in defiance of
their own union decisions. And Mr. Gaitskell found
an early opportunity to expel from the Parliamentary
Party a group of the best-known and most effective
left spokesmen, including Mr. Michael Foot and Mr.
Sydney Silverman.

While the Gaitskellite campaign was at its height,
in the summer of 1961, storm signals came from the
Government. Tory " freedom " was again working
itself out in a dangerously sagging economy. The
Chancellor of the Exchequer, Mr. Selwyn Lloyd,
announced a new squeeze-and-freeze phase, its central
feature being a " pause " in wage increases. Among
the first to feel the chill wind were the teachers,
already aroused by an inadequate salary award to an
unexampled readiness for strike action, which would
have been generally taken but for the pusillanimity
of the N.U.T. leadership. Soon the whole of the Civil
Service was in an uproar, particularly because the
" pause " involved a cynical breach by the Government of the long-established arbitration procedure.
Unrest equally swept the postal workers and Post
Office engineers ; there were angry demonstrations
and preparations for " go-slow " action. Tension
increased when the 120,000 electricity workers, despite
the " pause," won a substantial wage increase by the
threat of a strike, and when an official T. & G.W.U.
strike by London Airport loaders did likewise.

To accompany the " pause " the Government
sought to draw the T.U.C. leaders into a kind of
revived " Mondism," 1961 model, by proposing the
establishment of a joint Economic Development
Council, a supposed " planning " body. The universal
resentment aroused by the " pause " naturally forced
the General Council to handle this proposition very

gingerly at first; but eventually (January-February 1962) it agreed to join, nominating six representatives. Heading them was Mr. Harry Douglass, steel union leader and General Council economic spokesman, who had said, in a significant speech at the Portsmouth T.U.C.:

> If the Chancellor was worried about the situation, why did he not call in the General Council, put his facts on the table and say : " These facts belong to all of us, you and me. What shall we do about them ?"   This great Movement has never yet failed to face up to the facts of life.   The General Council has never failed to respond to an appeal for responsible action. . . . If we have the chance to co-operate in productivity, that we will do. We will make our demands, but let us demonstrate first that we are responsible and will accept the responsibility.[1]

Mr. George Woodcock himself was later much more specific. Saying that reluctance to join the Economic Council was due to resentment over the " pause," he added : " It would be wrong for the T.U.C. to allow peevishness and resentment, however justifiable, to be the decisive factor."[2]

With this situation developing the Labour Party conference met at Blackpool in October 1961. The Gaitskellite campaign had managed to swing three major unions away from their Scarborough position, the Distributive Workers, the A.E.U. and the N.U.R. In the case of the first two this had not been achieved by any decision on the straight issue at their own conferences, but by securing the endorsement of supposed " compromise " lines whose ultimate purpose was to cover a retreat from Scarborough. Thus

[1] T.U.C. Report 1961, pp. 375–76.

[2] Daily Mail, December 13th, 1961.

the official N.A.T.O.–nuclear policy carried by 4,526,000 votes to 1,756,000. But it was a Pyrrhic victory for Mr. Gaitskell; for conference went on to condemn foreign bases here—without which the official policy is meaningless—by majorities more than twice those received by similar motions at Scarborough. Training of West German troops in Britain was condemned by 3,519,000 votes to 2,733,000, and the U.S. Polaris bases by 3,611,000 votes to 2,739,000. Conference's loudest cheer greeted the veteran Mr. Emanuel Shinwell's " No war over Berlin " cry ; scarcely less loud was the applause for the parting shot from Mr. Robert Willis—that the left would " fight, fight and fight again !"

So Blackpool demonstrated, as was said at the beginning of this chapter, that the days of the old absolute right-wing domination are over. That in no way minimises the magnitude of the task confronting progressive trade unionists if they are to win the whole of the movement, industrially and politically, for their policy. The task is a double one, though both its aspects are linked.

First there are the trade union problems proper, some of them indicated in the Willis T.U.C. presidential address in 1959.[1] Amalgamation, the ending of inter-union competition and demarcation conflicts, what Mr. Briginshaw calls " streamlining," are urgent questions. The T.U.C. General Council should become,

[1] Serious legal threats have recently developed. The case of *Bonsor* v. *Musicians' Union* laid it down that a union could be mulcted in damages for a wrongful expulsion. *Rookes* v. *Barnard* brought back memories of Taff Vale and seemed to cut right across the 1906 Act ; the judgment awarded damages of £7,500 against officials of the Draughtsmen's union because they had threatened to call out their members at London Airport, in breach of their contract of employment, to maintain a closed shop. This judgment has rightly alarmed the entire trade union movement ; it went to appeal in February 1962.

what it was intended to be when it was devised in 1919
and what it has never been, the real General Staff of
Labour. The structure and functioning of the General
Council need complete overhaul, as does its method
of election—with the log-rolling and witch-hunting
which have long been notorious. That miners' general
secretaries of the calibre of Mr. Horner and Mr.
Paynter should be kept out of their normal place on
the Council just because they are Communists is
intolerable.

These trade union problems, however, need the
Socialist approach for their solution of which Mr.
Willis has spoken. This in its turn leads to the second
aspect of the movement's task, which involves the
whole question of the unions and politics. With the
leftward trends in the unions it is an astonishing
anomaly that the large and influential Trade Union
Group of Labour M.P.s should be a pillar of extreme
right-wing reaction (Mr. Charles Pannell, its secretary,
got a very rough house at Blackpool when he shouted
" show me a Communist, and I'll show you a crook ";
but the remark was not untypical).

Trade union backing will be crucial for the Labour
rank-and-file manifesto " This Way to Peace," calculated to provide a broad progressive platform and
being circulated throughout the movement at the
turn of 1961–2. Backed by sixty-five Labour M.P.s
and union leaders on its launching, this manifesto can
well mark a major step forward. In so advancing,
trade unionists will need to draw the full lessons of
this fundamental characterisation (written in 1960)
of the aftermath of 1945's crowning victory :

The Attlee–Bevin leadership proceeded to embark on
a programme of vicious anti-Soviet hostility from the
outset, the cold war, surrender of Britain to the United

States, construction of the atom bomb. . . . American bomber bases in Britain, colonial wars, N.A.T.O., the rebuilding of German militarism and colossal rearmament. When the bill for all this resulted in austerity, the reversal of social reforms and the wage freeze, the previous mass enthusiasm gave place to mass disillusionment. On this basis, not through their own virtues, the previously discredited Tories were able to creep back.[1]

Gaitskell–Brown are only an echo of Attlee–Bevin, whatever tricking out of policies " new thinking " or " re-thinking " has brought. Trade unionists will find their own true Signposts for the Sixties not in the non-Socialist, diluted document of that title paraded at the Blackpool conference, but in the militant, class, Socialist line that is its direct opposite.

[1] R. Palme Dutt, " Notes of the Month," *Labour Monthly*, October 1960.

CHAPTER 14: FROM "CONSENSUS" TO CONFRONTATION (1961-74)

Allen Hutt died without realising his intention to up-date the story of the struggles and development of British trade unionists and their organisation. Yet he would have rejoiced to recount the heroic battles and achievements of the past decade which he so brilliantly foresaw in the concluding sentence of the chapter with which he ended the fifth edition of this book. I feel privileged to have been asked by Allen, shortly before his death and when he was already aware that he lacked the physical strength to complete the work for this sixth edition, to undertake this task.

JOHN GOLLAN
London, August 1974

THE 1960's and early 1970's were years in which the crisis of British capitalism extended and political consciousness among the working class grew. The class struggle reached an intensity beyond anything experienced in the post-war period, if not in the entire history of British trade unionism. The events of the 1960s culminated in classic confrontations between the government and shipbuilding workers, engineers and coal miners which in turn acted as catalysts for further struggles.

In the early 1970's these struggles reached a level

which could only be described as a mass confrontation between the organised working class and the State, compelling governments to reverse policies to which they were publicly committed. They eventually led to the defeat of the Heath Government after the 1974 miners' strike.

This confrontation didn't just happen. It was the logical outcome of the political situation. The Report to the 32nd Congress of the Communist Party in November 1971, presenting a Marxist analysis of the balance of class forces and class interests, foresaw these developments. The Communist Party was the first political party to describe the rapidly mounting events in terms of " confrontation "—a word which since then has become commonplace in the country's political vocabulary.

> This government is big business personified. More than any recent government, it is trying to put the full burden of Britain's problems on the working class. Its room for manoeuvre is limited because of the crisis of the capitalist system, and of mounting working class resistance. As a result, there is class confrontation. In this confrontation our class is going to win.
>
> Report to 32nd Congress C.P.G.B.,
> reported in *Morning Star*, November 15th, 1971

At the start of the 'sixties there was a growing recognition among those in power of British capitalism's inability to survive without internal government intervention and external foreign financial support. In order publicly to justify using the resources of the State to prop up failing capitalist enterprises through subsidies and government intervention, it was necessary to attempt to create a climate of " consensus " within industry. The aim was to give the trade unions, employers and government a corporate identity, to have them involved in an unholy alliance

dominated by the employers. But to achieve this
it was necessary for the government to control the
trade unions. The 1960's, particularly the later
years, were characterised by intense but abortive
attempts by governments to subjugate the unions.
These very attempts stimulated a consciousness
among workers which made government failure
inevitable.

In 1961 there was one of the relatively frequent
economic crises which had marked Britain's post-war
years. The German mark was revalued upwards
and short-term speculative money moved out of
Britain producing panic amongst economic policy-
makers. In July, the government announced a series
of emergency measures including a demand for a pay
pause. Wage increases were to be linked to changes
in the level of national productivity which the government, through its severe credit squeeze measures,
ensured would not move upwards. In other words, the
government enforced a wage freeze.

In February 1962, the Tory White Paper *Incomes
Policy: The Next Step* introduced the notion of a
" guiding light " whereby wages and salaries in 1962
were to be kept within the $2\frac{1}{2}$ per cent. figure by
which it was expected national productivity would
rise. Where the government was able to control
wages, namely those of its own employees, it adopted
an inflexible attitude. The National Economic Development Council was set up, a body which was to include unions, employers and government. After
much hesitation the T.U.C. General Council, in the
same month accepted an invitation to be represented
on it. The N.E.D.C. had no powers of compulsion.
It was an estimating, forecasting, advisory body
with the main aim of achieving a consensus between
the T.U.C., the employers and the government on

vital economic issues. Alongside the N.E.D.C. the
government established the National Incomes Commission to consider claims or disputes referred to it
by agreement between unions and employers, or,
where the parties could not agree, by the government
itself. The N.I.C., however, never really got off the
ground, since the T.U.C. refused to be associated
with it.

In 1962 there were strong protests against the
government's incomes policy. When 10,000 nurses
staged a march in London in April, workers in other
industries supported them with token stoppages.
Dock workers threatened strike action to get more
than the government-stipulated $2\frac{1}{2}$ per cent., and
achieved an eleventh hour victory. Many groups of
workers in private industry won increases above the
norm. Only public employees suffered to the fullest
extent from the government policy.

Workers in some industries were meantime suffering from other aspects of government intervention.
The contraction of the railways and the mining
industry, begun during the late 1950s, was having
destructive effects by the 1960's. By 1962 nearly a
fifth of the whole railway network, over 3,600 miles,
had been closed. This was part of a cutback started
by Dr. Beeching. The same thing was happening in
mining under the guidance of Lord Robens. Some
634,000 men had been employed in the mines in
1959. This figure was reduced to 536,000 by 1962.
Contraction, increased mechanisation, industrial reorganisation, with the inevitable consequences of
redundancy, job transfer, work speed-up and worsened
working conditions were common in the early 1960's.
All this took place within a succession of economic
convulsions of one kind or another.

When the Labour Party was returned to power in

October 1964, after thirteen years of Tory rule, it inherited the deep economic crisis which the Tories had made worse and the features of an incipient corporate state in Britain were emerging. Britain had an unbearable balance of payments deficit to which the new Labour Government responded in traditional manner by borrowing from foreign bankers. The bank rate was pushed up, a surcharge of 15 per cent was imposed on imports. The Labour Government then produced its own version of an incomes policy. The first stage was an appeal for voluntary co-operation. In December 1964 a Joint Declaration of Intent on Productivity, Prices and Incomes was signed by employers and the T.U.C. A conference of Executive Committees of affiliated organisations was held by the T.U.C. in April 1965 to consider the Declaration of Intent, and outlined the machinery to implement the incomes policy and the criteria for wage increases contained in the government's White Paper.[1] The conference was, however, influenced by its loyalty to a Labour Government and by the tenuous majority the government had in Parliament. It endorsed collaboration with the government by a large majority.[2]

An essential part of this " consensus " scheme was to reduce the number, extent and intensity of strikes, and here the real problem was the so-called unofficial strike. It was estimated by the Ministry of Labour that 95 per cent. of all strikes were unofficial, led by shop stewards or local branch officials. Public attention was directed to shop stewards, particularly those in the engineering industry. The Prime Minister, Mr. Harold Wilson, called for special

[1] White Paper on Prices and Incomes. Cmd. 2693.
[2] See *Militant Trade Unionism* by V. L. Allen, Chap. IV, The Merlin Press, London 1966.

measures in the motor-car industry. The T.U.C. and
the British Employers' Federation agreed jointly to
investigate unofficial strikes for one year from October
1964.

Then, in February 1965, the government set up a
Royal Commission on Trade Unions and Employers'
Associations, headed by Lord Donovan. The Tories
had demanded such a Commission but the Labour
Party had rejected it during the 1964 election. The
Labour Party went back on its pledge in order to
satisfy the international bankers that capitalist
Britain was credit-worthy.

When it established the National Board for Prices
and Incomes in April 1965, and appointed Mr. Aubrey
Jones, a former Conservative Minister and M.P. as
its Chairman, the government moved a stage nearer
to a statutory incomes policy. The Board had some
small initial impact by inducing employers and unions
to delay introducing wage increases while these were
under discussion. By the summer, however, it was clear
that the Board was not serving the government's
purpose. It was a very blunt instrument for controlling
the wage demands of unions. No one was surprised,
therefore, when the government approached the
General Council of the T.U.C. in September with a
proposal to give the Prices and Incomes Board a
statutory basis.

There was strong opposition in the T.U.C. to
statutory wage controls. The T. & G.W.U. led the
attack, supported by the white-collar unions, which
were growing in influence. In the 1965 T.U.C. the
General Council Report, giving limited support to the
government, was adopted by 5,251,000 votes to
3,312,000. The Report accepted " A limited degree of
statutory reinforcement " which gave wide powers
to the National Board for Prices and Incomes. These

included collecting evidence and calling witnesses. There had to be prior notification of intent to increase prices or charges, and likewise of claims relating to pay, hours or other major improvements. Any price, whether existing or proposed, and any claim or settlement, had " in the national interest " to be referred to the Board. And any price or pay increases had to be deferred.

The Labour Government which was returned with a narrow majority in 1964 was prepared to let the T.U.C. have another go at voluntary wage control for a limited experimental period, and the General Council then set up a special committee to vet pay claims. This concession, however, was merely a government delaying tactic. The Prices and Incomes Bill was published in February 1966. It contained no mention of dividends, yet the General Council of the T.U.C. supported it by 21 votes to 11 before it had even seen its precise wording. For the first time in British trade union history the government, and a Labour Government at that, had announced its intention to intervene in the collective bargaining process in peace-time. Four days after the publication of the Bill a General Election was announced.

With the Labour Government re-elected in April 1966, the pressure on the unions grew and took different forms. The Prices and Incomes Act became law in August. Its first part followed the earlier Bill, but it had a new second part which enabled the government to enforce a wages norm. The government was given new power to cut back on earnings because, it claimed, " the country needs a breathing space of twelve months in which productivity can catch up with the excessive increases in incomes which have been taking place."[1] Millions of workers suffered

[1] Harold Wilson in the House of Commons, July 20th, 1966.

reductions in their living standards as a consequence of this legislation. Nonetheless the trade union movement decided that the government's policy should be given a fair trial and at a Conference of Union Executives in March 1967, an overwhelming majority supported it.

At the heart of the Labour Government's incomes policy was the attempt to control shop floor wage-bargaining and this meant, in effect, the control of shop stewards. At first the emphasis was on methods of wage payment. The Prices and Incomes Board recommended the substitution of measured day-work for piecework as a way of stopping wage drift without adversely affecting output. Measured day-work greatly reduced participation of shop stewards in customary continuous local bargaining by providing high fixed earnings in return for a high level of output. Vauxhall's introduced it; then Rootes followed suit.

Most Government wages propaganda, however, was directed to productivity bargaining in which wage increases were only given in return for concessions by workers concerning so-called restrictive practices. Unions which could not get wage increases because of the government's freeze policy quickly entered into productivity agreements which became a façade behind which free collective bargaining took place. Between January 1st, 1967 and March 3rd, 1967, 289 productivity agreements had been reported to the Ministry of Labour. They became the Achilles heel of the wage freeze policy, for frequently no real productivity concessions were made by the unions. The employers were not unduly worried because often their main concern was to find a way of increasing wages simply to attract labour or retain it. Productivity bargaining became an enormous sham in which union leaders, employers, politicians, civil servants

BRITISH TRADE UNIONISM

and academics enthusiastically joined. Of course it was never admitted to be a sham. Both the P.I.B. and the Royal Commission on Trade Unions devoted much of their time to providing a rationale for productivity bargaining.

But the main concern of the Labour Government after it was elected was the trade union militants. Three years of unrelenting pressure from government and employers culminated in the White Paper, *In Place of Strife*,[1] which sought to make unofficial strikes illegal. The first major indication of the government's tactics was shown during the Seamen's strike in May 1966, which marked the start of a new wave of militancy among lower-paid workers. The Executive of the National Union of Seamen rejected an employers' package deal in April and called for a national strike for May 16th for a substantial wage increase and a 40-hour week. The government used all the propaganda weapons at its disposal to oppose the strike and to discredit the strike leaders. The Prime Minister broadcast the day the strike began, and stated that " if our urgent advice were not taken it would be the duty of the Government . . . to resist the action they (the seamen) have taken. Because this would be a strike against the State—against the community. But this isn't all. What is at issue here is our national prices and incomes policy; to accept this demand would breach the dykes of our prices and incomes policy. . . . "[2] The strike got 100 per cent. support among the seamen.

A State of Emergency was declared on May 23rd. A Court of Inquiry was set up under Lord Pearson, but the Seamen's Executive refused to accept its report as

[1] *In Place of Strife*, January 1969. Cmd. 3888.
[2] For a fuller treatment of the Seamen's strike see *We Want 40*, a C.P. pamphlet by Jack Coward.

a basis for negotiations. Other unions gave wide support to the seamen. Dockers refused to handle ships declared " black " by local strike committees. Foreign unions were asked to " black " ships diverted from British ports. Then Mr. Wilson, the Prime Minister,[1] endeavoured to use McCarthyite tactics by referring in the House of Commons to a " tightly knit group of politically motivated men " who were influencing the N.U.S. Executive, including members of the Communist Party Industrial Department headed by Bert Ramelson, and such leading Communist dockers and seamen as Jack Dash, Harry Watson and Gordon Norris. The mass media took up the cue and began their own insidious interrogations on TV and radio. At the end of June the Prime Minister tried again to destroy the unity of the Seamen's Executive by exposing and denigrating some of its members—Jim Slater and Joe Kenny in particular. These tactics utterly failed. The strike ended on July 1st with an increase above the norm and a 42-hour week. It is worth noting that eight years later one of Mr. Wilson's named men, Jim Slater, was elected General Secretary of the National Union of Seamen.

Labour's six month wage freeze was then followed by " restraint ", and the government's neo-Tory policies acted as a catalyst, generating militancy among white-collar workers as well as among the manual workers. Teachers began preparing for militant action in 1967. A long and bitter struggle for trade union reorganisation took place at Roberts Arundel, an American-owned firm at Stockport, Cheshire.[2] More than 20,000 dockers struck in

[1] House of Commons, June 20th, 1966.
[2] For a full fascinating description of this dispute see *The Million Pound Strike* by Jim Arnison with a foreword by Hugh Scanlon. Lawrence and Wishart, 1970.

September 1967 for a higher minimum wage and better conditions. Airline pilots began a series of 48-hour strikes, while manning disputes sparked off the A.S.L.E.F. drivers' work-to-rule. In this period the Transport and General Workers' Union was alone amongst the big unions in its opposition to government policy. A dramatic change in the alignment of progressive forces in the unions was presaged by the announcement on November 7th that Mr. Hugh Scanlon had been elected President of the Amalgamated Engineering Union in succession to Lord Carron. Militancy began to be reflected in the union elections at national as well as district level.

While the Labour Government's incomes policy restrained wages, inflation was not controlled, nor was Britain's economy made more viable. The power of the monopolies grew. Mergers and takeovers multiplied in 1967 and 1968—1966 was a record year, with bids totalling over £500 million. 1967 provided another record with take-overs by public companies alone worth more than £1,000 million. During 1967 the Board of Trade was asked to refer ninety mergers or proposed bids to the Monopolies Commission. No section of industry was immune to the monopoly take-over fever. It was accompanied by increasing insecurity and intensified labour conditions for the workers. Unemployment began to increase.

In this situation redundancy did not simply involve job transfer, for there was a shortage of jobs. Miners and other workers were forced to adopt new attitudes towards the contraction of their industries. In 1967-8, sixty-two pits were closed, which was more than in any previous year. The number of N.C.B. mines fell from 840 in 1956 to 376 in 1967, and the number of miners from 698,000 to 365,000. Full employment up till then had cushioned the impact of industrial change.

In 1968 the cushion was suddenly and crudely removed.

Some sections of the work force experienced greater and more dramatic repercussions than others. Women made up 37 per cent. of the employed population and earned on average about half of male average earnings. The movement towards equal pay had been imperceptible. Unions, though frequently in favour of the principle of equal pay for equal work, were slow in pressing for it. Employers wriggled out of commitments for equal pay by redefining the meaning of women's work so that it was not comparable in trifling ways with men's work. With increases in the cost of living, women's earnings became vital for the maintenance of families. When unemployment hit male jobs then women's work became of primary importance.

The situation of coloured immigrant workers also changed. Their very existence began to be defined as a problem for British white society, and racial discrimination became more open and extensive. White racism, fostered by neo-fascists, was encouraged by their worsening economic plight of the " poor whites." The greater the degree of unemployment, the more were coloured workers used as scapegoats and exposed to discrimination. They, like women, received little protection from the unions. The Race Relations Act in 1965 had made discrimination illegal in places of public resort, while the second Act in 1968 made discrimination illegal in housing, employment and the provision of goods, facilities or services. The problem with discrimination, however, was its detection and making legal prohibition a reality.

A group of workers who had been largely insulated from the mounting economic pressures was that of white-collar workers. In the late 1960's, however, they too were suffering lowered standards of life. Already many public servants had suffered the greatest impact of the government's freeze policy. In 1968 and 1969 they were increasingly forced to recognise that they could be protected only by collective action. The sharp social lines between manual and non-manual began to be blurred and much overlapping between the groups took place.

These increasing pressures on workers to organise and protect their interests coincided with a government determination to isolate and prohibit unofficial strikes. This created a contradiction which had widespread repercussions. The growing influence of shop stewards had become a matter for public debate when the Report of the Royal Commission on Trade Unions was published in June 1968. The Report was primarily concerned with the control of wage drift and, therefore, with the regulation of workshop bargaining. It argued: " So long as workplace bargaining remains informal, autonomous and fragmented, the drift of earnings away from rates of pay cannot be brought under control. Well-regulated company and factory agreements would enable companies to exercise effective control over their own wage- and salary-bills, and that in turn would make the control of drift a possibility." The Report was in effect an exhortation to company directors to take matters into their own hands and through the manipulation of company-based agreements to restrict the activities of shop stewards.[1] On one vital issue, however, the Report was explicit. It opposed further statutory regulation of industrial relations. Voluntary collective bargaining, the Commission believed, should remain intact. This belief was in sharp contrast to the policy of the Tory Party, set out in *Fair*

[1] See *Donovan Exposed* by Bert Ramelson. C.P. pamphlet, 1968.

Deal at Work, which recommended far-reaching legal controls over trade unions.

There were 175,000 shop stewards, according to the Commission, compared with about 3,000 full-time trade union officers. There was little doubt that shop stewards were handling a major part of trade union business. They were, however, identified primarily as strike leaders, and the causes of Britain's economic ailments were laid at their door.

Above all the Labour Government held this view. And *In Place of Strife*, was published as the Labour Government's answer to industrial relations. In essence their White Paper turned the proposals in the Royal Commission Report on their head. It recommended penal sanctions for unofficial strikers and a " cooling off " period for strikers such as was practised in the U.S.A. It suggested the establishment of a Commission for Industrial Relations which the government immediately set up under the Chairmanship of Mr. George Woodcock, former General Secretary of the T.U.C., who retired in 1969 and had been replaced by Vic Feather.

There was an immediate reaction against the main proposals. Several unions, including the A.U.E.W., and the T. & G.W.U. demanded the recall of the T.U.C.

The Liaison Committee for the Defence of Trade Unions, consisting of shop stewards and others, sponsored by the shop stewards' committees of some of the largest factories in the country, launched an imaginative campaign for the defence of trade union rights. A Conference it called in November 1968 had to change its venue twice to find a hall big enough to hold all the delegates elected from factories, pits, depots and trade union branches.

This overflow conference, the largest rank and file

gathering in the history of the British trade union movement, enthusiastically called for a day of industrial action on December 8th. The response surpassed all expectations; over a million workers downed tools and no national papers appeared that day. This was followed by further industrial action the following month in some of those cities which had not responded on December 8th.

These were the first large-scale strikes, not for wages, but against government legislation, demanding the withdrawal of a Bill already being debated in Parliament. They were strikes with profound political repercussions.

While initiated by the rank and file, this campaign had a great effect on the official trade union movement and the country as a whole. The T.U.C. began actively to oppose the Bill and demand its withdrawal.

An intense and bitter debate began between unions and the T.U.C., on the one hand, and the government, on the other, about the government's intention to approve *In Place of Strife* as a basis for legislation. A total of some quarter of a million workers struck on May 1st against the government's Bill. There were large protest marches in Britain's main cities. The General Council of the T.U.C. recalled Congress on June 5th, 1969, the first such special Congress for over forty years, to debate a *Programme for Action* against the government legislation. It opposed all penalties on trade unionists and suggested changes in the T.U.C. rules to permit the General Council to intervene in inter-union and in " unauthorised " or " unconstitutional " strikes, with the power to make recommendations or awards binding upon trade unions and their members. Congress supported the General Council report by 7,908,000 votes to 846,000. The Prime Minister was not con-

vinced, however, and stated that there was insuffi-
cient assertion of responsibility by the trade union
movement in the T.U.C. proposals. He added that the
problem would not be solved by the government's
abdicating its responsibilities.

The second reading of the Bill (April 1970), incor-
porating the White Paper proposals, was ultimately
carried in Parliament by 224 votes to 62: 55 Labour
M.P.s voted against and about 40 abstained.

Whatever the private thoughts of the members of
the General Council, they had to be suppressed in view
of the mood of the movement, which was unequi-
vocally and intensely against repressive government
intervention in industrial relations. The traditional
relations between the Labour Party and trade unions
were threatened by the Labour Government's determination to go ahead with its plans. The future of
the Labour Party was at stake.

The government was compelled to climb down. On
June 18th an agreement was reached between it and
the T.U.C. General Council based on the T.U.C.'s
Programme for Action. The government gave the
pledge that it would not interfere in industrial relations
with penal sanctions. The settlement, however, did
not produce a return to normality in the relations
between government and trade unions. The events
of the first half of 1969 made many trade unions more
deeply political. The government had been seen as a
partisan in industrial relations and a vulnerable
one at that. Workers were shown that they could
use their collective strength to force a government to
change its policy. This was a new factor in British
industrial relations. A battle had been won, but not
the war. With the advent of the Tory Government the
struggle had to be waged all over again, with even
greater consequences.

Two other events of importance took place in 1969.
First, London dustmen struck for a wage increase in
September. It was a strike which not only started a
mood of militancy among lower-paid workers, but
also injected a new radical attitude into wage claims.
During the whole of the post-war period unions had
been satisfied with marginal changes in wages and
hours. By and large they had refrained from demanding specific increases and merely requested " substantial " increases. This enabled many union leader-
ships to adjust downwards without having to justify
their actions to their members. The London dustmen
demanded and won a rise from a basic rate of £15 9s.
to £20 after a prolonged strike. This, for that time, was
really substantial, and for a period the figure of £20 per
week became a magic one for many groups of workers.

The other event concerned the miners. During the
1960's, due to the combined effects of the decline
of the mining industry and the implementation of a
day-wage structure in place of piecework, the in-
cidence of strikes in the industry declined significantly. In 1961, 733,000 working days had been lost
through mining strikes. From the middle of the decade
there was a sharp decline. In 1966, 118,000 working
days were lost, while in 1968 the figure had fallen to a
record low of 54,000. There had, however, been no
official national strike since 1926. Contrary to the
general impression, miners in the late 1960's were not
militant. But at the end of 1968 Lawrence Daly, a
left-winger, successfully opposed right-winger Joe
Gormley in the election to succeed Will Paynter as
General Secretary of the National Union of Mineworkers, following an intense campaign throughout
the coalfields about pit closures, wages and working
conditions. This was the beginning of a long and
intensive process of left development amongst miners.

The first major sign of awakening came in October 1969, when the N.U.M. Yorkshire Area Council called a strike in support of a 40-hour week for surface workers. The strike spread to other coalfields bringing out 130,000 men from 140 pits. Miners had suddenly rediscovered the power of the strike weapon. On October 30th, a special delegate conference of the N.U.M. voted to reject an N.C.B. wages offer. The mood of compromise and acceptance which had pervaded the coalfields for two decades was unquestionably changing.

Largely beginning with the strike of London dustmen, the incomes policy of the Labour Government collapsed. There was a flood of demands for wage increases, amounting to up to 25 and 30 per cent., and many strikes. More working days were lost through strikes in 1970 than any previous year since 1926. Many of the strikes were unofficial, but there were also some important official strikes involving school teachers, dockers and local government employees. The last group waged a six weeks' strike in the autumn. Miners had demanded an increase of £5 a week, but the National Coal Board conceded only half of this. In a pit-head ballot more than 55 per cent. of the miners voted for strike action. But because the N.U.M. rules regarding a strike ballot required a two-thirds majority, feelings in South Wales, Scotland, Yorkshire, Kent and Derbyshire ran high and unofficial strikes were called. By November 10th 125,000 miners were out. Following this, in December, an intense anti-union propaganda campaign was evoked by industrial action in the electrical power industry, with the millionaire press plumbing the depths with sudden hypocritical concern about the hardships of old-age pensioners. The unions ended their action with the promise of a Court of Enquiry.

The contradictions in the British capitalist system which had created pressures which led to the attempt to penalise strikers were thus neither removed nor reduced in intensity by the Labour Government's retreat in 1969. Britain was indeed moving in the late 1960's into the classic phase of incipient authoritarianism. It was only a matter of time before the question of imposing a statutory control over unions was raised again. This came after the General Election in July 1970.

In July 1970 Mr. Wilson's Government reaped the bitter harvest of alienation from its base, the grass roots of the Labour movement, as a consequence of its efforts to stabilise British imperialism at the expense of the working class and its ill-starred efforts to destroy the independence, sovereignty and traditional function of the trade union movement.

As we have seen, the storm this aroused, the mass struggles it generated, sparked off a bitter clash within the Parliamentary Labour Party encouraging a considerable number of M.P.s not normally aligned with the left to take a more militant stand. It was this combination of extra-Parliamentary struggle with Parliamentary struggle which became an irresistible force and compelled Wilson to withdraw the Bill— itself an unprecedented event in Parliamentary history. This was followed by a relaxation on wage restraint. But the damage was done. Large sections of the Labour Movement were disillusioned and looked towards self-reliance or militant industrial action rather than towards a Labour Government to protect their interests, particularly as the conduct of the elections of 1970 was devoid of any indication that Wilson had learned the lessons of 1964-70. The result was mass Labour abstentions and the return of a Tory Government on a low poll and minority vote.

What followed showed that Heath and his Ministers were as incapable of understanding what had happened in the 'sixties and the mood of the workers as was the Wilson Government. The new Tory Government, cock-a-hoop at its victory, was determined to succeed where Wilson had failed.

Their basic strategy was the same—to ease the problems facing British capitalism at the expense of the working class. Real wage cuts were to be achieved by the pincer movement of provoking an open confrontation with the workers, and by resisting as employers all reasonable wage claims in the public sector and exhorting the big employers in the private sector to follow suit. They encouraged mass unemployment through the so-called "lame duck policy"—allowing firms in difficulties to become bankrupt with consequent closures and unemployment. Thus they hoped to demoralise the organised working class.

As the guarantee that the organised working class should be unable to fight back, they bulldozed through Parliament their hated and equally ill-starred Industrial Relations Act. Tory wages and economic policy was presented as a return to "freedom"— the freedom of the market, relying on confrontation rather than statutory regulations to keep wages down.

Heath's Government, arrogantly blind to the courage, militancy, determination and ingenuity of the working class, was totally unable to understand the tremendous changes within the Labour movement over the decade. It wasn't long before the struggles provoked by the government developed an inner dynamic, imposing a series of fatal government defeats, forcing it to change course, and finally culminating in compelling a General Election resulting in the overthrow of the Tory Government and the return to office of Labour, albeit with a minority in Parliament.

We will only refer to the highlights of the stormy three-and-a-half years of Tory Government.

The Tory General Election manifesto contained the proposals for controlling unions which had been propounded in *Fair Deal at Work*. Before the election Mr. Heath had declared that the reform of industrial relations was at the heart of the Tory's economic strategy. There was virtually no discussion about this document during the election. But almost the first act of the Tories after winning the election was to issue a new government discussion document containing proposals for restrictive trade union legislation. The Tory aim was to place unions into a legislative straitjacket and destroy free collective bargaining. The proposals incorporated into the Industrial Relations Bill, published on December 19th, 1970, aimed to deprive unions of valuable immunities protecting the right to strike; to make the majority of collective agreements legally binding; to give legal protection to non-unionism; to prescribe a series of " unfair " practices for which unions and members could be legally penalised; to establish an Industrial Relations Court with the powers of a High Court; to make the closed-shop illegal and generally to discourage strike action by instituting compulsory strike ballots and a 60-day cooling off period. Some of the features of the Tory proposals were similar to those of *In Place of Strife*. But all of them had been tried before in the U.S.A. and other countries and had been found, by the Royal Commission on Trade Unions, to be largely ineffective.

The Tory Industrial Relations Bill was both aided and handicapped by the Labour Government's *In Place of Strife*. It was aided because the public had become accustomed to discussion about penalising strikers and controlling unions. The matter, therefore, was not seen as anything new. And because the Labour Government itself had made similar proposals it was difficult to take the Parliamentary Labour Party's opposition to the Tory Government Bill seriously. The Bill was handicapped because rank and file trade unionists under the guidance of the Liaison Committee for the Defence of Trade Unions had already tasted success in their campaign in rousing the whole trade union movement against Labour's proposals, and reacted immediately.

Mass stoppages in protest against the Industrial Relations Bill took place on December 8th, 1970, when about 750,000 workers took part. The General Council of the T.U.C. agreed on December 16th that lunch-time protest meetings on January 12th, 1971 could extend into working hours. On January 1st about 45,000 Midlands workers struck against the Bill, and on January 3rd the General Council launched a mass education campaign. At least half a million workers took part in the day of protest on January 12th. The Amalgamated Union of Engineering Workers decided to hold a series of one-day official strikes against the Bill.

The Tory Government's incomes policy which was eventually adopted was to depend on the operation of the Industrial Relations Bill. Unions in their legal straitjacket would be unable to operate freely and effectively in pursuit of wage claims. In the meantime, however, the government encouraged direct confrontation with unions in the belief that the latter could be defeated. This Tory incomes policy was known as " N-1 ", the N being the norm or previous wages settlement. Each confrontation was intended to reduce any wage settlement in relation to the

previous one until a level of no increase was reached.
The first major confrontation occurred in January
1971, when the Union of Post Office Workers called an
official national strike. The union had claimed a 15
per cent. wage increase and had been offered 8 per cent.
By February 1st, 215,000 postal workers had stopped
work. Although the postal service was closed, telecommunications continued with only minor disruption, thus reducing the effectiveness of the strike.
The U.P.W. paid too little attention to gaining the
support of the telecommunications unions and the
solidarity of the rest of the organised movement. In
consequence the strike lost its impact and the low-
paid postal workers suffered hardships to no avail.
After 47 days the strike was called off, virtually on
the Post Office terms.

Opposition to the Industrial Relations Bill gained
momentum during 1971. A vast march and demonstration organised by the T.U.C., involving according to
various estimates between 150,000 and a quarter of a
million people, took place in London on February 21st.
Over two million workers supported an A.U.E.W.
strike on March 1st. When a Special Congress of the
T.U.C. met on March 18th to condemn the Tory
Government's plans, about 3 million workers took
part in a one-day strike originally initiated by the
Liaison Committee for the Defence of Trade Unions
and officially supported by the A.U.E.W. and a number of other unions. The Special Congress decided on a
policy of non-co-operation with the Government over
the Bill. Unions were advised not to register as required by the Bill when it became law and not to
recognise agencies set up under the Act.

Despite the prolonged campaign, the government
made only small amendments to the Bill, and it
became law in August 1971. The National Industrial

Relations Court and the Comission on Industrial Relations were set up. The Court was presided over by Sir John Donaldson, a Tory Judge who has earned his place in trade union history by his penal judgments imposed under the Act. But far from being the end of the story, it was only the start of a crescendo of struggles which made the Act virtually ineffective and led to its eventual repeal by the subsequent Labour Government.

It was the fear displayed by the still right-wing majority of the T.U.C. leadership of a total confrontation, including the calling of a general strike to compel the government to repeal the Act, that encouraged the Tories to push it through Parliament.

But the T.U.C., recoiling from a general strike, did decide not to co-operate with the Act and to instruct trade unions not to register and not to recognise the Courts set up by the Act. A handful of small unions with a total membership of less than 7 per cent. of affiliated unions, were expelled from the T.U.C. for ignoring these instructions.

The first action against a trade union under the Act was the imposition of two fines totalling £55,000 against the largest union, the Transport and General Workers' Union, arising out of blacking by dockers of a container firm. The Union at first refused to attend the Court, for which it was fined £5,000—and then it refused to pay this fine for which it was fined a further £50,000 for continued contempt. However, the right-wing majority of the General Council, faced with this challenge, retreated and changed its attitude, allowing unions to attend the Court to " defend " themselves.[1]

Unfortunately the T. & G.W.U. acted on this new

[1] See *Heaton's Transport* v. *The T. & G.W.U.*, *Times Law Report*, March 30th, 1972, and subsequent reports on this prolonged case.

decision, attended Court, paid the fines and urged the dockers to stop blacking the firm.

London dockers, led by the militant shop stewards, Bernie Steer, Vic Turner and others, refused to bow to another Court order to stop picketing a further container firm. Five of them, including Bernie Steer, a Communist, and Vic Turner, who later joined the Communist Party, were arrested and committed to Pentonville Prison on July 21st.

The Liaison Committee for Defence of Trade Unions immediately called for a general strike to demand the release of the Pentonville 5, as they became known. Within hours tens of thousands downed tools; within a day the number rose to hundreds of thousands. The strikes snowballed. Rank and file pressure for industrial action became irresistible. The General Council of the T.U.C., in the middle of the week, on a motion of the A.U.E.W., was forced to call an official one-day general strike to commence on the Monday of the subsequent week.

But on July 26th, just five days before the general strike was due to start, the government capitulated, using the camouflage of the Official Solicitor. The dockers were released and carried shoulder high in a victory march through the streets of London. This lightning action was one of the finest episodes in British trade union history and a body blow against the Act.

Before this, on April 12th, 1972, the three railway unions imposed a work-to-rule and an overtime ban in support of their wages claim. The Industrial Relations Court proceeded to order a 14-days' cooling-off period—but in vain, since the subsequent negotiations broke down and the unions resumed their industrial action. The Secretary for Employment then applied to the Court for a compulsory ballot, as provided for under the Act. The unions appealed against this to the Court of Appeal; and in an interesting comment Lord Justice Blackley said: " In a sense under Section 142, the Court is a rubber stamp because unless you can show that the application was unjustified, the Court is bound to make an order. We do not know what evidence the Secretary of State had, and I cannot see any means by which he can be compelled to disclose it."[1]

This was the first and only time the Court put into operation the machinery of the Act regarding compulsory ballot. The result was disastrous for the government, since the ballot proved decisive—with 129,441 for the union action and 23,181 against. It was a result that everyone with any knowledge of such things knew would happen. And it was a further nail in the coffin of the Act.

Then the second largest union, the Amalgamated Union of Engineering Workers, was fined £55,000 for refusing to carry out a Court Order to enrol a scab in its ranks.[2] The A.U.E.W., true to its policy, refused to attend Court or pay the fine, and called on its membership to support the executive's stand. The membership responded. Over 750,000 engineering workers struck for a day.

While the Court through its agents had helped themselves to hundreds of thousands of pounds of union funds, this resistance in action to all intents and purposes stopped the use of the Act against the unions. Readiness to defy what the unions rightly condemned as class law in action, despite the Labour leadership's plea to "obey the law," put the government, the employers and the Court in ever-increasing

[1] *Times Law Reports*, May 18th, 1972
[2] See *Times Law Reports* November 9th, 1972 and December 8th, 1972, *Goad* v. *A.U.E.W.*

difficulties. For the first time in British legal history, millions of trade unionists defied a law and a Court and made both unworkable.

Employers meantime connived to break the law. They bought off declassed individuals with large sums of money not to use the law against the unions for fear of the subsequent mass industrial action. Even a nationalised industry, the National Coal Board, " illegally " fired a miner who left the union rather than face a strike to maintain the closed shop, which was illegal under the Industrial Relations Act.

Simultaneously with the struggle against the Act, big industrial battles flared up. Shortly before the government reaffirmed its determination to try to control the unions, a struggle between the Clyde shipyard workers and the government began. This epic struggle of the Upper Clyde Workers—it started in June 1971 and lasted 18 months— became famous throughout the world, and the workers' spokesman, Jimmy Reid, a household name. It not only reversed government policy but strongly influenced diverse and historic new forms of industrial action in the trade union movement.

It marked a new stage in the fight for the extension of industrial democracy and a genuine step in achieving at least a measure of " workers' control " in the only way feasible within the framework of capitalism. The traditional working-class slogan of " the right to work " was transformed from a long-term aspiration into a practical reality.

Faced with a decision by management and the government to shut down the Upper Clyde yards, to force liquidation and to dispose of the equipment and the valuable sites for speculative redevelopment— the workers refused to accept. They developed the novel form of the "work-in. " The shop stewards with the approval of the whole work force took "control of the gates." Nothing could leave or enter the yards without the shop stewards' permission. The logic behind this form of struggle was to prevent the sale of equipment, to prevent redundancy, to ensure that the equipment, machinery and labour force remained intact and to retain the viability of the yards while compelling management and the government to reverse the decision to close the yards.

A tremendous campaign of solidarity—nationally and internationally—was developed through these long months of struggle. The shop stewards' control of exit and entry frustrated the plans to run down the manpower, while the solidarity funds enabled the payment of workers declared redundant who remained in the yards and shared in the work.

Management and the government were forced to capitulate and advance sufficient funds to retain the yards as a viable concern both for shipbuilding and oil-rig building, and no workers were forced out of jobs. This successful action by the Clyde workers to reverse management decisions inspired scores of others faced with closures to challenge management's decisions and force a change in investment and reorganisation policies.

Workers of Briant Colour in London—a printing establishment faced with a similar situation of closure —occupied the works in June 1972, kept management and the Receiver out of the plant, and ran the plant eight months by printing leaflets, posters, pamphlets and books for the Labour movement. As a result the buyer of the bankrupt firm, who intended to close it down and sell the land for speculative redevelopment, had to negotiate with the shop stewards, abandon his dreams of an " easy fortune " and run the plant as a printing works employing the whole labour force. This battle went on until February 1973.

Further examples over the next two years were the struggle against the giant Thorn Electric firm to close down one of its plants, Fisher-Bendix, employing 800 workers in Liverpool, the long occupation of the famous Triumph Motor Cycle works. When the Beaverbrook Press shut down the Scottish *Daily Express* in 1974, the workers occupied the plant, formed an Action Committee and obtained a conditonal government promise of £1,750,000 to publish a co-operatively owned independent daily paper.

These are but a few examples of how workers' struggle and confrontations with the employers compelled the latter to negotiate over such areas as investment plans, and to permit manning problems to enter into the area of negotiations, making them subject to mutual agreement with the organised workers who thus achieved a real role in decision-making.

" In the first six months of this year there were 57 sit-ins costing more than half a million working days," a highly reputable firm of industrial consultants reported in a study published in 1973.[1] The consultants concluded: " Many of the redundancy sit-ins were successful in achieving part or all of their main objectives, the prevention of threatened closures and redundancies taking place. The workers involved in the sit-ins are convinced that the factories would have been closed if they had not sat in, and most companies confirm that there would have been total shut down."

Since then it is estimated that at least another thirty plants were saved from closure. In addition there were

[1] *An Analysis of Sit-Ins*, Metra Consulting Group, 1973.

numerous examples of successful struggle to force management to change plans on methods of work, discipline and production methods.[1]

In the Upper Clyde struggle, which inspired so many other actions, the key to success was the unity of the left—Communists, Labour and militants of no party affiliations. Their spokesman, Jimmy Reid, and his colleagues travelled up and down the country to offer the benefits of their experience to many of the occupied factories threatened with closure.

Discontent among the miners grew rapidly after the unofficial and partial strike in 1971. They were emerging from decades of demoralisation due to the combination of the disastrous policies of Labour and Tory governments in running down the industry and decades of right-wing leadership of the union.

The general changes in the movement towards the left and the consistent work at rank and file level led to considerable changes in the leadership at national as well as coalfield level. Mick McGahey defeated his right-wing opponent for the Vice-Presidency (joining the left-wing General Secretary, Lawrence Daly), having been narrowly beaten earlier by Joe Gormley for the Presidency. Left-wingers A. Scargill, Owen Briscoe and Communist Peter Tait won the Presidency, General Secretaryship and National Executive seat of the Yorkshire Area—the largest and hitherto right-wing dominated coalfield. Communist Joe Whelan wrested the Notts coalfield seat on the N.E.C. for the first time from the right-wing. This was the setting when the N.U.M. 1971 National Conference met and adopted the Scottish resolution

[1] For a detailed description and assessment of the U.C.S. struggle see *U.C.S.—The Fight for the Right to Work* by Alex Murray. C.P. 1971, and *The U.C.S. Work-In*, by Willie Thompson and Finlay Hart, with Foreword by Jimmy Reid, Lawrence and Wishart, 1972.

for a big wage increase which included the instruction to use industrial action to realise it.

Thus the miners' claim, including a big wage increase and a reduction in hours, was the first major test of the Tories' policy of confrontation on the wages front. On government instructions the claim was rejected by the Coal Board. The miners countered with a prolonged ban on overtime. When this failed to achieve their objective, a recommendation for an all-out strike resulted in the necessary majority. The miners had changed their strike ballot rule from a previous two-thirds majority to a 55 per cent. majority. The ballot registered 59 per cent. for strike action.

The miners' strike started on January 9th 1972. It marked a milestone in working-class struggle, not only because of the victory won, but equally because of the new forms of struggle forged in the course of it, the degree of solidarity which developed, the humiliating defeat inflicted on the government, and the effect it had on the pattern of wages struggle and future government policies.

As was to be expected from the miners, the strike was solid from the very first day. For its part, the government was relying on huge coal stocks at pit yards and power stations to starve the miners into submission, especially as the N.U.M. was short of funds and not in a position to issue strike pay.

Solidarity appeals from the miners met with an immediate response throughout the movement. The response of the General Council of the T.U.C. was less than had been expected, but it did issue a call to the movement not to " cross the miners' picket line." The railwaymen responded admirably and not an ounce of coal was moved by rail. But the problem that faced the miners was the movement by blackleg road haulage firms of coal, coke, some oil and hydrogen essential to keep the power stations functioning.

With their "flying picket" squads the miners revolutionised normal picketing. The "flying pickets" became the effective key to victory through the solidarity and support of the working class, although the police massed their forces to break them up, pitched battles were provoked and numerous arrests of miners took place.

The turning point in the strike came with the Saltley power station showdown in Birmingham. With over 1,000 police massed to prevent the hundreds of miners from picketing strike-breaking lorry drivers, Birmingham car workers and engineers called for a total solidarity strike in the city's factories and in serried ranks with Union banners marched on Saltley to join the miners' pickets. They forced the massed police from three counties to capitulate and to order the shutting down of the depot. It was the beginning of the end.

This decisive show of solidarity brought home to Heath that the confrontation he had sought and got had rebounded against him. His first attempt to extricate himself from utter defeat was to appoint a Court of Inquiry headed by a High Court Judge, Lord Wilberforce, combined with an appeal to the miners to call off the strike pending the report of the Court.

But the miners were not fobbed off. While agreeing to give evidence to the court, the strike went on and the "flying pickets" increased their activity. Under pressure of the continued strike the Wilberforce Report went a long way to meet the miners' demands and was far in advance of what the miners would have settled for before the strike. It was rejected by the miners.

Heath was reduced to pleading with the miners' leaders at 10 Downing Street, and finally capitulated. The final settlement included many additional demands not in the original claim. On Monday, February 28th, the miners called off the strike.

This total victory of the miners killed stone dead the government's incomes policy of N-1. Millions of workers soon followed the miners and, perhaps for the first time since the war, real wages of the working people rose to an apppreciable extent. The building workers in July 1972 called the first national official strike in their history for a £10 increase and a reduction in hours, using most effectively the technique of " flying pickets " initiated by the miners. After a bitter ten weeks' battle they too, on September 14th, won the major element of their claim.

These struggles forced the government to change its policy of resisting wage claims by confrontation and to resort to a legally enforceable incomes policy by enacting the Counter-Inflation Act (1972) and the setting up of a Pay Board and Prices Board. To enforce legal ceilings on wage and price increases they issued various Orders in Council, which became known as Phases I, II and III of the Tory Incomes Policy.

But while the methods were changed, the objective was not. The Tories were determined to break the morale of the workers and destroy the ability of the trade unions to struggle.

Six months after the building strike, in the non-industrial area of North Wales in 1973, twenty-four building workers were arrested and charged under the Conspiracy laws with offences arising out of the militant picketing during that strike. The " Shrewsbury 24 " and the movement to defend them against the patently trumped up charges rapidly developed. The

Shrewsbury case was intended to intimidate the working class and to counter successful picketing.[1]

Heavy jail sentences were imposed on some of the twenty-four, with the leading militant shop steward, Des Warren, receiving three years and others lesser terms and heavy fines. The courageous behaviour and speeches of Warren and Tomlinson from the dock and the campaign of the Shrewsbury 24 Defence Committee and the Liaison Committee for the Defence of Trade Unions caused the passive U.C.A.T.T. right wing leadership to give active support to the demand for the men's release. The General Council of the T.U.C. met the Home Secretary to press this. Warren and Tomlinson as a result were eventually removed from an ordinary jail to an open one. Finally Warren and Tomlinson were released on bail pending appeal, although they had been refused bail at an earlier stage.

This important case underlines the need to safeguard the right to picket and win immunity of trade unionists from charges of conspiracy under Common Law or the Conspiracy Acts.

By late 1973 the miners were again faced with the government's determination to deprive them of wage increases to safeguard their 1972 gains. The Coal Board, bound by the Counter-Inflation Act, offered them all that was permitted under Phase 3 of the Tory incomes policy—a fraction of their demand for £35, £40 and £45. But the miners were in no mood to be blocked by the Tory Phase 3, any more than they had been by the former version of N-1. Once again a ban on overtime was followed by an all-out strike.

Heath now responded with the unprecedented step of ordering a three-day week. Most of industry was

[1] For the full story of this case see *The Shrewsbury 3* by J. Arnison, with an introduction by B. Ramelson. Lawrence and Wishart, 1974.

ordered to shut down for two days a week to save power station stocks, with great harm to the economy as a whole. The three-day week was introduced, as soon became obvious, chiefly with the political objective of breaking solidarity with the miners by fears that the strike would bring about the collapse of the whole economy, cuts in earnings and mass unemployment. Heath was attempting to panic the people into hostility against the miners. And in this he was aided by the panic-mongering of the mass media. Only the *Morning Star*, successor to the *Daily Worker*, was the staunch daily supporter of the miners among the daily press, keeping the public informed of the facts and mobilising support for the miners. It has performed the same service in all the battles, and spear-headed the fight against the Industrial Relations Act.

Like the Bourbons, Heath forgot nothing and learned nothing from 1972. As in 1972, the miners had the sympathy of the public. Heath's frantic determination to avenge himself for the crushing defeat they had inflicted on him in 1972 misfired and an even more bitter defeat awaited him. He again tried the stratagem of an Inquiry combined with an appeal to call off the strike pending its findings—only this time it was the government Pay Board instead of a Wilberforce-type Court of Inquiry that was given the job. Once more the miners refused to co-operate.

Heath then decided on the desperate measure of seeking a mandate to defeat the miners and " teach the workers a lesson." He prorogued Parliament and called a General Election for February 28th, 1974, while the strike and the three-day working week were still on.

Wilson, to his discredit, joined Heath in letting it be known that he would like to see the strike called off for the duration of the election. The miners continued the strike, however—although the loco drivers, who were also involved in industrial action at the time, acceded to Wilson's plea and called their action off.

The 1974 election had no precedent in British political history. It was the first time a government had resigned in the middle of a major strike, claiming that " it could no longer rule." The Tories posed as the central election issue: " Who is to run the country—the Unions or the Government?" Every effort was made to create a Red Scare, in typical McCartheyite style, with the Communist Party, and in particular Mick McGahey, N.U.M. Vice-President and member of the Communist Party's Political Committee, as the chief bogymen. Wilson, Prentice and some other Labour right-wingers contributed their mite of assistance by joining in the witch hunt.

But the labour movement in 1974 had matured considerably from the days when they were easy prey to Cold War propaganda. Far from getting a mandate to bash the unions, it was Heath who was sent into the wilderness. *The Times* commented editorially " This has been an historic dispute. It is the first time that an industrial stoppage has provoked a General Election and indirectly brought about the downfall of a Government."[1]

A new Labour Government took office pledged to repeal the Industrial Relations Act, restore free collective bargaining, extend public ownership and bring about " a massive redistribution in the balance of wealth in favour of the working people." Its first act was to free the Coal Board from the restrictions of Phase 3 in its negotiations with the miners. The miners gained increases of 30 per cent. and returned to work victorious at the beginning of March.

In the meantime Tory legislation was still in force.

[1] *The Times*, March 7th, 1974.

While the Industrial Relations Act had been rendered virtually ineffective by the mass movement, nevertheless Sir John Donaldson missed no opportunity to inflict harm on the trade unions when he thought he saw the chance.

As we have noted, the outstanding role in the struggle against the Act, and which made its repeal inevitable, was undoubtedly that of the principled, consistent opposition of the A.U.E.W. At no time during the operation of the Act did the A.U.E.W. recognise the Industrial Relations Court, and it refused to attend, or to pay any fines even when threatened with the total sequestration of its funds and assets arising out of the notorious Con-Mech judgment.[1]

This last important action against the A.U.E.W. by Sir John Donaldson exposed both his die-hard hostility and impotence. He had ordered the total sequestration of the A.U.E.W. funds on May 3rd, 1974 because of the union's refusal to pay the damages awarded. The A.U.E.W. responded with a decision for an all-out unlimited general strike of all engineering workers, the first such call in the union's history. The country was faced with what could have become a total shut down in a matter of days and at most a week. Without A.U.E.W. maintenance workers, no modern plant, power station or railway could continue to function.

Pressure to pay up was exerted on the A.U.E.W. from all sides, including from Michael Foot, the newly-appointed Minister of Employment. But when the union refused to succumb to these pressures, there was a repetition of the judicial farce which had taken place during the case of the Pentonville 5. Sir John

[1] Con-Mech was a small engineering firm which claimed damages through the N.I.R.C. over a strike for union recognition.

Donaldson changed his mind and decided to accept the payment of all outstanding fines, damages and costs against the A.U.E.W. by a group of "anonymous donors," though only the day before, when that offer was made, he had rejected it.

During the first week in July 1974 Sir John tried yet another action against the A.U.E.W. and found against the union. This time, however, contrary to his usual practice and in full knowledge that his judgment would be ignored by the union, he gave judgment not to be effective until mid-August, knowing that before then his Court would cease to exist and this judgment would lapse.

And indeed, July 25th became a Red Letter Day in Labour history. On that date the Tory Pay Board was abolished and Sir John Donaldson read his own obituary on the shutting down of the National Industrial Relations Court. It was the culmination of a seven-year campaign to eliminate all attempts to invoke legal sanctions against the unions, against collective bargaining and industrial action.

At the time the Court was set up all the Fleet Street leader writers and industrial correspondents announced that the unions were to be dragged screaming into the twentieth century. On its demise the *Financial Times*, July 22nd, 1974, wrote: " Few tears for the death of the N.I.R.C." The unions had warned that this would be the case. They were right. The government, the press, the lawyers and the Courts were wrong. Struggle had decided the issue. On July 31st the Industrial Relations Act was repealed, although the Act repealing it contained a number of wrecking amendments from the ever anti-union House of Lords. These outlawed the closed shop, established a right not to belong to a union, made it illegal to participate in solidarity actions both at home and with fellow workers abroad, and interfered in the internal affairs of unions by laying down restrictions on the exercise by unions of discipline and electoral procedures of their choice. The T.U.C. sharply condemned these Lords amendments.   So the unions still have much to do to restore full trade union freedom. With what has gone before, who can doubt that these provisions will be defied, just as they were under the Industrial Relations Act?

The general advance to the left in the unions, both with regard to policy and leadership, was reflected not only in more progressive economic, industrial and social policies, but also in international affairs.

A more active role was played by the T.U.C. in the fight to eliminate nuclear bases in Britain, for drastic cuts in arms expenditure, active support for the democratic forces in Spain, the condemnation of apartheid and the Greek Colonel's regime.

Removal of the bans against Communists in the trade union movement resulted in scrapping the Proscribed Organisation List of the Labour Party, and some advances in establishing relations with the trade unions in the socialist countries as well as with Communist-led unions in capitalist countries.

In 1972 Jack Jones succeeded right-wing Lord Cooper as Chairman of the International Committee of the General Council and in July 1973, together with Vic Feather, he led a high-powered T.U.C. delegation to the U.S.S.R. An invitation for a reciprocal visit from the U.S.S.R. trade unions was issued.

In 1973 the T.U.C. under Mr. Len Murray, its new General Secretary, continued to play the major role in establishing a European Confederation of Trade Unions in the teeth of opposition from the reactionary West German T.U.C. and the French Force Ouvrière. In framing the constitution of the E.C.T.U. the aim was to unite all European trade unions regardless of political trends or international affiliations. On July 9th, 1974 the Italian C.G.I.L. was admitted to membership.

A similar development was beginning to take place on an industry basis. The European Metal Federation came into existence previously to co-ordinate trade union work within the Common Market countries. The A.U.E.W. decided to affiliate, and mainly as a result of its efforts, and the vigorous fight put up by its President, Hugh Scanlon, the Metal Federation was being transformed into an all-European organisation open to all unions in Europe. That the basis for a united trade union movement capable of confronting the menace of the multi-national firm has now been laid was primarily due to the determination of the British T.U.C.

Earlier in 1974 there was a very successful international conference of railwaymen held in Moscow attended by all European unions. For the first time trade unionists from "East" and "West" Germany, the German Democratic Republic and the German Federal Republic, met and discussed common problems with all other railwaymen. So successful was this conference that the decision to follow it up with another conference was unanimously agreed.

These developments towards international trade union unity have tremendous political significance and create the essential conditions to develop international solidarity and struggle against the octopus-like multi-national firms.

It is generally acknowledged that the key role in making these developments possible was played by the T.U.C.

In this chapter it has been possible to give only a very brief summary of the highlights of a decade of industrial action that has no parallel in the rich history of British trade unionism.

It was a decade which saw a great quantitative increase in the class struggle, whether measured by the number of strikes, days lost, numbers involved or duration of major strikes. In 1971 there were 13.5 million days of strike action. In 1972 this rose to 23.9 million. What is of even greater importance, the struggles were qualitatively in a different category compared with the past and will have a lasting political as well as an industrial impact on the pattern of development of the trade unions and the political perspective of the fight to transform capitalist society.

It was a decade that saw a growth in membership and a big advance in the process of uniting the fragmented structure of the unions. While the membership has grown from 8,299,393 to 10,001,419 the number of unions has been reduced from 183 to 126.[1]

It was a decade that saw the unionisation of white-collar and professional workers, who are showing daily that they are as militant and potentially political as the traditional manual workers.

Likewise there was a growth in women's membership. And the fight for equal pay and opportunities for women was stepped up. An outstanding example was the strike of women machinists at Fords in 1968, which went a long way to establishing equal pay there. And again, in an industry where women make up the overwhelming majority of workers, the clothing strike in Leeds in 1970 waged a long and sharp struggle to reduce the differentials between men's and women's pay.

Overall, women in this decade played a full part in

[1] These are the latest published figures available, although since the 1973 Trades Union Congress there have been further union amalgamations.

all the industrial struggles, whether for wages or against the Industrial Relations Act.

And this growth in the militancy and maturity of women workers led to the Labour Government's Equal Pay Act, and created the conditions which influenced the Labour Government to introduce in 1964 the Bill for equal opportunities for women.

It was a decade which saw the traditionally passive workers—the unskilled and those in the public and civil service sectors—develop a militancy and readiness to take industrial action second to none.

It was a decade that saw the beginning of a process that will no doubt lead to an end of the right-wing grip on the trade union movement. For left leaders have now emerged at every level in the trade unions, including a considerable group on the General Council itself.[1]

It was a period which witnessed a rapid development of the democratisation of the trade union movement. With the solitary exception of the E.E.P.T.U. all bans and proscriptions have been ended and there has been a big development in rank and file participation. In a number of unions shop stewards are now involved officially in national negotiations and the practice of prior approval by the membership before a settlement is signed is spreading.

Rank and file bodies are playing a growing role— no longer branded as subversive but accepted by the movement as healthy developments. On a national

[1] A few examples: Jack Jones in the T. & G.W.U.; Hugh Scanlon, A.U.E.W.; Eddie Marsden, C.E.U.; Ken Gill, T.A.S.S.; Greaves, Tobacco Workers; George Guy, Sheet Metal Workers; Jim Slater, Seamen; and the powerful group in the Miners referred to earlier. On the General Council, Sapper, Parry, Doughty, Jones, Scanlon, Daly, Urwin, Patterson, Briginshaw, Ken Gill and Jim Slater. And Alex Kitson, John Forrester and Joan Maynard in the Labour Party E.C. from the unions.

scale there is the Liaison Committee for the Defence of Trade Unions, and at industry level such committees and movements as those grouped around the Builders' Charter and the Printers' Charter, or around such rank and file papers as *Flashlight* (electrical workers), the *Engineers' Voice* and the *Power Worker*, to name but a few. Indeed, the interaction of the rank and file bodies and the official movement is characteristic of the whole period.

With State intervention in industrial relations and the State itself emerging as the other side in many disputes, strikes and industrial unrest are compelled to assume a political significance and the old reactionary efforts to compartmentalise industrial and political action are rapidly disappearing. Workers are no longer inhibited from taking industrial action because it has a political connotation; this shedding of such inhibitions has great political significance for the future.

All the actions against the Industrial Relations Act or in defiance of the Counter-Inflation Act were obviously in part political and had to be so as the government was acting politically against the unions.

But this tendency has gone even further. There has been official industrial action in support of pensioners and the N.U.P.E. strike, superimposing upon a wage claim the further demand for a rapid phasing out of private beds in National Health hospitals. These are matters which go beyond immediate industrial aims. The official industrial action against the French nuclear tests, and against sending aircraft to Chile are examples of what is a new phenomenon for the British labour movement (except for the *Jolly George* incident over half a century ago)— strike action on issues of political policy.

There has likewise been a greater awareness on the

part of the trade unions of the need to exert their power to change the policies and leadership of the Labour Party.

We are witnessing the institutionalising of the Liaison Committee of the T.U.C. and the Labour Party—a regular meeting of the General Council with the N.E.C. of the Labour Party as well as the leadership of the Parliamentary Labour Party—replacing the defunct National Council of Labour as an important body shaping Labour policy. It was this body that was largely responsible for the main guide lines of Labour's election manifesto in February 1974.

As a corollary of this political advance of the trade union movement and its growing realisation of the need to shape political policy, greater attention is now being paid to the election of the trade union members of the N.E.C. of the Labour Party and the selection of Constituency Labour Parliamentary candidates. For the first time since its foundation the majority of trade union members on the N.E.C. of the Labour Party are lefts, and a number of trade unions are becoming more discerning too in the M.P.s they sponsor.

It cannot be said that the right-wing grip has yet been broken, or that the right wing is not fighting back and will not continue to do so—or, for that matter, that all in the left see the road ahead clearly and have become freed of the dead hand of the past. Yet there can be no doubt that the last decade of struggle, and its continuance today, proved and is proving itself one of the most momentous in the history of British trade unionism. The application of its lessons can be even more decisive in the next decade.

INDEX

261

262 INDEX